D1367075

Praise for *Coming to Concurrence: Addressable Attitudes and the New Marketing Productivity*

Coming to Concurrence is a riveting analysis of what's going on in today's consumer marketplace. The marketing insights in this book are deep and profound. In particular, the Yankelovich innovation of Addressable Attitudes is an important advance that marketers like me have needed and wanted for years. This book should be required reading for every serious marketer.

Jody Bilney
Executive Vice President and Chief Marketing Officer
The Charles Schwab Corporation

. . . Yankelovich's mighty triumvirate of Smith, Clurman and Wood . . . have laid out a path by which we can improve people's lives and improve marketing effectiveness—simultaneously. In ten years, this book— and the sea change it will have sparked—will be hailed as a milestone. . . . The war is over. The consumer won. And Yankelovich offers us marketers a guide to the peace.

Chuck Donofrio
Chief Executive Officer
Carton Donofrio Partners, Inc.

Yankelovich accurately assesses the serious decline in marketing productivity and offers a means of reversing it. By using familiar tools in a novel way, they give brands the opportunity to achieve new degrees of reach and connection.

Christopher Ireland
Principal and CEO
Cheskin

This is a must-have addition to a marketing bookshelf. It deals with today's number-one marketing issue: marketing productivity. More and more, customers are tuning out marketing messages due to lack of personal relevance. This provocative new book addresses two key issue marketers face today: communications saturation, and the consumer's rejection of these marketing communications. It is a call to action challenging conventional marketing approaches. Tapping into the gold mine of Yankelovich MONITOR, and mixing with the keen observations of the authors, this thoughtful and thought-provoking book generates insights and uses this information to yield practical marketing actions.

Larry Light
Executive Vice President, Global Chief Marketing Officer
McDonald's Corporation

With *Coming to Concurrence,* the Yankelovich team has defined the biggest problem for marketers today. But the real powers of the book are the lessons marketers can learn to turn this crisis into a giant opportunity to improve marketing performance. The powerful examples of companies empowering customers to take control should convince even the slowest learners of the value of concurrence—getting in sync with customers.

Frederick Newell
CEO SEKLEMIAN/NEWELL
Author of *Why CRM Doesn't Work*

Prepare to be enlightened. This book offers groundbreaking insights into perhaps the greatest challenge facing marketers today—customers desperately want to be loyal, but don't feel their loyalty is being earned by most companies. The authors prove why marketers must transform their thinking and actions to show customers how much they care and, once again, give them a reason to believe.

Scott Robinette
President, Hallmark Loyalty, A Hallmark Company
Co-author of *Emotion Marketing*

The Marketing Tool Makers at Yankelovich have done it again. Readable, relevant and insightful, *Coming To Concurrence* is another bestseller for the team of J. Walker Smith, Ann Clurman and Craig Wood.

Paco Underhill
CEO Envirosell Inc.
Author of *Call of the Mall* **and** *Why We Buy*

Finally, a refreshing and bold departure from rusty conventions in marketing. Walker, Ann, and Craig have found a way to use their absolutely unique knowledge about the evolution of societal behavior to evaluate the effectiveness of marketing. In *Coming to Concurrence* they have developed new, meaningful ways to convey marketing messages in a fashion which is more reciprocal, empowering, participatory, and in better harmony with today's realities.

Erik Vonk
Chairman & CEO
Gevity HR, Inc.

Coming to Concurrence truly captures the new road map to breakthrough brand building, and brand rebuilding, too. The practice of concurrence marketing outlined in this book is so critical that the CMO title should be changed to Chief Concurrence Officer. As usual, Yankelovich has given us tomorrow's headlines today. This book is a must-read guide to the future of marketing.

Ed Winter
CEO
TracyLocke

Coming to
CONCURRENCE

ddressable Attitudes and the New Model for Marketing Productivity

J. Walker Smith

Ann Clurman

Craig Wood

RACOM
COMMUNICATIONS

Published by
Racom Communications
815 Ridge Ave.
Evanston, IL 60202

Cataloging in Publication information is available from the Library of Congress

ISBN 0-9704515-8-X

Editor & Publisher: Richard A. Hagle
Text and Cover Design: Sans Serif Inc.

Printed in the United States of America

I learned marketing at Texize.
If I can be even half as good, my career will be a success.
Thanks to all for the unstinting lessons about work and life.
—J. Walker Smith

For my mother and father, whose love and
wisdom will be with me forever.
—Ann Clurman

To Holly, Kendall and Kate, for bringing love,
laughter and balance to my life.
—Craig Wood

Contents

Acknowledgements

It goes without saying that it is impossible to give thanks to everyone who has fired our imaginations over the years. But, certainly, it is our clients, past and present, from whom we have learned the most. We want to thank all of our clients for the opportunities they have given us to do interesting work and to make lifelong friends.

Our special, heartfelt gratitude and thanks go to Marsha Everton, CEO of Pfaltzgraff, and David Merlo, Vice President and Chief Marketing Officer of Principal Bank, for their help with and contributions to this book.

A few people played a big part in making this book happen. Thanks to Ray Schultz, editorial director of *DIRECT* magazine, for giving us the idea for this book and for introducing us to our publisher, Rich Hagle, to whom we owe many thanks for his support, hard work and guidance throughout this process. Thanks to Mike Hail, CEO of Yankelovich, our boss as well as our friend, who made this book happen by giving us the time to work on it and by supporting us with unflagging enthusiasm, encouragement and hearty cheer all along the way. Thanks, too, to Steve Lerner, Executive Chairman of Yankelovich, who has long been an unwavering advocate and close friend and whose generous spirit and business acumen are an unending source of inspiration to us.

The directors of Yankelovich have been long-time supporters of the company and its vision. They have led us with a steady hand at the wheel and they have been our comrades in arms whenever the situation has required it. In addition to Mike and Steve, many thanks to John Struck, Bruce Schnitzer, Archie Purcell and Brad Esson. Thanks as well to Jim Cain, CFO of Yankelovich, our steadfast ally and colleague. Thanks to Kevin Brown, Vice President of Sales for Yankelovich, whose tenacious work ethic and patient determination motivate us all. Thanks to Steve Bodhaine, COO of The Segmentation Company, whose creative insights constantly stretch our thinking. Thanks to Taffy Fitzmaurice for her unfailing legal perspicacity.

Every employee of Yankelovich has had an impact on this book. The company's culture of study and action is unlike any other and continues to bring out the best in everyone. Thanks to all. Many people at Yankelovich helped to get this book completed, several of whom went the extra mile. Kerry Fulton and Barbara Roldan generated all of the graphics and brought their creative genius to the process. Legions of facts and figures were doggedly and indefatigably compiled and checked by Carrie Manross, Don Winter, Dana Mazzucco, Heather Whitehead, Garret Negri, Simon Kaplan, and Cathy VonFange. And endless ideas have been kicked around and shared with Noel Dunivant, Thomas Mills, Holly Moore, Gayle Davey, Amy Schafrann, Mary-Kay Harrity, David Bersoff, Christine Baskin, Susan Simpson, and Meredith Gilfeather. The publicity and marketing have been brilliantly handled as always by Margaret Gardner and by our team at Bliss, Gouvernour & Associates, John Bliss, Elizabeth Sosnow, Danielle Rumore, and Keenan Hughes. Bart Noble answered the call when asked, as usual, and Sandy McCray never lets the miles keep her ideas from steering us in the right direction. Thanks as well to Barbara Caplan, Kristen Harmeling, Sharon Romer and Peter Rose for their thought leadership and commitment to excellence. And though they are longer a part of our team, Pam Riker, Todd Neal and Steve Kraus made an impact that still reverberates in the pages of this book.

Our partners at several of the innovative, exceptional firms that work closely with Yankelovich helped with many of the ideas in this book. Brian Hankin, founder of (r)evolution partners, has long been a friend, colleague and collaborator, and his help on this project was as unsparing as always. Thanks to Brian and his partners (our officemates, too) Brad White and Sutton Bacon. Thanks to David Wilson, our neighbor and CEO of FGI, for always rallying round and being a staunch supporter of our efforts. Thanks to Christopher Ireland, Principal and CEO of Cheskin, and her outstanding crew of cultural experts for keeping us on our toes with provocative ideas and insights. Thanks to Gary Laben, President and CEO of KnowledgeBase Marketing, and his team for always delivering excellence in every aspect of our relationship.

Many other colleagues have given us crucial help and support throughout the years. Thanks to Richard Levey, senior writer for *DIRECT* magazine, Leslie Bacon, group publisher of *DIRECT* magazine, Deborah

Grassi of Acxiom, Stephen Kimmerling, formerly of the Direct Marketing Association, and Coy Clement of clementDIRECT.

And last but certainly not least, thanks to all of you, our readers, for giving us the chance to share our thoughts and ideas. We hope they serve you well.

A special word of thanks from Walker:

There would be no book for me, indeed, no life at all without Joy to whom I owe more thanks than I can ever say. My parents and sisters, nieces and nephew, keep me honest and whole. Max, Steve (N.C.), Jim, Steve (S.C.), Jeff, Scott, you guys are the best. And then there's Fred. What can I say? I owe a special word of thanks to Steve Greyser, who made time to share his counsel and perspective early on in this process. Ken Bernhardt's thoughtful friendship came through again in the clutch. Jim Crimmins unselfishly shared his data and ideas. Bill Moult forgave me for leaving him the lurch, but then he has always been a faithful friend and colleague. Jim Spaeth answered every email with yet more charts and insights. Everyone at CORD took great pains (ouch) to vet much of the early thinking behind this book. Carolyn Neal and Carol Coletta along with Geoffrey Redick have generously given me forums in which to hone my thoughts and refine my voice. Roy Carlisle continues to teach me how to write, and run, too. Bronco, Roger, and Cindell put up with my fretting during yet another Grand Canyon river trip in the midst of yet another book project. Carol, you were dearly missed. Thanks to all. And special thanks to Ann and Craig for making this book a joy to write, a pleasure to read and a delight to share with others.

A special word of thanks from Ann:

I am indebted to Florence Skelly, Arthur White and Dan Yankelovich, whose vision and integrity continue to inspire me. To Judy, Bruce and Ari who nourish me, I send my love. To Delia deLisser, Babi Satzman, Gina Schulman, Denise Larson,

Nelida Willoughby, Virginia Sadock, Jennifer Aaron, Raquel Lorenzo, Billy Steel, Paul O'Halloran and Michelle Ramoni whose patience, spirit, and humor strengthen me, I send my deepest affection and gratitude.

A special word of thanks from Craig:

To Tandy Wood, Jeff Wood, Allison Wiener and Laurie Wood for your love and unending support. Special thanks to Kyle Craig, Tim Toben, Jaye Gamble, Sandy Schmidt and Ellen Whitener for imparting your business acumen over the years, whether you were conscious of it or not. And thanks to Raegan May for helping a good friend keep things in perspective.

For more information, visit the
Concurrence Marketing Resource Center.

www.ConcurrenceMarketing.com

The Concurrence Marketing Resource Center contains
additional case studies, links to additional information
and tools, periodic white papers, contact information
for consulting advice, and other relevant resources.

A Bigger Bang for the Buck

This book is about the biggest problem facing marketing and marketers today, marketing productivity, the consumer resistance that is creating this problem, and the shift in marketing practice that is the only viable solution.

This book is about making marketing more productive—about getting a bigger bang for the buck. But this book is not a typical "marketing productivity" book. It's not about making marketing work. Marketers are completely conversant in all the tricks of the trade. Nowadays, though, what marketers do to make marketing "work" doesn't always make marketing "work" more productively. In fact, it often reduces marketing productivity—and productivity is what counts because productivity is more important than efficacy alone when it comes to building value in a business.

THE MARKETING EDGE

The most interesting thing about marketing today is that the biggest problem facing marketers is also their biggest opportunity: Consumer resistance to marketing is a disaster in the making, yet there has never been a better time to win record levels of consumer loyalty and commitment. As smart marketers know, problems always create opportunities for companies willing to break the mold and do something different. So the current mix of problems and opportunities is not as much of a paradox as it sounds. The best time to secure enduring competitive advantage is when the marketplace is in turmoil. Now is that time.

Simply put, consumers are fed up with marketing saturation and intrusiveness, so marketers have the chance to create competitive advantage for their brands through better marketing practices. Better marketing is not just better promotion of a brand, it *is* a better brand.

Marketers who respond to consumer resistance with Precision, Relevance, Power and Reciprocity instead of more marketing saturation and intrusiveness will come out on top. This means customer-centricity in both word and deed, not the process-centricity that characterizes most marketing organizations. Marketers think in terms of the 4P's–product, place, promotion and price—but these are all about marketing processes, not consumers. Marketers must start thinking in terms of consumers, and that means replacing the 4P's with this new combination of P's and R's—P&R^2 ^{SM}. Precision, Relevance, Power and Reciprocity will take marketing to the next level.

P&R^2 provides the four cornerstones of Concurrence Marketing^{SM}. Concurrence means two things. First, it means synchrony or agreement. Second, it means collaboration or cooperation. Precision and Relevance are about getting in agreement or in sync with consumers in both targeting and messaging. Power and Reciprocity are about cooperating or collaborating with consumers in product design and marketing execution. Marketing saturation and intrusiveness are not about concurrence. Only concurrence can build the kinds of customer relationships that are needed to reverse the ongoing declines in marketing productivity.

Marketing productivity is measured as the customer response generated per marketing dollar spent. The consensus of evidence, both anecdotal and quantitative, is clear. Marketing productivity is in rapid decline. A dollar spent today buys less response—and a smaller audience—than the same dollar spent in the past. Many factors are at work:

- Specialized niche media have fragmented the audience, so mass media buying efficiencies have been significantly eroded.
- More competition has diluted the dominance and customer loyalty once enjoyed by many brands, so more must be invested in sustaining relationships.
- People are less dependent upon advertising for information, so advertisers have to invest more to get people to watch and read.

- People are savvier and more knowledgeable about marketing tactics, so constant innovation is required.
- Marketing clutter has significantly increased, forcing marketers to spend more and more in order to be heard above the noise.

Another factor is at work as well: The growing consumer resistance to marketing. Marketing resistance is both a cause and an effect of the current marketplace environment. More fragmentation, competition and clutter have led to more marketing. Barraged with a growing deluge of ever more intrusive marketing, people have begun to adopt ways of insulating themselves from marketing. As consumer resistance has become more widespread and more sophisticated, marketers have saturated the marketplace with even more marketing. This cause and effect has created a destructive feedback loop that is spiraling out of control. As more marketing chases more resistant consumers—or, to put it another way, as spending rises while response declines—marketing productivity deteriorates at an accelerating rate.

Above all else, marketing resistance is the challenge that marketers need to tackle first. Marketing resistance is not the only cause of today's marketing productivity crisis, it is now the single biggest barrier to resolving this crisis.

Most of the attention being paid to declining marketing productivity focuses on rising costs. This is important, but as long as consumers resist marketing, actions to address the other factors affecting marketing productivity will be piecemeal solutions. For example, reaching a fragmented audience in a more efficient way is essential because it reduces costs, but as long as viewers or readers are resisting the marketing that reaches them, declining marketing productivity will remain a problem. Nominal costs (i.e., actual dollars spent) may be reduced, but response will keep dropping.

LOVE HATE

Brands are built on relationships with consumers, and marketing is one of the primary ways in which brands establish and nurture those relationships. Growing consumer resistance to marketing is a red flag about

Figure I.1: **Illustrative Measures of Marketing Performance & Productivity**

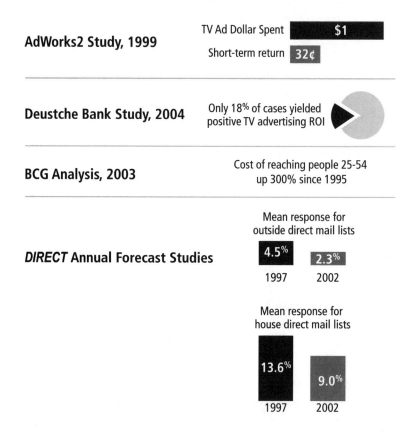

the state of these relationships. Marketing resistance strikes at the very heart of what makes brands strong and valuable.

People have always had a love/hate relationship with marketing and advertising. Even as marketing resistance has grown to epic proportions, people continue to enjoy entertaining ads and fun events sponsored by marketers. Paradoxically, people feel as much affection for marketing as dislike. (Or to put it another way, people love advertising but hate marketing.) This might seem like encouraging news, but it's not. The proper balance between love and hate is a lot of the former and just a little of the latter. And so it was 40-plus years ago. But not any longer.

While people feel the same as ever about the things they love about marketing and advertising, people now feel much more annoyed and aggravated by the things they hate. Intrusiveness is the culprit. Marketing and advertising have remained informative and entertaining while becoming omnipresent to the point of oversaturating every aspect of people's lives. The consumer response to this supersaturation is resistance.

Spammers and telemarketers usually get the blame for marketing resistance. Other marketers support efforts to rein them in. But curbs on spam and telemarketing won't bring an end to marketing resistance. People are just as annoyed with the intrusiveness and oversaturation practiced by traditional marketers and advertisers. People want a fundamentally different kind of exchange with marketers. But most traditional marketers are no more interested in living on a two-way street than are spammers and telemarketers. Yet, a completely new approach is imperative. So, that's what the smartest old-line marketers are working on right now.

THE BROKEN MODEL: BEYOND THE 30-SECOND AD

On February 5, 2003, the former President and COO of the Coca-Cola Company, Steve Heyer, took the stage at the Beverly Hills Hotel to kick off the inaugural *AdAge* Madison & Vine Conference. His keynote address was a marketing manifesto announcing an end to traditional marketing thinking at Coke and proclaiming a new vision of purpose and practice for the future of marketing.

Heyer began by reciting the obligatory litany of challenges facing traditional marketing. As a result, he declared that Coke would no longer turn "reflexively" to TV advertising. TV ads, he said, are no longer the best way to connect with people, so old-style marketing is over. Heyer even cautioned those working in Hollywood and on Music Row to stay away from using traditional marketing for their products lest they, too, get hurt by its declining effectiveness.

Heyer made special mention of consumer resistance, noting that consumers now have an "unrivalled ability" to avoid advertising. With smart consumers in command of the technology to edit or opt out of marketing, Heyer said that the time had come for "transformational" change.

The future of marketing is about ideas, Heyer said, ideas that link consumers with brands through entertainment. Coke is an idea about refreshment and connection. The entertainment vocabulary, not the traditional marketing tag line, is the best language in which to communicate that idea to consumers. At this intersection of Madison and Vine, more collaboration among marketers, agencies and entertainment companies is essential. All must come together around a core idea with the power to inspire passion for a brand among consumers.

Brands must deliver enduring experiences that enrich people's lifestyles beyond the mere act of consuming a product. Brands must touch people at many points, not just during commercial breaks. The only way to do this in the consumer-controlled, experience economy of tomorrow, Heyer said, is to entertain, which is why Heyer called entertainment the "new media."

Heyer's manifesto is not about spam and telemarketing. It is about the failure, if not the utter structural irrelevance, of traditional marketing. Marketing in the old-fashioned way no longer engages people, so people are ignoring it, blocking it and looking elsewhere. Jury-rigged fixes won't help. A complete transformation is needed.

The word out of Coke is that it is time for marketers to start thinking differently about the future of marketing. The same message is coming from no less a company than the venerable Procter & Gamble (P&G)—like Coke, one of the most storied marketing powerhouses of all time.

On February 12, 2004, a year after Heyer's highly publicized speech, Jim Stengel, the Global Marketing Officer of P&G, made his own headlines. Stengel stood on the dais at the Loews Royal Pacific Resort in Orlando, Florida, for the American Association of Advertising Agencies (AAAA) Media Conference and gave the marketing industry a grade of C-minus. Like Heyer, Stengel pulled no punches in declaring that traditional marketing is "obsolete" and "broken." Stengel voiced concern that marketers had made little meaningful progress in coming to terms with that.

In addition to the familiar litany of challenges, Stengel made special note of consumer empowerment and marketing resistance. He was particularly outspoken in his insistence that marketers shift to a permission-based marketing paradigm—not just online marketers and telemarketers, but all marketers. Not only are consumers taking control; consumers should be given *even more control*. Marketing should either be so compelling that consumers ask for it, or it should not be presented to consumers at all. Stengel's acid test for any ad or marketing initiative is whether or not a person would "choose" to watch or view it.

Stengel said that marketers must focus on "life beyond" the 30-second TV spot by connecting with consumers in a holistic way. Stengel cited examples of P&G products for which the marketing support has been shifted away from a total reliance on traditional marketing vehicles. A broader lifestyle focus is needed; and to accomplish this, Stengel, echoing Heyer, called for a collaborative effort that combines the competencies of marketers, agencies and media companies.

As an example of P&G's commitment to new ways of marketing its brands, Stengel cited Tremor, which is a new marketing service developed by P&G to tap into the power of word-of-mouth among teens. Begun in 2001, Tremor uses a proprietary formula to identify influential teens between the ages of 13 and 19 and then recruits them to join Tremor's panel. Tremor panelists are unpaid, but they get lots of samples, merchandise, coupons, and new products. P&G counts on them to spread the word by telling their friends. And P&G relies on them for feedback about new product ideas, logos, packaging copy, and product prototypes. From product inception to launch to on-going management, P&G's whole business approach has changed.

Tremor is now being used by many other companies, too, including Coke, AOL, Kraft, Toyota and the International Dairy Foods Association. Tremor was used in 15 campaigns in 2003 and will be used for 20 in 2004. Sony Electronics even dropped its print and radio ads for Net MD in favor of Tremor word-of-mouth. [1]

Coke is looking outside of traditional marketing as well. Coke Red Lounges are now open in many malls across the country. These are places filled with music, videos and movies—as well as Coke products—that have become gathering places for teens. Coke has stepped up its involvement in sports, music and the Internet. For example, a Web site in Spain enables teens to create a personal virtual apartment. An interactive music Web site in the U.K. called MyCokeMusic.com is second only to Apple's iTunes Web site in terms of number of downloads. MyCokeMusic.com has proven so popular that Coke is rolling it out across Europe.[2]

Skeptics scoff at these experimental efforts by Coke, P&G and others by pointing out that they account for little more than a drop in the bucket of the total marketing spending done by these companies. As things stand today, this is true. But what's more relevant is that Coke and P&G have renounced traditional marketing as part of their future. Their initial efforts today are merely the start of bigger long-term efforts to completely reinvent the model that guides the marketing of their brands.

Indeed, it's the model that's broken. Advertising and marketing vehicles themselves are not so much the problem as the model by which they are put to use. The time has come to tear the existing model down to the ground and lay a new foundation on which to erect a consumer marketing model for the future.

P&R^2 is that new foundation. Concurrence Marketing is the new model.

BOOK TOUR: CONCURRENCE MARKETING AT A GLANCE

This book is about the core principles of Concurrence Marketing that must guide marketing in the future as well as the specific marketing capabilities and tools needed to make these ideas work.

- Chapter 1 digs into the growing consumer resistance to marketing. The scope of resistance and its impact on marketing are reviewed. Additionally, the results of a special study on marketing resistance conducted by Yankelovich Partners in early 2004 are presented and explored in detail.
- Chapters 2 through 5 describe the new consumer priorities that are fundamentally reshaping people's expectations and lifestyles. These changes are not wholly compatible with the sort of marketing that has enjoyed a heyday since the end of World War II. Understanding the new consumer is the essential first step in making marketing more productive. Findings from the Yankelovich MONITOR®, the longest running tracking of consumer values and lifestyles, are included.[3] Chapter 2 reviews trends affecting targeting precision. Chapter 3 reviews

trends affecting message and product relevance. Chapter 4 reviews trends affecting the balance of power between consumers and marketers. And Chapter 5 reviews trends related to the reciprocal value that people expect in exchange for their scarce time and attention. In short, these four chapters are about the trends giving rise to the need to shift to a Concurrence Marketing approach rooted in the principles of P&R².

- Chapters 6 and 7 introduce the outlines of the new Concurrence Marketing model. Chapter 6 examines the impact of consumer resistance on marketing productivity and critiques saturation-oriented marketing approaches. The strengths and weaknesses of other new approaches like permission marketing are examined as well. In Chapter 7, the results of a special study into the marketing beliefs and attitudes of marketing directors conducted by Yankelovich Partners in 2004 are reviewed in detail. The attitudes of consumers and marketers are contrasted and the gap between expectations and performance is assessed for insights into making marketing more productive.

Chapter 7 also presents the basic concepts of Concurrence Marketing. The four cornerstones of Concurrence Marketing are better marketing *Precision*, better marketing *Relevance*, more *Power* for consumers, and more *Reciprocity* for consumers. Although these four things may sound familiar, the familiarity is in name only. As will be evident, the four things called for here represent far-reaching changes in current marketing practice. This chapter contrasts the old model with the new model and introduces the tools of Addressable Attitudes[SM] and Insights Integration[SM] that are needed to make this shift in marketing practice. Currently, companies do marketing research, build customer databases, rent prospect files, and so forth, and then analyze each separately, as if they were not about the same consumers. Insights Integration entails the systems, skills and organizational philosophies it takes to craft a complete and integrated picture of consumers. Not just integrating data, but integrating insights and having smarter ideas about what to do by putting behavioral and demographic data in perspective. Addressable Attitudes are attitudes linked to specific names and addresses. Addressable Attitudes enable direct marketers to move beyond the limitations of ignoring attitudes for lack of addressability and they enable brand marketers to apply what they know about attitudes in more productive, execution-oriented ways. Since Addressable Attitudes are a completely new breakthrough in marketing capabilities, relevant details about modeling and analytics are provided.

- Chapters 8 through 11 lay out specific opportunities for doing more productive marketing that responds to new consumer values and priorities. Marketing productivity can only be restored by following the new principles tied to P&R^2, Insights Integration and Addressable Attitudes. Detailed case studies are presented to show how smart marketers have been able to capture competitive advantage by utilizing the principles and tools of Concurrence Marketing. Chapter 8 presents opportunities and case studies related to marketing precision. Chapter 9 does the same for marketing relevance. Chapter 10 discusses opportunities and case studies related to consumer power. Chapter 11 focuses on consumer reciprocity.

- Chapter 12 pulls together the lessons and information presented in this book into a summary of key requirements for Concurrence Marketing. This is not a paint-by-numbers model. Marketing is always more complicated than that, no matter what principles are guiding the process. This chapter provides a list of reminders about what's needed for marketers to re-engage resistant consumers through Concurrence Marketing.

This book articulates a point of view that has been percolating within Yankelovich for several years. Yankelovich has been closely monitoring the evolution of the marketplace and has seen that a different way of thinking is required. In response to client needs and the new shape of the marketplace, the company itself has moved beyond merely tracking trends and now offers a variety of full-blown marketing solutions "to deliver measurable breakthroughs in marketing productivity for our clients." In fact, that is the Yankelovich mission statement verbatim.

Yankelovich has restructured its lines of business around a single-minded corporate focus on delivering marketing productivity solutions because that is the biggest issue facing marketers in the years ahead.

However, while this book draws on relevant client experience and research knowledge, it is not a capabilities presentation for Yankelovich. This book pulls together the insights and thinking of many different observers, both inside and outside Yankelovich, to provide an overarching synthesis of what needs to be done to make marketing more productive.

TRUTH BE TOLD

Marketers are out of sync with consumers—not because of bad products but because of bad practice. This reality is no less true for small businesses than for multinational corporations, no less relevant for impulse purchases than for major purchases, no less applicable to pharmaceutical companies than to consumer packaged goods companies. The way consumers want to hear from marketers is not the way marketers talk to consumers. As a result, disharmony prevails and declining marketing productivity is the result.

When marketers hear this kind of criticism, they tend to focus on the bad news and get defensive. That's shortsighted. There is huge potential in today's marketplace. All the things that people dislike represent new business opportunities. Indeed, it has always been that way in marketing. Bad products create opportunities for better products. So, too, does bad marketing create opportunities for better marketing. The bigger the problems, the bigger the opportunities.

Concurrence Marketing is both completely different from traditional marketing and just the same as traditional marketing. Getting in sync with consumers is what marketers have always tried to do, but the feedback from consumers today is that the old-school ideas of Precision and Relevance need polishing up. The challenge, though, is that standard marketing practice works against Precision and Relevance by encouraging saturation and intrusiveness. So, to re-learn the old lessons of Precision and Relevance, marketers must first break some bad habits.

At the same time, marketers will have to learn two new things: Power and Reciprocity. This means unlearning old lessons as well as breaking bad habits. The consumer who was happy for marketers to be in control and to offer nothing in return for the time spent with marketing is no more. Yet, the one-way model persists even in marketing that professes to be cutting edge. Online pop-up ads are just more of the same force-fed communication. Targeted TV (also known as addressable TV) is nothing but a better address book unless new principles guide how it is used. Beware of marketing innovations that go knocking on consumers' doors with the same old heavy hand. They don't provide opportunities, only the same old wine in a new bottle.

There are new tools to master in making this shift to Concurrence Marketing. Attitudes need to be addressable parts of marketing execution systems. Insights need to be integrated into marketing processes. Otherwise, the same old marketing saturation and intrusiveness will continue to create consumer resistance and reduce marketing productivity.

Information technology has forever changed the marketplace. The traditional marketing models were built to sell to consumers who had no voice and no control. That consumer is now a relic, so the old marketing models are, too. Today's networked consumers are re-engaged with other consumers in conversations that are instantaneous, hyperlinked and highly informed, and becoming more so every day. Because people are able to talk to other people so much more easily, product owners and interested buyers often know more about a product than the company that makes it. Because people have the ability to control the media they use, new expectations and new relationships rule the marketplace.

Businesses that continue to lecture rather than learn to converse will face an uphill battle against more resistance, not to mention more sophisticated resistance. Fighting this resistance will sap the productivity from marketing—more spending chasing declining response. People want to be treated with respect, which means not overwhelming people with imprecise and irrelevant clutter. It also means offering people Power and Reciprocity. It means addressing marketing only to people with the right attitudes. And it means practicing marketing based upon insights about people. Insights about people as they live their lives, not about people as consumers. Insights about lifestyles, not shopping styles. Insights about treating people as people, not as category users.

People are not marketing constructs. They live rich lives lush with connections, commitments, dreams, aspirations and everyday practicalities. The most powerful brands are those that resonate with people in their lives, not those that talk down to people as if they were a category user or a media demographic. As advertising great David Ogilvy once famously remarked, "The consumer is not an idiot, she is your wife."

Marketing constructs have an insidious tendency to make marketers forget that consumers are people. For example, everybody uses soap (we hope), but no one thinks of himself or herself as just a soap user. Yet, that's how soap marketers often look at people. Similarly, spray cleaner marketers look at many of the same people, but see them only as spray cleaner users. Automobile manufacturers see the same people only as car buyers. Restaurants see the same people only as diners. And so on. People use all of these products, and more, not because people are category users but because people live full, rich lives and these products enhance their lifestyles.

The problem is that the model guiding marketing thinking is driven by constructs. People want to shop and buy, but people do not want to be marketed to as constructs—as consumers of some category of goods and services. Instead, people want to shop and buy in ways that make them collaborators in the creation of meaning in their lives. And if marketers won't cooperate, then people will continue to resist.

Lifestyles matter more than ever in designing effective marketing programs, and concurrence not saturation or intrusiveness is the appropriate design. Marketers must provide Precision, Relevance, Power and Reciprocity. Marketers must master Addressable Attitudes and Insights Integration. Marketers must practice the art and science of what they do in ways that engender engagement not resistance. Because this is the only way of making marketing more productive.

NOTES

1 Melanie Wells, "Kid Nabbing," *Forbes*, February 2, 2004.

2 Dean Foust with Brian Grow, "Coke: Wooing the TiVo Generation," *Business Week*, March 1, 2004; and Shelley Emling, "Coke Site a Hit in Europe," *The Atlanta Journal-Constitution*, July 14, 2004.

3 The Yankelovich MONITOR was launched in 1971. A two-hour door-to-door interview, with an additional leave-behind to be completed overnight, among 2,500 nationally representative respondents is

conducted between January and March each year. Additionally, five times each year, telephone re-contact interviews are completed with nationally representative subsamples of the original sample. MONITOR covers a wide range of consumer values ranging from attitudes about brands, shopping and leisure to opinions about family, self and spirituality. Additionally, the AmeriLINK® consumer data file of KnowledgeBase Marketing® has been merged with the MONITOR data to provide a unique and comprehensive database of information on attitudes, behaviors, demographics and lifestyles. MONITOR is reported in an annual State of the Consumer management summary as well as weekly MONITOR Minute emails and bimonthly MONITOR LIVE teleconferences. The MONITOR consulting group also delivers proprietary analyses and marketing solutions. MONITOR clients include all types of businesses, but consist primarily of Fortune 500 consumer marketing companies and marketing services firms.

SECTION I
The World to Come

Marketing Smog

Too often, saturation tactics are the knee-jerk response by marketers to competition, clutter and resistance. But consumers, barraged with a growing deluge of ever more intrusive marketing, have begun to adopt ways of insulating themselves from marketing. Consumers do not want an end to marketing; they want better marketing. Consumers are demanding a different marketing model.

2003 was a tough year for marketers, noteworthy for one day in particular. On Friday, June 27, 2003, President George W. Bush stood in the White House Rose Garden with Federal Trade Commission Chairman Timothy Muris and Federal Communications Commission Chairman Michael Powell to announce the opening of the Federal Do-Not-Call Registry. Denouncing "the stranger with the sales pitch" who interrupts dinner or a parent reading to his or her child, President Bush called telemarketing "intrusive" and "annoying" and declared, "We're taking practical action to address this problem." The symbolism of announcing the Do-Not-Call Registry in the Rose Garden was unmistakable: Stopping unwanted telemarketing calls has become a top national priority, commanding attention at the seat of world power—not to mention, perhaps, that leading the charge against telemarketers is now a popular political position that wins votes.

The public response to the opening of the Federal Do-Not-Call Registry was immediate and overwhelming. Within the first two hours,

250,000 numbers had been registered either at a special Web site or via a toll-free number. By noon the first day, 370,000 numbers had been registered and the Web site was being hit 1,000 times a second. In the first 14 hours, registration was up to 635,000 numbers. By the end of four days, 10 million numbers had been registered—an average rate of 29 numbers per second. Response was so strong that the system itself was nearly swamped. But despite any problems people may have had in getting through, they refused to give up.

Over 62 million numbers were registered in the first 12 months, a figure roughly equivalent to the 66 million people who buy something from telemarketers each year. Dislike for telemarketing is not confined to a small cult of raving anticonsumerism activists; it's a widely held opinion, even among marketers themselves.

Of course, the antipathy that people feel toward telemarketers is nothing new. Results from a survey conducted by Yankelovich in 1999 on the eve of the new millennium found telemarketers tied with Jerry Springer as the number one thing that people wanted to leave behind in the old millennium, with 73 percent saying so.

THE REAL MESSAGE LEFT BY "DO NOT CALL"

It's not just telemarketing that people find intrusive and annoying; it's all forms of direct marketing. Research completed for *DIRECT* magazine by Yankelovich in 2003 found that well over 80 percent feel inundated by all forms of direct marketing including direct mail and email and that more than 60 percent regard the sale of mailing lists as a serious invasion of privacy.

And it's not just direct marketing; it's all forms of marketing. For example, when asked in the Yankelovich MONITOR about things needing more government regulation, advertising is right up there in the top five along with four things that can kill—air pollution, water pollution, toxic waste and nuclear safety.

Survey results like these might tempt one to conclude that people have come to a life-and-death view about dealing with advertising and marketing. Yet, the situation in the consumer marketplace is more complicated than that.

Certainly, people are outspoken in their loathing for highly intrusive marketing that assaults them with a nonstop barrage of come-ons and high-pressure arm-twisting. But nobody wants to put the brakes on the marketplace. People just want to be able to shop without having to fend off a constant barrage of marketing. Pushy, hard-sell marketing means more disruptions and irritations for people who are already pressed for time and, oftentimes, under lots of stress. So, over the past few years a new perspective has been bubbling up about the best way to deal with marketers and advertisers, a view that sometimes boils over into the kind of fierce response precipitated by the opening of the Federal Do-Not-Call Registry.

THE SOCIALIZATION OF MARKETING RESISTANCE

People have always had a love/hate relationship with marketing and advertising. But lately, public sentiment has gotten much worse at the hate end of the continuum, making it a lot harder and a lot more expensive for marketers and advertisers to continue with business as usual.

Resistance to marketing has moved from the fringe to the mainstream. Marketing resistance is something that everybody does and thus something that people have come to see as normal. The irony is that this growing disaffection with marketing has created a growing opportunity to market products to resist marketing. The list is as extensive as the kinds of marketing media: audio signals to disrupt telemarketing calls; digital video recorders that enable viewers to skip commercials; satellite radio that broadcasts without commercials; spam killers; pop-up ad blockers; information services about intrusive ads and marketing; and, as they used to say in those late-night commercials, much, much more.

The consumer shift from passive consumption to active involvement and resistance is a profound change in the marketplace. In an August 2, 2004 *Business Week* story on the marketplace phenomenon of "Cult Brands" and the consumer passion associated with them, Peter Weedfald, Senior Vice President for strategic marketing and new media at consumer electronics company Samsung, was quoted as saying, "Consumers are empowered in a way that's frightening"—frightening, indeed, for traditional marketing practice.[1]

Marketers of all sorts are vulnerable. Marketers have always taken it for granted that the general reaction to marketing and advertising would be engagement and interest. Nowadays, resistance is an increasingly likely reaction. And the tipping point was reached in 2003.

The DMA worried aloud that the 2003 Do-Not-Call Registry would be the first step down a slippery slope of regulations and restrictions. This prescient observation came to life later that year when the growing outrage over intrusive marketing finally prodded regulators and legislators to take additional action.

At year's end, on December 16, 2003, President Bush signed into law the CAN-SPAM Act (Controlling the Assault of Non-Solicited Pornography and Marketing Act of 2003). While this law has been heavily criticized as watered down and insufficient, it was another step down the slippery slope of regulation in response to marketing resistance. The greatest significance of the CAN-SPAM Act wasn't its existence as much as the timing: 2003 was the year in which the amount of spam being transmitted each day finally exceeded the amount of legitimate email.

Other anti-spam efforts during 2003 were even more aggressive. State Attorneys General in Missouri and New York filed high-profile lawsuits against spammers and the Attorney General in Virginia filed felony charges against two of the most prolific spammers. Microsoft, AOL, Earthlink and Yahoo, among others, filed dozens of private lawsuits against spammers. In his annual address to the Comdex technology show in Las Vegas on November 16, 2003, Bill Gates promised more far powerful software tools from Microsoft to battle spam.

In 2004, more high-profile lawsuits by big Internet service providers were filed. And to beef up efforts against spammers, consideration was being given to paying bounties to people who reveal to authorities the identities of spammers breaking the law.

On another front, the HIPAA (Health Insurance and Portability Accountability Act of 1996) Privacy Rule went into effect on April 14, 2003, requiring stricter protection of the privacy of all health-related consumer-specific data, requirements that affect marketers as much as health care providers. Every visit to the doctor since then has included a few extra minutes in the waiting room reviewing and signing a form acknowledging receipt of notification of that physician's new privacy policies and procedures.

During 2003 marketing practices as a whole came under greater scrutiny because of public health concerns about the epidemics of obesity and diabetes, especially among children. Not since the heyday of the public health debates about tobacco have marketers been under such a powerful microscope. Peter Jennings sharpened the edge of the public health debate about obesity in an hour-long *Primetime Monday* special that aired December 8, 2003 entitled "How to Get Fat Without Really Trying." Jennings examined agricultural subsidies and marketing practices. He argued that food marketers introduce many more products that are bad for people than are good for people. And he suggested that by increasing the number and size of their products, food marketers have actively encouraged people to overeat, especially kids.

Jennings concluded that parents are "outnumbered and outfinanced by marketers." As a result, Jennings wondered whether children shouldn't be protected from advertising for unhealthy foods just as they are shielded from cigarette advertising. This is precisely the sort of rallying cry that many people are ready and willing to take up because it resonates with their increasingly aggressive sensibility of marketing resistance.

Surveying the flood of legislation and the burgeoning marketplace of products designed for marketing resistance, the words of Ted Levitt, the emeritus marketing guru at the Harvard Business School, come to mind: "Customers don't buy products. They buy solutions to problems."[2] This is the most important insight ever penned about marketing, and it is the way to understand the attitudes people have about marketing today. With so many marketing resistance products now available for sale, it is apparent that many people have come to see marketing as a problem in need of solution.

MARKETING SATURATION

It's not difficult to understand why people feel like they are under siege by marketers. Figures vary, but in the 1970s it is estimated that the average person was targeted by 500 to 2,000 ads each day. The latest estimate is 3,000 to 5,000 per day. The top end of this 30-year increase is an astounding 10-fold boom in daily ad exposure from 500 to 5,000. But even the smallest estimated increase from 2,000 to 3,000 is still a very sizable

50 percent growth in daily exposure to marketing and advertising. These growth figures are hard to fathom until one thinks about all of the places where brand logos, promotions and ads show up these days, including:

> Network television. Cable television. Public television. Broadcast radio. Magazines. Newspapers. Free shoppers. Pagers. PDAs. Cell phones. Billboards. DVDs. Neon signs. Email. Popups. Faxes. Matchbook covers. Ticket stubs. Theater programs. Car valet receipts. Turnstile handles. Floor mats. Mugs. Caps. Mouse pads. Napkins. Ashtrays. Pens. Pencils. Notepads. City buses. Bus stops. Hanging straps. Taxicabs, inside and out. Racecars. Race tracks. Sports arenas. Bowling alleys. Watches. Currency. Shopping bags. Shopping carts. Receipts. Postcards. Bulletin boards. Municipal buildings. Classrooms. School cafeterias. School buses. Crawls. Utility poles. Sidewalk graffiti. T-shirts. Sweatshirts. Team uniforms. Jockey's pants. Tattoos. Waiting rooms. Theater lobbies. Movie previews. Videotapes. Blimps. Hot air balloons. Skywriting. Decals. Bumper stickers. Bar windows. Store windows. Restaurant menus. Egg cartons. Stadium seats. Airport gates. Airplane seats. Airline ticket jackets. Urinals. Bathroom stalls. Highway rest stops. Web sites. Floor tiles. Credit cards. Elevators. Gas pumps. Yard signs. Sports arenas. Office buildings. Farm animals. Pets. Passenger cars with specialty paint jobs or magnetic signs. Telephones. Telephone books. Telephone booths. Delivery vehicles. Golf balls. Golf tees. Golf holes. Video games. ATMs. To mention just a few.[3]

A famous Atlanta adman, Joel Babbitt, once lamented the unutilized billboard space on the sides of the stray dogs wandering the streets of Atlanta, adding in passing that Newfoundlands ought to be able to command a higher rate than Chihuahuas because the brand name could be bigger. Apparently, an Amsterdam agency, StrawberryFrog, saw the same opportunity because it used so-called dogvertising throughout Europe as a way to promote the 2002 introduction of the Sony Ericsson T300 cell phone.

When Babbitt was running marketing for the 1996 Olympics in Atlanta, he proposed promoting the games with a gigantic metallic billboard placed into geosynchronous orbit around the Earth that would be visible to three-quarters of the world's population for several hours every day. His idea was quickly shelved, but don't bet against it in the long run.

Indeed, don't bet against every available blank space, no matter how unusual or insignificant, getting covered with an ad or a brand logo (Fig. 1.1). A New Jersey company called Beach'n Billboards imprints ads and logos onto long stretches of sand at popular beaches. In 1999, Casa Sanchez, a San Francisco Mission District restaurant, offered free lunch for life to anyone willing to get a permanent tattoo of its Jimmy the Cornman logo. In 2000, a Kansas couple received $5,000 from an online music company called the Internet Underground Music Archive for naming their newborn son Iuma, which is the acronym for the company's name. At least three couples have named their newborns Espn, after the ESPN cable channel.

Even food isn't safe from marketing. An industrial designer has invented a toaster wired to the Internet that sears an icon with the day's weather forecast onto people's toast. A sun, a cloud or a raindrop. It won't be too long before brand logos and promotions start showing up on people's breakfast foods.

When blank spaces can't be found, they are created. Many radio stations now use a system called Cash that compresses the running time of shows through real-time editing of silent spots and pauses, thereby freeing up to six more minutes per hour for commercials. Not to be outdone, TV sports broadcasters now project digital images of brand logos onto playing fields and sideline barricades.

Additionally, TV networks and radio stations keep chipping away at programming time to make room for more commercials. Over the past several years, a minute or more has been carved out of programming time in each TV daypart. Similarly, during the last decade, radio stations have increased the number of commercial minutes each hour from 10 to 12 minutes to as many as 24 minutes, with most stations playing over 15 minutes of commercials each hour.[4]

Although TV networks eventually reach a limit on the number of ads that can be broadcast, they can still offer product placements within shows for more advertising opportunities. In 2002, ABC and Revlon went

Fig. 1.1: **A Marketing Bag**

In advance of the race, pre-registrants for the 2004 Cooper River Bridge Run in Charleston, SC, April 3, 2004, received a plastic bag in the mail. On one side of the bag were the brand logos for race sponsors Chick-fil-A and Bi-Lo. On the other side of the bag were the brand logo and tagline for local newspaper sponsor *The Post and Courier*. The bag was filled with:

- A **race bib** and four safety pins.
- A **timer chip**.
- A **t-shirt** with the Chick-fil-A and Bi-Lo logos underneath the 2004 race design on the front and logos on the back for Chick-fil-A, Bi-Lo, Principal Financial Group, *The Post and Courier*, Aquafina, Prevecare, and Sprint.
- An **informational paper** with the Chick-fil-A and Bi-Lo logos on the front , an ad for *The Post and Courier* on the back, and a race graphic on the back with brand logos overlaid on it for Chick-fil-A, Bi-Lo, Principal Financial Group, *The Post and Courier*, Prevecare, Sprint, Aquafina, Fazoli's, Wachovia, Boston Bill, Ion, SpiritLine Cruises, Imax, Fountain Walk, Gilligan's Steamers and Raw Bar, Fit For Sports, The Sportman's Shop, Try Sports, One More Mile running, Hurricane Marketing Group, WCSC Channel 5, Bayer, the Medical University of South Carolina, Sabre Advertising, National Sporting Goods, R&M Sporting Goods, Sports N More, and Outback Steakhouse.
- An **informational piece** with a **coupon** for Bayer aspirin.
- A **coupon** for The Extra Mile.
- A **coupon** for Fazoli's.
- A **coupon** for The Terrace.
- A **coupon** for California Dreaming.
- A **coupon** for EAS AdvantEdge Carb Control Bars, only good at Bi-Lo.
- A **coupon** for Gilligan's Steamers and Raw Bar.
- A **coupon** for Subway.
- A **coupon** for Try Sports providing a choice of one of three promotional offers.
- A **coupon** for Sunfire Grill and Bistro.
- A **coupon** for Carolina Ice Palace.
- A **coupon** for Cisco's Café.
- A **bookmark** for Prevent Child Abuse South Carolina, listing the names, phone numbers and cities of its 10 affiliates in the state.
- One Pinnacle Jeff Gordon **trading card** with a Pepsi brand logo.
- A paper **door hanger** for Reliv.
- A **promotional piece** with a return card for more information about Viagra from Pfizer.
- A **promotional piece** for Hibby Runs the City Blindfolded benefitting the Association for the Blind, with brand logos for Superior Transportation and Coast 92.5 FM.
- A **promotional piece** announcing a drawing at the Piccolo Spoleto Custom House Concert for a Mercedes Benz from Baker Motors, with proceedings benefitting the Charleston Symphony Orchestra.
- A **promotional piece** for the Savannah River Bridge Run, sponsored by Enmark and accepting online registration at www.active.com, with more information available from a person at Fleet Feet Savannah.
- A **promotional piece** folded in half with "Important Information Inside" and "Do Not Discard" printed on both sides announcing a weekly contest for a cash prize at the race's Lead Car sponsor, Palmetto Car & Truck, with brand logos for each of the Palmetto Car & Truck Group companies – Palmetto Ford, Palmetto Mazda, Palmetto Jaguar, Mama's Used Cars, Thrifty Car Sales and Featherlite Trailers.
- An **application** for the Myrtle Beach Marathon, Relay, 5K and Fun Run, with brand logos for race sponsors NASCAR Speed Park, RBC Centura, Ripley's Aquarium, Bi-Lo, Dasani, Myrtle Beach Trips and House of Blues, along with the Myrtle Beach city seal.
- An **application** for the Virginia Beach Rock 'N' Roll Marathon, with logos for the State of Virginia, the city of Virginia Beach, Reebok, SunTrust, Jabra, Geico Direct, GNC, Power Bar and Avis, with announcements of other races and events including P.F. Chang's Rock 'N' Roll Arizona, the Country Music Marathon & Half-Marathon, the Suzuki Rock 'N' Roll Marathon and the Verizon Wireless American Music Festival.
- A one-half ounce **sample** of John Frieda Sheer Blonde volumizing spray.
- An 8 milliliter **sample** of Biore.
- A **sample** pack of four spearmint Altoids.
- An 8.8 milliliter **sample** of Bullfrog.
- A **sample** pack of one Biore Cleanse blemish fighting cleansing cloths.
- A **sample** pack of one Aleve caplet.
- One 25 gram **sample** size Balance gold energy bar.
- A 2.8 gram **sample** of Icy Hot.
- Two **samples** of Wyler's Light powdered drink mix, one for Lemoade flavor and one for Cool Raspberry flavor.

! That's **30-plus** branded items in the bag, with **over 100** product, brand and organizational logos and mentions.

a step further and in a deal worth millions, arranged for Revlon to be written into the storyline of ABC's popular soap opera "All My Children."

These examples barely scratch the surface, and this recitation could go on and on; but it only takes a few examples like these to see clearly the essence of marketing as it is practiced today. It is all about dominating consumers and the marketplace by saturating people with marketing and advertising everywhere they turn. What begins as a straightforward, textbook effort to create exposure for a brand quickly degenerates into an out-of-control feedback loop in which every successive level of marketing exposure and saturation has to be trumped by an even greater level of saturation. The end result is a marketplace filled with ever more marketing messages shouting ever louder to be heard above an ever more deafening cacophony of competing voices. Eventually, all that people can hear is a piercing din of noise, so after searching the dial and finding nothing agreeable, people just give up and turn it off. Marketing saturation leads inevitably to marketing resistance.

Precise targeting and relevant messages are the two fundamental elements of good marketing. A saturation approach flies in the face of such good practice because it is about domination, with little or no regard for precision; hence, relevance falls by the wayside as well. Moreover, a saturation approach presumes that marketers are in control and that almost all of the value accrues to marketers. Nowadays, though, people want greater power and reciprocity. And they can get it.

It goes without saying, of course, that alienating people runs counter to everything that marketers hope to accomplish. But the intense, rising competition for people's limited time, attention and budgets leads even marketers with the best intentions down a troubled path. All kinds of marketers, not just the most intrusive spammers and telemarketers find saturation too tempting to resist.

2004 YANKELOVICH MONITOR STUDY ON MARKETING RESISTANCE

Marketing resistance is widespread and growing. Yet, little research has studied this phenomenon directly. A groundbreaking MONITOR Omni-Plus study[5] provides marketers with a baseline understanding of consumer attitudes toward marketing practices.[6]

This study examined marketing practice from a marketing perspective. The objective was to look at marketing in the same way that marketers look at any other product or service. What are people's needs, wants, dissatisfactions, complaints and aspirations with respect to marketing? Given that, what can marketers do to meet those needs and wants, and what must they do to remedy those dissatisfactions and complaints? How can marketers make marketing practice fit the ways in which people aspire to live their lives? What is the opportunity for greater marketing success from improvements in marketing practice?

This study wasn't undertaken to look for justification for restricting marketing. The purpose of the study was to identify the things that marketers can do to make marketing better, thereby making marketing more productive. The essential first step is identifying and owning up to the problems and weaknesses that keep marketing from realizing its full potential. This can be difficult for marketers, though, because it is hard to look for the silver lining in the dark storm cloud when that cloud is thundering directly overhead.

Marketers fear that bad news about marketing will be misinterpreted and misused, perhaps even opening the door for more regulation. But the regulatory train has already left the station, so the best way to keep it from stopping at Madison Avenue is to confront the evidence head on and fix the problems, not to mention to take advantage of the opportunities for progress and growth; i.e., to be the solution, not the problem. It is worth remembering that there is always enduring competitive advantage to be had whenever there is widespread consumer discontent. For savvy marketers, this bad news is a great opportunity.

Advertising agencies and other marketing services firms have always been very good at coaxing their clients into facing up to bad news about their products and services and then coaching them about what to do to create good news. This same discipline is needed when it comes to marketing practice. Agencies must do for themselves what they do so brilliantly for their clients.

The urgency for a new approach is immediately apparent in the results of the 2004 MONITOR study on marketing resistance. The overwhelming majority of respondents expressed a negative opinion about marketing. Sixty percent agreed that their opinion of marketing and advertising has become much more negative than it was just a few years ago. Sixty-one percent said that the amount of marketing and advertising has gotten out of control. Seventy percent said that they tune out advertising more than they did just a few years ago.

Even worse, a sizable percentage of respondents said that marketing and advertising are a detriment to their quality of life. Forty-five percent said that the amount of marketing they are exposed to detracts from their experience of everyday life, and 36 percent said that their shopping experiences are less enjoyable because of all the pressure to buy. Even benign marketing gets hurt by association in today's marketplace. Fifty-three percent of respondents said that spam has turned them off to all forms of marketing and advertising.

A basis of comparison is available from a major study completed on behalf of the AAAA in 1964 regarding attitudes toward advertising.[7] The Yankelovich research did not use the same question as the 1964 AAAA study. Instead, a measure of overall opinions was calculated from four multidimensional scales. Two scales measured favorable attitudes: Positive Scale and Empowering Scale. Two scales measured unfavorable attitudes: Annoyance Scale and Resistance Scale. People with high scores on both favorable scales and low scores on both unfavorable scales were counted as having a wholly positive view. People with high scores on both unfavorable scales and low scores on both favorable scales were counted as having a wholly negative view.

While a direct comparison of the 1964 AAAA study to the 2004 Yankelovich study is complicated by differences in data collection, question wording and scaling, a worsening of opinions is unmistakably clear nevertheless. The percentage with mixed opinions did not change, but the percentage holding a positive attitude declined and the percentage holding a negative attitude increased substantially (Fig. 1.2).

The reason for this worsening of attitudes is no mystery. It is the exponentially greater level of marketing saturation and intrusiveness. Again, the 1964 AAAA study provides an illuminating base of comparison (Fig. 1.3).

Both studies found respondents mentioning the same two principal benefits from marketing and advertising—the social benefit of helping the economy and the personal benefit of providing useful information. And while perceptions of the information value of advertising have increased somewhat from 1964 to 2004, the top dislike has increased significantly.

Figure 1.2: **Overall Attitudes About Marketing**

1964 AAAA Advertising Attitudes Survey		2004 Yankelovich MONITOR Marketing Resistance Survey	
Favorable view	**41**%	**28**%	Wholly positive
Mixed view	**34**%	**36**%	Neutral/mixed view
Unfavorable view	**14**%	**36**%	Wholly negative

Figure 1.3: **What Makes Marketing Good and Bad**

1964 AAAA Advertising Attitudes Survey		2004 Yankelovich MONITOR Marketing Resistance Survey	
BENEFITS:			
Advertising raises our standard of living	**71**%	**75**%	Marketing and advertising are good for the economy
Reasons why people like advertising: Information-related reasons	**57**%	**68**%	Marketing and advertising give me useful ideas about how to make my life better
DISADVANTAGES:			
Reasons why people dislike advertising: Intrusiveness	**40**%	**65**%	Constantly bombarded with too much marketing and advertising

Clutter and intrusiveness have grown, so, unsurprisingly, the percentage of respondents citing this dislike has also grown by a sizable amount.

The fervor with which people are resisting means that the impact on marketing productivity is considerable. Sixty percent of respondents described themselves as a person who tries to resist or avoid being exposed to marketing and advertising. Sixty-nine percent said that they were interested in products to block, skip or opt out of exposure to marketing and advertising. Or to put this finding another way, the size of the market for marketing resistance products is seven out of ten people.

Consumer resistance to marketing is a defining characteristic of today's marketplace. Contrast the overwhelming percentages of self-confessed resisters in the 2004 Yankelovich survey with the mere 15 percent in the 1964 AAAA study who held the ardent opinion, somewhat comparable to today's resistance, that advertising needed attention and change.[8]

The proper way to look at these findings is not to dwell on the negatives. Rather, it is to look for the opportunities to capture competitive advantage by delivering what consumers want and need. After all, this is how marketing works. Marketers solve problems for consumers, and there's no reason why this shouldn't apply to marketing practice as much as to products and services. Concurrence Marketing is the new model for competitive advantage.

THE MODEL IS BROKEN

Consumer resistance to marketing is not simply about bad marketing. Bad marketing makes it worse, but the basic way in which marketing works—the model—is at the root of consumer resistance. The saturation tactics of domination are standard marketing practice. So is intrusiveness, yet this is the very thing that consumers dislike the most. So, consumer resistance is not symptomatic of bad marketing; it's symptomatic of all marketing following the current marketing model.

Indeed, more often than not, bad marketing is nothing but standard marketing practice carried to an extreme. Spammers and telemarketers follow the same principles of interruption and intrusiveness that all marketers follow. Spammers and telemarketers are just more aggressive when putting these principles into action. The challenge is not bad marketing per se but the marketing model itself.

The results from the 2004 Yankelovich study show that marketing resistance has moved beyond the passive resistance that is a standard element of the current marketing model. Self-selection is expected, which is why marketing saturation and intrusiveness are normal practice. If people don't care to watch an ad or some other form of marketing, the marketing model assumes that they will just ignore it. Saturation and intrusiveness are designed to penetrate this veil of indifference and disinterest.

Even 40 years ago, though, this assumption was being challenged. In their book on the 1964 AAAA results, Bauer and Greyser referenced pioneering work by Bauer demonstrating that people are active processors of advertising, which often leads to outcomes that advertisers don't anticipate or desire. Active involvement has increased substantially since the early 1960s as marketing saturation and intrusiveness have increased. Nowadays, people aren't simply turning away or driving a hard bargain; they are taking active steps to close off the channels of communication. The marketing costs to reopen channels or to develop new pathways severely impact marketing productivity. Put it another way: The old marketing rule-of-thumb that it costs five times as much to sell to a new customer as it does to make a repeat sale offers an interesting, even if unsettling, measure of the real cost of causing customers to tune out because of saturation marketing.

The prevailing marketing model does not operate to engage people in active relationships. Instead, marketing saturation and intrusiveness are undertaken to overwhelm people in order to dominate their reactions and behaviors. Most marketers don't think of their actions as browbeating consumers, of course. Marketers value consumer goodwill. But the one-way flow of communications and control in the standard marketing model entails a presumption of domination that does not readily accommodate active involvement and interaction (Fig. 1.4).

Marketers act as if they were involved in a game of wits. It's all about cunning and craftiness, not empathy and concern. No surprise, then, that consumers play it as a game, too. The problem for marketers is that they can't outwit consumers anymore.

The current marketing model has worked well in the past, but its days are numbered. Going forward, the current model will suffer from a continuing decline in productivity because the conditions underlying its past success are long gone. The most important change is the impact of technology. In the past, no matter what people felt about marketing and advertising, they lacked the means to do anything about it because marketers had all the power. Technology has completely changed that, yet the marketing model that continues to guide marketing practice is based upon the old balance of power.

To put it even more strongly, absent the new technologies of marketing resistance, there would be no crisis of marketing productivity. Whatever dissatisfaction people may have had for marketing in the past, there was little they could do about it. But the technologies to resist marketing

Figure 1.4: **From Dominion to Concurrence**

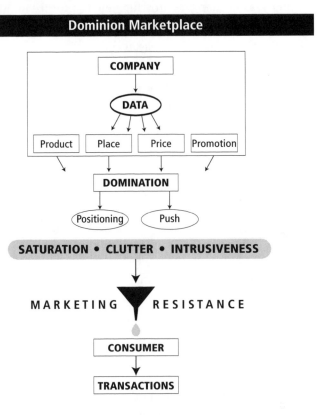

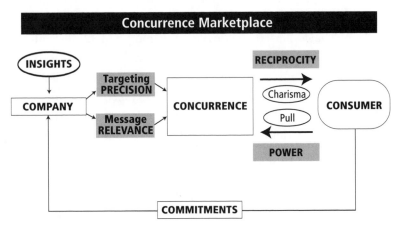

have changed that forever. And these technologies will only get better, if for no other reason than the growing demand for them. Marketers who fight resistance with more saturation and intrusiveness will lose the battle against the technologies of resistance.

Indeed, these technologies have raised the bar for marketing. Consumers have learned that it is now technologically feasible to get only what they want, so that is what they are demanding from marketers.

But more than technology has changed. The ways in which people live and shop have changed radically, too. American society is more heterogeneous, and consumer tastes have splintered, which makes active involvement more important to people. It is the only way that people can ensure that they get exactly what they want.

People don't depend on marketing as much as before to learn about products and services. People are smarter than ever—literally, better educated—and have fingertip access to hundreds of sources of information. People have more street smarts, too, having been schooled by decades of exposure to every marketing trick in the book.

There was a time when advertising was an indispensable source of information. There was a time when people could take the time to linger and browse. There was a time when marketing novelties were newsworthy. No longer.

People's lifestyle expectations and aspirations have changed, too. People have grown accustomed to a more prosperous public life and people's pantries, drawers and driveways are filled with more stuff than ever before. People have started looking for meaning and fulfillment beyond more things to buy, so emotions, experiences and aesthetics have become the central sources of competitive advantage while reliability, performance and functionality have come to be taken for granted. People are demanding more from marketers than great products alone. People want a better experience with a product's marketing. Otherwise, they see marketing as an unnecessary and unwanted imposition on their scarce time and resources.

However, people don't want to quit shopping. Marketing resistance does not presage an end to consumerism or even a moderation of demand. People enjoy the comforts and satisfactions of the products they buy, and they want as much of that as they can afford. But people no longer take it as a given that they must be at the mercy of marketers in order to enjoy these things.

People do not want an end to marketing. People understand that the answer to a flood is not a drought. People just want marketing that is less annoying, less intrusive, less dominating, less saturating, more respectful and more informative. People want some relief from the dense marketing smog that covers everything in their lives with a brand logo or a marketing come-on. People want a different marketing model.

The challenge for marketers is to find a new model that doesn't penalize them for changing their marketing practices. No marketer should risk self-destruction by pulling back. And the 2004 Yankelovich research data on consumer resistance don't point in that direction. Rather, the findings show clearly that marketing based on better principles will be more productive. The old principles are making marketing less productive. The old tools guided by new principles will work better.

Marketing has become the white noise of modern life, a background hum left over from the big bang of the last fifty years of consumerism to which the law of entropy now applies. Without new thinking and fresh energy, it won't be long before it all goes cold.

SUMMING UP

- Consumers feel besieged by marketers. A marketing smog blankets people's lives. Active marketing resistance has moved from the fringe to the mainstream. Fighting resistance with saturation and intrusiveness is a losing battle. The technologies available to consumers are now too powerful and too widespread.

- The one-way flow of control in traditional marketing entails a presumption of domination that does not fit the active involvement that consumers want today.

- Consumers do not want an end to marketing. They want marketing that is less intrusive and more respectful. People want a better experience with marketing.

- The old marketing model is broken. Marketers need a model rooted in new principles that will re-engage people and reignite their affection for marketing.

NOTES

1 "A Farewell to Ads?" *The Economist,* April 17–23, 2004.

2 Theodore Levitt, *The Marketing Imagination* (Free Press: 1983).

3 Apparently, even military service offers no escape from the arm-twisting of high-pressure marketing and selling. In a July 20, 2004 *New York Times* story entitled, "Going Off to War, and Vulnerable to the Pitches of Salesmen," reporter Diana Henriques wrote about the open and often poorly supervised access that many insurance companies have to sell their products, many of which are inappropriate, to the "captive audience" of men and women in uniform.

4 As this book was going to press, Clear Channel Radio, owner of more than 1,200 radio stations nationwide, announced reductions ranging from 6 to 12 minutes per hour in the number of minutes allowed for commercials. During late 2003 and early 2004, Infinity Broadcasting, owner of about 185 radio stations, also reduced the number of commercial minutes allowed each hour for some of its stations. See Nat Ives, "A Radio Giant Moves to Limit Commercials," *New York Times,* July 19, 2004. These actions are laudable, yet there is still a net increase over time in the total amount of radio advertising per hour.

5 This study was a 15-minute re-contact telephone interview from February 20–29, 2004, among 601 nationally representative empanelled MONITOR 2003 respondents, 16+ years of age.

6 This research was first presented by J. Walker Smith at the AAAA Management Conference at the Miami South Beach Ritz-Carlton on April 15, 2004. See Stuart Elliott, "The Media Business; Advertising: A Survey of Consumer Attitudes Reveals the Depth of the Challenge that the Agencies Face." *New York Times,* April 14, 2004.

7 This study was a door-to-door survey among a nationally representative sample of 1,846 respondents. It is described more fully in *Advertising In America: The Consumer View* (Harvard Business School Press: 1968) by Raymond Bauer and Stephen Greyser.

8 The authors of the 1964 AAAA study noted that even this 15 percent figure was probably too high an estimate of the size of support for governmental regulatory action. See pp. 383–4. Which means that the size of active resistance today is an even greater multiple of the past.

Nano-Casting

Nano-proliferation is here to stay. The explosion of demographics and alternative media is being amplified by an accompanying explosion of attitudinal differences. Demographics don't provide as much information as they used to. Marketers must catch up to this nano-marketplace by shifting from systems that rely so heavily on demographics to systems that utilize a broader base of information, attitudes in particular. Marketers must master the art and science of nano-casting. Only then will marketers have the means of being precise enough to reverse the unwelcome trends of growing clutter and declining marketing productivity.

The mass market is long dead and gone. Its successor, the micro-market, is now dying, too. In its place, a nano-market is rapidly coming of age—an explosive proliferation of consumer segments, tastes, preferences, media and lifestyles that is splintering the marketplace into infinitesimally small pieces that are beyond the capacity of traditional marketing systems to recognize, much less adequately service and satisfy.

Not that all marketers would agree that mass marketing has lost its usefulness. Some argue that the economics of many products still depend upon efficiently and affordably reaching very large blocs of people. Only the traditional mass media, network TV in particular, can deliver audiences big enough to make those numbers work.

But that ability is waning. While it's true that mass media can still deliver huge audiences, the question is the value of those audiences. Despite their relative size, mass audiences are shrinking and are more expensive to bring together than in the past. More importantly, nano-proliferation in the consumer marketplace means that the mass audience delivered by the mass media is an increasingly heterogeneous group with a large and rapidly evolving variety of needs and wants. The mass content appeal of the mass media belies a massive multiplicity of lifestyles. Hence, even with a mass audience watching or listening, marketers must still figure out how to nano-cast their messages.

A uniform mass message must connect with everyone, but in today's nano-market this means stretching the message too thinly to provide adequate coverage for anyone. Even in the heyday of mass marketing, marketers knew that mass messages lacked deep personal relevance for any particular individual because mass messages had to speak to the lowest common denominator. Nano-proliferation has forced marketers to go in search of even lower common denominators in order to connect with today's far greater diversity.[1] As a result, the relevance of mass marketing messages for individual people is getting even more tenuous, which increases the frequency with which marketing of all sorts is perceived as clutter.

The challenges facing mass marketing are true for micro-marketing as well. In the audiences they reach, both mass marketing and micro-marketing sweep up lots of people who have no interest in the messages being communicated. Although marketing messages do get delivered to the right people, these messages are increasingly likely to get delivered to the wrong people, too. As it has become more difficult to reach the right people, many marketers have responded by completely saturating the marketplace so that their messages can't help but get through. The result is clutter and intrusiveness to the point of active consumer resistance.

The customary concerns expressed in recent years about the splintering of the marketplace focus on two factors—media vehicles and demographics. But there is another factor, too, one that is hidden from view, yet one with an enormous multiplier effect. More specifically, the demographic changes now transforming American society are creating an even greater diversity of attitudes. Because for every change in demographics, there are multiple changes in attitudes.

Of course, demographics still provide information, but much more information is needed to navigate today's marketplace. Nano-casting requires more precise information.

The old rule-of-thumb that demographics are a "good enough" proxy for attitudes is a poor operating assumption in today's marketplace. Yet, traditional marketing systems are solidly rooted in demographics as the fundamental basis for targeting as well as the primary instrument of marketing delivery and marketing measurement.

Marketers want to communicate and sell to people with the right attitudes—people who actually need and want the product. But they don't measure attitudes in ways that can be utilized to buy media or pull direct marketing lists. Demographics are measurable, cheap and accessible, so demographics have been used instead. When marketing to everyone in a demographic group, marketers have relied on the presumption that even though many people in that group will not have the right attitudes, people with attitudes receptive to their brands will be part of that group.

As long as demographics and attitudes retained at least some correspondence, marketers could afford the built-in inefficiencies of using demographic proxies for attitudes. But the waste from communicating with people who do not have the right attitudes becomes too expensive when demographics and attitudes sharply diverge, and this is what is happening today.

The marketing imprecision that is so resented by consumers today is due more to the deteriorating performance of marketing systems that rely upon demographics (and other descriptive data) than to any insensitivity or immoderation on the part of marketers themselves. With demographics no longer as definitive or as affordable as before, marketers must move beyond demographic proxies and develop new systems that capture the precision of working directly with attitudes. In fact, in this manner, marketers will get more value from demographics.

THE MULTIPLICITY MULTIPLIER

The changes in demographics begin with the fact that more demographic groups of all sorts are becoming sizable and important, which introduces a greater variety of attitudinal needs, wants, preferences and tastes into the marketplace. In addition, most demographic groups—the emerging groups in particular–are all characterized by an increasing variability of attitudes. To put it in statistical terms, the attitudinal variance among groups as well as the attitudinal variance within groups is increasing. It's a double whammy: There are more demographic categories, and the people within any given demographic category are more dissimilar attitudinally. This multiplicative increase in the variability of attitudes erodes the connection between demographics and attitudes that enabled marketing systems to work efficiently and productively in the past.

The divergence of demographics and attitudes hurts marketing economics in two ways. First, people with the right attitudes are spread across many more demographic groups instead of being clustered together in one demographic group. Reaching people with the right attitudes entails buying media to reach many different demographics instead of just a single demographic, and this is often a less efficient media buy. Second, the response to messages communicated to any particular demographic group will be lower because the greater diversity of attitudes means a lower likelihood of reaching people with the right attitudes. The greater likelihood that people will see or hear marketing of little or no relevance means that they are exposed to more clutter, and the resulting resistance worsens the overall environment for marketing even more.

Not that demographics have lost all marketing utility. Demographics continue to be useful, but the weakening connection between demographics and attitudes means that marketers must now employ more than demographics in marketing planning and marketing targeting, attitudinal information in particular. This means marketing systems that are based on attitudes. Attitudes must be the new platform for marketing execution. Direct marketers have been able to go beyond mere demographics in developing targeting models because they work with databases that include additional descriptive and transactional information. That's fine as far as it goes, but this additional information isn't enough. The imperative of shifting one's focus to be more inclusive of attitudes applies no less to direct marketers because all types of descriptive data now work less productively as proxies for attitudes.

Consumer profiles from Yankelovich MindBase® show the risks and inefficiencies that come from presuming too much knowledge about attitudes simply on the basis of demographics.[2] Consider adults living in households with children under the age of 18, a favorite target group of many marketers because these adults buy a wide array of household products and make decisions about finances, housing and travel that entail the needs of many people. Presumably, one of the best ways to appeal to these adults is to show warm, loving family scenes. After all, these are adults with kids at home, so emphasizing the affection and devotion of parents for their children is thought to be a message that will resonate across the board.

As it turns out, this is not the case. Through the individual scoring that can be done with MindBase, the attitudes of all adults with children under 18 can be profiled. These MindBase results show that about two-thirds of adults living with children under 18 have family attitudes that can be roughly described as warm and fuzzy. For these adults, images of parents displaying some type of love and affection for their kids is good marketing.

However, warm, fuzzy imagery is bad marketing for the other one-third of adults living with kids under 18. The family attitudes of these adults are better described as dutiful. They view family more as a responsibility than as a source of emotional warmth and support. The family images that resonate persuasively with them should emphasize responsibilities and obligations.

These MindBase results mean that from the get-go it is a certainty that one-third of a marketing budget is misspent if it is spent sending marketing messages with warm, fuzzy family scenes to the broad demographic target of adults living with children under 18. Yet, traditional marketing systems cannot prevent this surefire waste.

This simple example shows in miniature what nano-proliferation means for the consumer marketplace. A single demographic frequently masks multiple attitudes. With more demographic groups, there will be more diversity of attitudes. And the number of attitudes associated with any particular demographic group is growing by leaps and bounds. Each new or more prominent demographic group makes its increasing presence felt with multiple attitudes, not just one.

The emerging discrepancies between demographics and attitudes are bigger than the gaps that marketers managed to live with in the past.

The continuing dependence on demographics for marketing execution in the face of the increasing discrepancy between demographics and attitudes is already making marketing worse: Clutter is growing and efficiencies are declining.

AN UNMARRIED HOUSEHOLD

Marriage is a dwindling institution in American society. In the fifties, about 80 percent of all households were some form of a married household. Today, it's just over 50 percent and projected to be less than half by 2010. The traditional American family of two adults living at home with kids under 18 is less than one-quarter of American households for the first time in American history and is projected to be just one-fifth of American households by 2010 (Fig. 2.1).

With the shift to unmarried households of single people and single parents comes an increasing demographic diversity because unmarried households include a greater variety of household types. For example, over the last 20 years, households headed by single fathers who had never married were one of the fastest growing types of households. From 1985 to 2002, the number of children living with single fathers who had never married grew from 260,000 to 1,239,000. Children living with single fathers who had never married grew from 17 percent of

Figure 2.1: **American Household Composition**

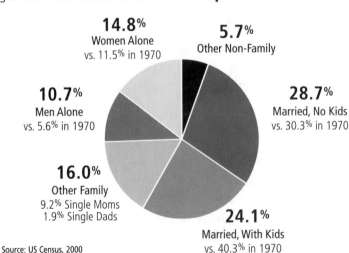

14.8% Women Alone vs. 11.5% in 1970

5.7% Other Non-Family

10.7% Men Alone vs. 5.6% in 1970

28.7% Married, No Kids vs. 30.3% in 1970

16.0% Other Family 9.2% Single Moms 1.9% Single Dads

24.1% Married, With Kids vs. 40.3% in 1970

Source: US Census, 2000

those living with single fathers in 1985 to 38 percent in 2002. Of course, these households are only a small portion of single parent households and only a fraction of all households, but that is precisely the point. The growth of unmarried households means a greater variety of household types, many of which only account for a small numbers of households.

This diversity of household structure extends to many types of households. For example, it is estimated that there are 160,000 households consisting of gay couples with children. These households include approximately one-quarter of a million children. Roughly another million children live with a single gay parent.

The diversity of household types chips away at the relative uniformity of household needs and priorities that used to characterize the marketplace when it was dominated by the nearly ubiquitous presence of married households. But the bigger challenge for marketers is the multiplicity multiplier of attitudes. Unmarried households are not only more varied in types of households, they are far more diverse in terms of attitudes, too.

Marriage is a lifestyle that tends to create relatively more agreement of opinions. This is not to suggest that all married people think alike, only that marriage has been dominant for so long that institutions, mores and expectations steer married people to a greater degree than unmarried people. Consequently, with the shift from married households to unmarried households comes a greater variety of ways of looking at things.

Single people live in many types of households, so they have a greater variety of lifestyle needs than married people. Single people live a more socially unscripted lifestyle than married people, so their perceptions and opinions are subject to fewer constraints and expectations. Single people have more options available to them when they are faced with pressures to conform or fit in. So, unsurprisingly, there is a greater variability of opinions among unmarried people than among married people.

An analysis of Yankelovich MONITOR data confirms that the attitudes of unmarried people show significantly more variance than the attitudes of married people, even after taking age into account. This is to say that on any given question in the MONITOR survey, the attitudes of married people show less disagreement than the attitudes of unmarried people.

To assess the differences in the variability of attitudes between married people and unmarried people, all of the key MONITOR attitudinal dimensions were assessed simultaneously. This analysis examined 174 different attitudinal dimensions, including attitudes about brands, shopping, business, corporate reputation, community, self-reliance, technology, family, children, home, investments, nutrition, the Internet, leisure, media, health, self-perceptions, religion, fads, pop culture, stress, simplification, travel and work. The percentage of married and unmarried households varied by age, so this analysis looked at differences in the variability of attitudes within broad age cohorts.

The findings from the statistical analysis are overwhelmingly clear. Across all age groups, unmarried people have significantly greater variability in their attitudes across all areas of interest to all types of marketers. Hence, as unmarried households make up a larger portion of the marketplace, soon to be the majority, attitudinal differences are becoming much greater than they were in the past when married households dominated. Consequently, household demographic proxies do a much poorer job of identifying an audience with a shared set of needs, tastes and preferences (Fig. 2.2).

In order to do cost-effective marketing in this environment, marketers need more than demographics (or descriptive profiling data of any sort). In particular, marketers must begin to target directly on the basis of attitudes, which means doing such things as buying media or pulling lists on

Figure 2.2: **Opinion Variance by Household Types**

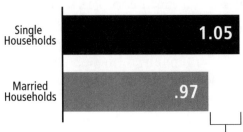

Index of Attitudinal Variability*

Single Households **1.05**

Married Households **.97**

This difference is statistically significant at the 95% level of confidence.**

*Indexed against average within group variance across 174 MONITOR questions.
**Using Box's Test of Equality of Covariance Matrices testing the null hypothesis that the observed covariance matrices of the attitudinal variables are equal across groups.

the basis of attitudes rather than on the basis of demographics or demographic models. This requires a different way of doing marketing because existing marketing systems are unable to link attitudes to the names and addresses in marketing databases or to the dayparts in media calendars.

Clutter will worsen, too, until marketers start to target directly on the basis of attitudes. More diversity of attitudes within each demographic group means that many more people are going to receive marketing in which they have no interest simply because they share a type of household structure, or some other demographic characteristic, with people who do have an interest.

Shifts in household structure are but one part of the exploding demographic diversity occurring in today's marketplace. The biggest part of diversity is related to race and ethnicity. And the growth of Hispanics is having an even bigger impact on the multiplicity of attitudes in the consumer marketplace.

THE MULTICULTURAL MAINSTREAM

In 1980, minorities accounted for 20.4 percent of the U.S. population. By 1990, it was 24.4 percent and by 2000, it was 30.9 percent. Whites no longer constitute a majority in California, Hawaii, New Mexico, and the District of Columbia. This will be true of Texas, too, by 2025.

Projections are that, by 2030, minorities will be 39.9 percent of the U.S. population. After 2040, whites will not only be declining in relative terms, they will be declining in absolute numbers as well. More whites will die each year than are born.

In just two decades, the demographic make-up of U.S. society has shifted from a society in which whites completely dominated to one in which whites are but one group among many (Fig. 2.3).

Hispanics are the largest minority group in America, surpassing African-Americans during the first half of 2003. The growth rate of Hispanics is accelerating. Hispanics grew 13 percent between 2000 and 2003, over four times the rate for the population as a whole. Already, Hispanics account for the largest part of year-to-year population growth and the Census Bureau estimates that by no later than 2050, America will have the second largest number of Hispanics of any nation in the world. Only Mexico will have more.

Figure 2.3: **Minority Population Growth**

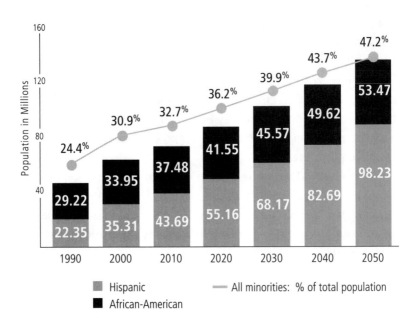

Source: U.S. Census

In 1990, the buying power of African-Americans was estimated to be $318 billion compared to $222 billion for Hispanics. By 2003, it was $688 billion and $653 billion, respectively, a difference nearly two-thirds smaller than the gap in 1990. By 2008, the buying power of Hispanics is projected to be $1.014 trillion compared to $921 billion for African-Americans.

However, the impact of Hispanics is not apparent in these aggregate figures. Talking about Hispanics as if they all come from a single cultural heritage is misleading. Indeed, the term Hispanic itself (and Latino, too) is misleading because it glosses over the wide-ranging diversity of geographies, nationalities and cultures that exists among Hispanics.

The vast majority of Hispanics living in America come from Mexico or have Mexican roots, but Hispanics from other countries and cultures are an important part of the mix, too (Fig. 2.4). As Hispanics become a bigger part of society, diversity and multiculturalism will be even more pronounced because of the cultural diversity that exists among them. This

Figure 2.4: **National Origin of Hispanics**

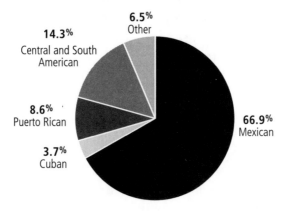

Source: US Census 2002

will be felt differently in different parts of the country, thus exacerbating the nano-proliferation of the marketplace. Cubans in Miami, Salvadorans in Washington D.C., Puerto Ricans in New York, and Mexicans in Texas, L.A. and Chicago will make the impact of the growth in Hispanics unique to each locale. Like household structure, demographic changes in race and ethnicity come with a multiplicity multiplier.

A big part of the impact of Hispanics from every background and heritage is the Spanish language. Results from the Yankelovich Multicultural Marketing Study® (MMS)[3] show that whites, African-Americans and Hispanics agree on the top two cultural elements worth preserving, but the third item preferred by each group reveals distinct interests. For Hispanics, it is the Spanish language.

Other MMS results show the importance of language to Hispanics. Sixty-two percent of Hispanics agree that the Spanish language is more important to them than it was five years ago. While the majority of Hispanics prefer English as their language of choice for every situation, English is the language of choice at home for only 37 percent. Language is thus an additional component of the new diversity sweeping through the consumer marketplace. Establishing a meaningful rapport with Hispanic consumers requires that marketers appreciate and speak to the Spanish language as a cultural artifact that influences the attitudes and preferences of Hispanics.

Altogether, the elements of race, ethnicity and language have made multiculturalism the mainstream in every context and arena. Mainstream culture increasingly reflects the influence and leadership of minority cultural elements.

The growing presence of minorities changes how people think about everything. People today live in a world in which difference is the norm. And not just race and ethnicity. Everyday, in every high school lunchroom, or in every high-rise office building for that matter, people see long hairs, short hairs, bald heads, skinheads, buzz cuts, braids, dreadlocks, mop-tops, ponytails, beehives, do-rags, hijabs, and more.

No matter where people click to, whether surfing the Web or channel surfing, there is a glut of difference from which to choose. There is a TV show or a Web site for every possible predilection. Hit sitcoms now find laughs in all kinds of household settings that were virtually invisible or unheard of in the past: *Will & Grace* for gay lifestyles; *Friends* for young single lifestyles; *George Lopez* for middle-class Hispanic family lifestyles.

Not that unconventional program choices have never been available or that African-American, Hispanic or gay characters and performers have never enjoyed mainstream success. But the choices available to people today are considerably greater. Take sports. It's not just the AFL or the NFL anymore. Or the ABA or the NBA. Now, it's the NFL's NFC or the NFL's AFC or Arena Football or World Football. It's the PGA or the Champions Tour or the LPGA. It's ESPN or ESPN2 or Fox Sports. It's MLS or World Cup or WUSA. It's satellite TV packages with sports contests from all over the country that can be watched from anywhere in the country. These few examples barely scratch the surface, but it doesn't take much to illustrate the key point that difference is the most common thing about the experience of life in today's marketplace.

A MIXED BAG

As difference has taken over the mainstream, people's attitudes have become disconnected from mere demographics. Demographics don't provide as much information as they have in the past. A difference in appearance no longer means a difference of opinion. What people look like on the outside (i.e., demographics) means less than it used to about what people are thinking on the inside (i.e., attitudes).

Demographics still matter, but not as much as before as people look beyond characteristics like race and ethnicity for new ways to think about what race and identity mean for their choices in the marketplace. People are reaching for opportunities to transcend the traditional categories that have fixed their identities and limited their choices. People are redefining their expectations and preferences to reflect the new possibilities now within their grasp. Demographics are no longer a personal characteristic with a reliable connection to someone's lifestyle. The permission people feel to be different dissolves the traditional bond between demographics and attitudes.

Out of difference comes the urgency to create a unique experience for oneself. So, people steer themselves in the direction of the technologies and media that enable them to do so, which has led to the fragmentation of the audience for mass media. However, the biggest impact of the new media is not in how one puts a media plan together. The biggest impact is attitudinal.

Nowadays, ethnic cultural elements have powerful appeal for audiences of all types, cutting across all racial and ethnic groups, and working well in combination with many different cultural elements. In a marketplace in which difference is the ordinary, everyday experience, ethnic culture has wide-ranging power and multicultural fashions, music, symbols and identities have strong crossover appeal. White people no longer have "white tastes." Black people no longer have "black tastes." Demographics don't predict attitudes as well in a world in which multiculturalism is the mainstream.

Consider the Caribbean soul rap, "Who Let The Dogs Out," that became a fan anthem at ballparks and stadiums all across the country in 2000 and 2001. The Baha Men were a 20-year old nine-piece band from the Bahamas with worldwide renown (including five consecutive platinum albums in Japan) everywhere but in America until they released their version of a remake of a Caribbean soca song called "Doggie." The Baha Men made the song's chant into a more prominent refrain, added a rap at the end and then watched as the song became all the rage all over America, garnering them a Grammy award in 2000. The song that became a national craze is the product of a multicultural mix of influences, backgrounds, people and styles.

Or like the high-energy, adrenaline-pumping hip-hop song, "Let's Get

It Started," used by ESPN to promote its schedule for televising the 2004 NBA Playoffs and then later used by ABC to open its coverage of each game of the 2004 NBA Finals. This song is a remake of "Let's Get Retarded" from the multi-platinum CD "Elephunk" by the Black Eyed Peas, a group of three black West Coast, breakdancing male rappers, Will.I.Am, Apl.De.Ap and Taboo, and one white California female vocalist, Fergie, who used to star in kid's TV shows, commercials, and movies and who used to sing in a girl pop group called Wild Orchid.

The Black Eyed Peas first achieved breakthrough notice with a hit single about 9/11 recorded with Justin Timberlake, the white male pop star who was the youngest member of 'N Sync and who used to date fellow Mouseketeer Britney Spears. The "Elephunk" CD has been both praised and criticized for dabbling in a wide variety of musical styles.

ESPN used "Let's Get It Started" in four TV spots that featured an eclectic mix of people and celebrities—the band itself, a boys choir, musician Carlos Santana, former NBA stars Kareem Abdul-Jabbar and Bill Walton, and ABC sitcom stars Jim Belushi and George Lopez. The song that was used to promote a televised sports event of crossover interest and appeal was the product of a multicultural mix, both ethnic and mainstream, of performers, celebrities, professional connections and experiences, and musical influences.

This dynamic of cultural recombination to create crossover success involves all types of cultural elements, not just race and ethnicity. Like the breakout success of the *Left Behind* series of apocalyptic Christian novels written by Tim LaHaye, a co-founder of the Moral Majority, and Jerry Jenkins, a writer-at-large for the Moody Bible Institute, a biographer of many public figures, and writer of the comic strip "Gil Thorpe." Since the first book in the *Left Behind* series was published in 1995, over 62 million copies have been sold, clearly a success for an Evangelical Christian product that broke out of conventional cultural categories.

In a marketplace in which racial and ethnic minorities are growing and in which all types of niche cultural phenomena are crossing over traditional boundaries, marketers must work smarter. There are no old standbys to fall back on anymore. Demographics have splintered into pieces that are being recombined in greater varieties. People who look the same demographically are less likely to think the same attitudinally. And the big crossover successes that do generate a positive universal response are harder to predict because they are built from shared tastes and interests that show little correspondence to the demographics that drive marketing systems.

THE FUTURE IS CABLINASIAN

The cultural collage that characterizes more and more of the consumer marketplace seems to confirm the truth of the recent joke about a world in which the best rapper is white (Eminem) and the best golfer is black (Tiger Woods). These sorts of demographic categories mean less than ever. Tiger Woods knows this better than anyone.

After Tiger won the Masters Golf Tournament for the first time in 1997, he appeared as a guest on "The Oprah Winfrey Show." At one point during their conversation, Oprah asked Tiger if it bothered him to be referred to as an African-American golfer. Tiger said that it did and then added that in many ways he didn't think of himself as black. Tiger noted that his father is half black, one-quarter American Indian and one-quarter white and his mother is half Thai and half Chinese. Tiger said that growing up he had invented a word to describe himself—Cablinasian, a word with a syllable or two from each of the words Caucasian, black, (American) Indian and Asian.

Tiger's description of himself as Cablinasian was highly controversial, even garnering a soft rebuke from Colin Powell who said, "In America, which I love from the depths of my heart and soul, when you look like me, you're black." But Tiger's answer to Oprah's question showed deeper insight than his critics understood. Tiger recognizes that the black-and-white checkerboard of the past has been supplanted by the mix-and-match collage of today and tomorrow. Tiger's generation has come of age during the period in which racial and ethnic categories have been undergoing enormous change. The emerging world is not one of more racial and ethnic groups sharing the stage but one of a pervasive and unapologetic intermingling and redefinition of racial and ethnic categories. The future is Cablinasian.

For the first time ever, the 2000 Census allowed people to check more than one box for race. Nearly 7 million people did so, 42 percent of them under the age of 18 and 54 percent of them under the age of 25. One in 16 Americans under 18 has a multi-racial heritage. In some areas of the country, one in six new babies is multi-racial. Already, more than 25 colleges and universities have multi-racial student organizations. This phenomenon is so widespread that it is not really a new trend anymore. Certainly not after the Sunday newspaper supplement *Parade* featured multi-racial kids in a cover story on July 26, 2003 entitled, "The Changing Faces of America."

Traditional racial and ethnic categories have not been repudiated or abandoned. Many observers would argue that racial and ethnic self-awareness is stronger than ever. But the burgeoning presence of multi-racialism and multi-ethnicity is causing people to rethink the meaning and relevance of traditional racial and ethnic identities. Over time, this will further undermine the marketing utility of traditional demographic categories. More importantly, multi-racialism and multi-ethnicity are re-inforcing the sense of permission that people feel to be different, irrespective of traditional demographic classifications.

The year Tiger won the Masters, Nike, one of his major sponsors, re-launched a TV ad from the year before in which kids of all races, cultures and ethnicities, dressed in every kind of clothing, carrying every kind of golfing equipment, are shown parading off to play golf. As each kid passes the camera, he or she stops to stare directly into the lens and de-clare, "I am Tiger Woods." Kids from all types of backgrounds are shown identifying with Tiger because Tiger's appeal transcends these traditional demographic boundaries to engage kids of every sort and bring them together attitudinally notwithstanding the surface differences that might have kept them apart in the past.

Admittedly, this was just advertising, but like all great ads this commercial had a deep, authentic resonance that rang true. Demographics can't keep people of like minds from coming together because demographics don't define people as much as they did before. The marketplace is Cablinasian.

Tiger has not ignored the pioneering sacrifices of the African-American golfers who paved the way for him. Tiger has paid tribute to them throughout his career, but he has rejected the notion that an old-time demographic category, whether white, black, Indian or Asian, utterly defines his demographic identity.

In fact, a multi-racial, multi-ethnic sensibility is the new chic. Celebrities and sports figures with multi-racial, multi-ethnic heritages like Greg

Louganis, Derek Jeter, Halle Berry, Vin Diesel, Lisa Bonet, Jessica Alba, Christina Aguilera, Jennifer Lopez, Benjamin Bratt, Lenny Kravitz, Nia Peeples, Mariah Carey, and Cameron Diaz demonstrate the potency of personas that defy and redefine traditional ethnic and racial categories. One way to draw a crowd these days is to show off a new skin that reveals a whole new way of thinking.

THE ECHO BOOM

The generation that has come of age in the midst of growing demographic diversity is now a major factor in the marketplace. This is the generation that has never experienced a society in which marriage was the norm. This is the generation that has never experienced a society in which whites are an overwhelming majority and in which racial and ethnic categories are static and sharply defined. This generation is the Echo Boom of the nearly 106 million people 25 years old and younger who are making their presence felt in the marketplace through their cultural leadership and through their estimated $150 billion to $175 billion in buying power.

Echo Boomers are unlike any generation before them because the diversity of experiences, styles and inventions that characterizes them makes it difficult to lump them together as a generational cohort. Like all generations, Echo Boomers have shared a number of common formative experiences, but these experiences have encouraged them to value and seek pluralism and diversity.[4]

The Yankelovich Youth MONITOR® provides an in-depth look at the values and attitudes of young people, 6 to 17 years old, that can be tracked back as far as 1985 when today's thirty-something generation of GenXers were the same age.[5] Additionally, the Yankelovich MONITOR interviews respondents 16 years of age and older, which provides key information about older Echo Boomers. The findings reveal a generation that is more distinct from prior generations than Baby Boomers were from their parents.

Echo Boomers are the first generation to come of age with instantaneous, technologically facilitated access to everything that has ever been printed, produced, written, recorded and filmed. Echo Boomers not only assume access to everything, they presume that they will be able to mold it and manipulate it to reinvent it in whatever ways they see fit. They feel complete and unfettered permission to be different.

An interesting example of how young people are asserting control over the things that make up their lives is the online fad of a few years back inserting the phrase, "All Your Base Are Belong To Us" (AYBABTU) into all kinds of images and Web sites. It's a nonsense phrase that comes from a video game called Zero Wing that was developed in 1989 by a now-defunct Japanese company. The English translation of the introduction was very poor and included many odd sentences, one of which was an ominous message from an enemy called Cats, who intoned, "All your base are belong to us."[6]

The phrase began to attract notice in late 1998 when it appeared on a Web site that posts odd phrases from video games. By 2000, AYBABTU had become an insider's joke among online gamers and Web programmers. In February 2001, an animated music video was released that featured the phrase. This triggered an AYBABTU craze. Suddenly, the phrase was being inserted or hidden in everything everywhere, online and off-line.

College students painted the phrase on bridges, hung banners with the phrase, spelled out the phrase on campus lawns with rocks, projected the phrase onto the side of a dorm with laser lights, and spread leaflets and posters with the phrase all across campuses nationwide. The phrase was referenced six times in the nationally syndicated comic strip "FoxTrot." On an episode of the TV game show "The Chair," a contestant was given four choices for the last word of the Pledge of Allegiance: all, your, base, belong. AYBABTU had become the first streaking or goldfish-swallowing craze of the 21st Century.

By late 2001, the AYBABTU craze had simmered down, but it has not disappeared. People keep concocting pranks and April Fool's jokes with it, and references to AYBABTU continue to pop up online and in video and multiplayer games.

The most interesting part of this mass infatuation with AYBABTU was the use of software tools to modify pictures and images of products and brand logos to include the phrase. Thousands of pictures appeared online (and can still be viewed by Googling the phrase). This was more than just doing something rebellious or zany; this was taking control of a marketing image and reinventing it to fit one's own purposes and interests.

Satirists have done this for centuries, of course, but the AYBABTU craze was not the handiwork of a few madcap humorists; it was a shared experience in which everyone could participate. Access was open to anyone and most of the fun came from seeing how one inventive idea would spark the next. What people were sharing was the "doing of the thing," if you will, not the "consuming of the thing." This kind of unprecedented access and opportunity is what the Echo Boom generation has come of age taking for granted. Young people expect to be in control, to be able to participate, and to do so in any way they like, no matter how different or unexpected.

Echo Boomers are steeped in participatory activities and opportunities. Chat rooms and instant messaging keep people in constant contact with their friends. Social networking Internet services link people to dozens of others in a virtual exchange of interaction and connection. Email messages get modified with commentaries, highlights, edits, links and other mark-ups before being answered or forwarded. Fan fiction Web sites enable people to recreate their favorite TV shows according to their own narrative inventions. Multiplayer online games bring players together from all over the world. Blogs (Web logs) give people a voice of their own and make instant publishers out of everyone. Flash mobs and bluejacking are participatory experiences facilitated by a shared use of wireless technologies. Peer-to-peer file-sharing systems make it possible for people to trade music files directly with one another. Wireless devices allow people to send pictures and text messages from anywhere. Digital cameras and photo editing software systems enable people to actively manage images. Online polls and dial-in numbers allow people to cast votes for things like the MVP of the NBA Finals or the winner on *American Idol*. TiVo and ReplayTV give people the ability to invent personalized viewing experiences according to their own schedules and tastes.

Echo Boomers take it for granted that technology enables them to participate in one way or another in anything and everything. Echo Boomers have never known anything else. The idea that people should be able to create whatever they want for themselves is something that they take for granted in all aspects of their lives, including race and ethnicity.

Echo Boomers are surrounded by more diversity than any generation before them. For people 70 years of age and older, the ratio of white people to people of color is five to one. For people 40 years of age and younger, the ratio is two to one. For kids 10 years of age and younger, the ratio is 1.5 to one. Echo Boomers have never known anything but widespread racial and ethnic diversity.

Echo Boomers are difficult if not impossible to typecast in traditional terms. It's hard to understand them solely on the basis of descriptive characteristics. Difference is pursued. The traditional and the radical live more comfortably side by side with this generation. After all, it was Echo Boomer Miss Vermont who sported the first navel ring in the 1997 Miss America Pageant, the same year that Miss Pennsylvania was rumored to have a tattoo, although she wouldn't say where.

Echo Boomers feel comfortable with a fluidity of identities and the ability to mix and match in any combination at will, without worrying about the dividing lines that have traditionally enforced consistency, stability and compatibility. It takes attitudes in addition to demographics, not demographics alone, to understand them.

Yankelovich Youth MONITOR results show that Echo Boomers feel less bound by convention compared to kids of the same age 16 years ago. Young people today have a lot of confidence in their own judgments and abilities, and they don't trust other people to always have a better idea. Echo Boomers understand the extent to which technology has enabled them to be more independent and self-directed (Fig. 2.5).

None of this means that Echo Boomers have severed their relationships with others. Indeed, the kind of generation gap between kids and their parents that was true of Baby Boomers is not true of Echo Boomers. Young people today report close family ties, and parents of Echo Boomers mention the influence and roles that kids play in household decisions. Echo Boomers are a more empowered generation, a unique formative experience that means they are going to be even more aggressive than their Baby Boomers parents in rewriting the rules as they get older.

Echo Boomers expect that everybody should have the ability to jump right in and reinvent anything and everything. These kids think that fitting in is just one choice among many, not a mandatory duty that restricts one's options. These kids will reinvent the meaning of demographics as much as they are reinventing everything else, if indeed demographics will continue to mean anything at all as leading edge Echo Boomers age into their early thirties over the next few years.

Figure 2.5: **Attitudes of Echo Boomers**

16-25 **67**% I think my IQ is higher than average

12-17 **62**% I'm smarter than most kids my age

12-17 **76**% Trust my own judgment a lot

16-25 **80**% (Among those online) Having access to the Internet has helped me do more things on my own that in the past I needed the help of others to do

---

6-17 **Influence everyday items such as:**

	1997	2003
Sneakers	72%*	83%
Snack foods	66	76
Cereals	62	74
Soft drinks	57	65
Movies to rent	53	77
Cookies	53	62

And big-ticket items such as:

	1991	2003
Vacation	37%	49%
The family car	12	22
Home electronics**	9	40

12-17 Say their parents have asked them to go online to find info about products and services

46% 2001 ▶▶ **55**% 2003

12-17 It's more important to fit in than be different from other people

67% 1987 **47**% 2003

16-24 Relate more to authenticity than integrity

38% 1999 **57**% 2003

12-17 Things very important to you: Always telling the truth

70%

16-24 I want to spend more time exploring my spiritual side

50% 2001 ▶▶ **60**% 2003

Signs of success & accomplishment: Being in control of your life

64% Xers 1993 ▶▶ **76**% Echoes 2003

People should live for themselves rather than for their children

40% Xers at 16-23 1994 ▶▶ **29**% Echoes at 16-23 2002

*1999 data
**9-17 year olds only
Source: Yankelovich MONITOR and Yankelovich Youth MONITOR

MARKETING PRECISION: THE NANO-MARKETPLACE IS THE NORM

Demographics have already started to fail marketers. It's harder for messages to find their mark, and when they do, it's only at great expense.

Attitudes must play a more central role in marketing execution. Attitudes have always been important to marketing strategy, but not to execution. Marketing execution has been the exclusive preserve of demographics. Attitudes must now play a role, too. Attitudes need to be deployed by name and address just like every other variable used for marketing execution.

Nano-proliferation is here to stay. The explosion of demographics and alternative media is being amplified and complicated by the accompanying explosion of attitudinal differences. Marketers must catch up to this nano-marketplace by shifting from systems that rely so heavily on demographics to systems that utilize a broader base of information, attitudes in particular. Marketers must master the art and science of nano-casting. Only then will marketers have the means of being precise enough to reverse the unwelcome trends of growing clutter and declining productivity that plague marketing today.

SUMMING UP

- Nano-proliferation means that the consumer marketplace is increasingly characterized by an exploding multiplicity of lifestyle needs and wants. Nano-casting is required for marketing precision. This means a bigger role for attitudinal data in targeting and marketing execution systems.
- Not only are there more demographic groups in today's marketplace, the diversity of attitudes within each demographic group is greater. The shifts in household structure from married to single households means more diversity of attitudes. The growing presence of minorities means more crossover of ethnic influences on the marketplace at large. People feel more permission to be different.
- Difference is the most common thing in today's marketplace. The expression and manifestation of difference is in a Cabli-

nasian style. This will grow with the emergence of Echo Boomers, the first generation to come of age fully empowered by technology and unconstrained by the traditional expectations and divisions of demographics. Niche cultural phenomena are crossing over traditional boundaries, making demographics obsolete as a reliable indicator of attitudes.

• Marketing execution systems are rooted in an assumption of correspondence between demographics and attitudes. But demographics no longer work well as a proxy for attitudes. Marketers must begin to use attitudes in building targeting models and utilizing marketing execution systems. Otherwise, clutter, consumer resistance and marketing productivity will continue to be serious problems.

NOTES

1 The terms diversity and multiculturalism are used in this book in their dictionary meanings only, not in their politically charged meanings and connotations. Diversity meaning a multiplicity of forms and variety; multiculturalism meaning the simultaneous presence of many cultures or sub-cultures at once, often but not always combined in some way or mixed together.

2 Yankelovich MindBase is the first service that overlays attitudinal information onto customer files and third-party lists. MindBase scores each record, whether an individual or a household, with a code signifying membership in one of several attitudinal groups. This scoring is based on a series of models that are highly predictive and that do not require time-consuming and expensive survey data collection. Once assigned to a MindBase group, each individual or household can then be directly linked to the 4,000-plus attitudinal data points tracked by the Yankelovich MONITOR. In this manner, attitudes get overlaid onto each record in behavioral databases.

3 The Yankelovich Multicultural Marketing Study is an annual, nationally representative survey among African-Americans, Hispanics and non-Hispanic Caucasians, ages 16+. A 20-minute telephone interview is followed by a 60-minute self-administered questionnaire

completed by mail or Internet, at the preference of each respondent. Interviews with Hispanics were conducted in the language of choice of each respondent. The 2003 Study was conducted in collaboration with Cheskin and Images USA. Tracking is available back to 1994 for Hispanics and 1995 for African-Americans.

4 Yankelovich Partners pioneered the study of generations for marketing applications. One of the firm's founders, Florence Skelly, coined the term Baby Boomers. The Yankelovich MONITOR was launched in 1971 on the basis of pioneering work done in the 1960s to understand the role of youth in creating and leading value change in society and the marketplace. An in-depth look at generational marketing issues is available in a critically acclaimed book written by two of the authors of this book, J. Walker Smith and Ann Clurman, called *Rocking The Ages: The Yankelovich Report on Generational Marketing* (Harper-Business: 1997).

5 The 2003 Yankelovich Youth MONITOR is based upon 1,468 in-home interviews with children 6 to 17 years of age. A nationally representative base sample of 1,189 was supplemented by over-samples of 109 African-American children and 170 Hispanic children. One parent or adult legal guardian of each child interviewed for the Youth MONITOR was also interviewed in order to provide direct comparisons of the attitudes of children and their parents. The Youth MONITOR has been conducted approximately every other year since it was first pilot tested in 1985.

The Claustrophobia
of Abundance

Marketing must deliver the intangibles. Marketing cannot be so narrowly focused on communicating the value of a brand that it runs afoul of what people want. Marketing must deliver value by enriching people's lives. In this sense, marketing itself is the value of a brand.

There are stirrings of restlessness in the consumer marketplace. The evidence of a shift in consumer priorities is everywhere. But it's more than changing tastes. It's an ebbing gusto for buying with abandon.

This declining fervor for mindless materialism does not mean that people are deserting the marketplace. People are not dropping shopping, but they are approaching it differently. People are becoming more exacting and more discriminating as well as more resistant to marketing. People are demanding more from marketers before they shop, and this means a higher cost of doing business in the traditional way. Yet, it also means strong growth opportunities for savvy marketers willing to change and adapt in parallel with the evolving marketplace.

SUPER-ABUNDANCE

Super-abundance defines our times. Not that every individual has too much of everything or even enough of the essentials. But in society at large if not at home in private, people's lives are crowded with stuff.

Store shelves are full to bursting. Retailers are ubiquitous: online, on TV, on the phone, at the door, around every street corner. Popular culture from hip-hop to sitcoms to action flicks to celebrity lifestyle magazines venerates stuff in word, deed and setting. The media pour out a 24/7 stream of dazzling, beckoning images of glittering material goods. Super-abundance characterizes everything that people see, hear, learn or do. However, this overwhelming abundance, for so long the shared aspiration behind the hard work and sacrifice of so many generations, has reached the point of super-saturation.

Surrounded by so much, nothing much is special anymore. Special things carry less meaning, so marketers have to invent new ways to restore some degree of scarcity in order to make things exclusive and valuable again. Limited editions and exclusive promotions as well as limited-time retailing have been used to do so. Target opened a store in Rockefeller Center for six weeks in 2003 to publicize its new women's clothing line designed by Isaac Mizrahi. It had a floating store on the Hudson River just for the holiday season that year, too. Vacant is a worldwide retailer that opens stores for only one month in empty spaces in large cities selling limited-edition brands and products. The Airline Song opened a merchandise store for nine weeks in New York to coincide with its launch in 2003. A second Song store was open for two months in Boston in early 2004. But these kinds of efforts only go so far in an overstuffed marketplace.

The experience of super-abundance doesn't breed resentment or revolt, but it does put a much sharper edge on the longing for something more than just more stuff. So, even as people keep accumulating more stuff, they are looking harder than ever for meaning and purpose in the material glut. Marketing in the same old way won't measure up to people's new desires and expectations. In a world of super-abundance, people have different needs than they had in the less abundant past and hence people are seeking different benefits from the products they buy.

In particular, with so much being so affordable, people are looking beyond materialism. The result is a burgeoning interest in nonmaterial values, an interest that is intensified by the dawning realization among more and more people that money and material things do not bring happiness or fulfillment. People do not want to give up material things; rather, they want to accumulate plenty of nonmaterial things to go along with all of their stuff. People no longer accept that nonmaterial values require material sacrifices. The quest for lots of both at once means that marketing success is going to require a new approach to the practice of marketing.

QUALITY, INTANGIBLES, TIME

First priorities have shifted from quantity, tangibles and money to quality, intangibles and time.[1] Not that people are walking away from more tangibles and money, only that things per se have been eclipsed in importance by quality, intangibles and time.

The road warrior and the dot-com entrepreneur, the role models of success in the recent past and the kinds of people willing to give up as much time as it takes in order to make as much money as possible, no longer inspire emulation or even respect. People want to restore balance to their lives in order to enjoy the intangibles that mean the most to them. This isn't easy to do, but people are trying anyway because the values of quality, intangibles and time are the core constituents of the new definition of success.

Overwhelmed with material abundance, nearly 60 percent of respondents to the Yankelovich MONITOR agree that they "do not need any more material possessions." The *Dallas Morning News* reported on August 8, 2000 that the number of self-storage facilities tripled between 1982 and 1999. It is literally true that people have more stuff than they know what to do with. Sixty-seven percent of MONITOR respondents agree that while they "may not be as well off in the future as they have been in the past, it may be better for [their] moral character and [they] may even be happier." Or to put it another way, the vast majority of people agree that life would be better and more satisfying with a greater emphasis on the intangibles.

But don't mistake this wistful sentiment for a harbinger of a mad rush to plunge into more austere lifestyles of voluntary simplicity. People aren't going to give up their big houses or nice cars to build new lives centered on intangible satisfactions. People like nice things and material comforts, and they will continue to stock up on as many of these things as they can afford (even if they have to put them into storage). Few people are willing to live with any less. But they want something more than just more stuff. Indeed, the only stuff they want more of is stuff that brings them something more. People are desperate to create a harmony of materialism and fulfillment in their lives. People want more of the intangibles that can give meaning to the claustrophobic surfeit of stuff that crowds their lives. Intangible rewards are now people's top priority.

MasterCard's "Priceless" campaign is the best example of advertising that reflects this shift in first priorities. MasterCard understands that the most effective way to pitch a credit card these days is not to focus on the stuff you can buy but to make a strong emotional connection with all of the intangibles that money can't buy. Things are important, but things that deliver or are associated with people's new priorities are the things in which people will have the greatest interest. The enduring power of this campaign, begun in 1997, is testimony to the growing strength of the new values now guiding people's decisions and ambitions.

MasterCard is not alone. Citigroup's "Live Richly" campaign, launched in 2001, strikes a similar chord. Money matters, but other things matter more. Life's real riches are family, hugs, romance and smiles. Good health is one's greatest asset. A 2003 Jeep print ad shows a man with his dog along a wilderness riverbank. The ad reminds people that self-worth is not the same thing as net worth. Being well off means keeping money in perspective. The foreground of a 2001 Chevy Malibu print ad features a father holding his infant son. The car is relegated to the background where it sits with a coat draped through the window of an open back door. This is not the usual beauty shot of a car. The father-son cameo in the foreground communicates a more compelling message about the brand.

Throughout the decade of the 1990s, the Yankelovich MONITOR tracked a steady decline in the percentage of people citing material luxuries as signs of success and accomplishment (Fig 3.1). While valuable, they are no longer special. Over this same period of time, the percentage defining success in terms of intangibles like "being satisfied," "being in control" or "having a good marriage" grew dramatically. Today's look of success is a satisfied, stress-free smile not a bejeweled designer outfit.

In a similar vein, the Yankelovich MONITOR has tracked a huge jump in the percentage of people saying they believe to at least some degree in something mysterious like "spiritualism"—from the low teens during the

Figure 3.1: **Status Symbols**

Signs of Success and Accomplishment:	1991	2003
Satisfied with life	63%	79%
In control of life	57	76
Good marriage	62*	69
Travel for pleasure	52	42
Expensive car	38	23
Prestige stores	20	11**
Expensive jewelry	18	11

*1993 MONITOR
**2001 MONITOR
Source: Yankelovich MONITOR

Figure 3.2: **Belief in Things Unseen**

Believe in at least to some degree:	1976	1998
Spiritualism	12%	52%
Faith healing	10	45
Astrology	17	37
UFOs	24	30
Reincarnation	9	25
Mysticism	2	15
Voodoo	1	9

Source: Yankelovich MONITOR

"Age of Aquarius" to just over half at the height of the dot-com boom (Fig. 3.2).

Other surveys show this, too. A 1997 *Worth* magazine survey of people with a net worth of at least $2.5 million found that the thing they would be willing to pay the most to get was "a place in heaven." Even though they were only willing to pay an average of $640,000 for a place in heaven (who knows what the rest of the bankroll is being saved for!), it beats the mere $55,000 they thought "being President" was worth; and it is a valuation that finds currency in the lifestyle priorities now topping people's lists.[2]

As people look around for products that fit their new priorities, more of the same is not what they want. Half of Yankelovich MONITOR respondents say they already own lots of things they "never really use," and over the past several years the interest in new products has dropped markedly in every product and service category. Fewer than half express any interest in making time to shop and browse—not because people don't want to shop but because what's available for sale doesn't fit the bill.

SLOW FOOD

Several emerging lifestyle movements offer a glimpse into this new sensibility. The Slow Food movement is one. Begun in 1986 by Italian food and wine author Carlos Petrini in conjunction with a protest against the opening of a McDonald's restaurant in Piazza Spagna in Rome, Slow Food was expanded into an international movement in Paris in 1989. The movement's logo is a snail and its mission is a reaction against the haste and overprocessing of contemporary life, particularly in food and dining. The Slow Food movement promotes local foods, crafts and beverages, especially wine, and publishes cookbooks and restaurant guides.

In 2000, the Slow Food movement was broadened to include Cittaslow or Slow Cities. Thirty-three Italian cities banded together to form a group dedicated to safeguarding a more traditional and less harried style of city life. A municipality can be designated as a Slow City only if it conforms to 50 different requirements like banning car alarms, promoting organic farming and creating centers where visitors can taste local foods in natural surroundings.

The Slow Food movement emphasizes the values of quality, intangibles and time. It encourages slow, reflective living along with all of the authentic elements that go with that. Yet, neither the Slow Food nor the Cittaslow movement preaches an end to or even a slackening of commerce. Instead, what both movements promote is a shift in tastes and preferences. The cities that have joined Cittaslow, for example, hope to benefit from joint marketing to promote tourism and local products.

While Slow Food can claim only a very small number of card-carrying members—75,000 worldwide with 12,500 in the United States—it is the tip of a booming marketplace iceberg, particularly in the United States. The Organic Trade Association reports that annual U.S. retail sales of organic foods have skyrocketed to $11 billion from $1 billion in 1990. A report on its Web site projects 2007 sales of $30.7 billion. Made-to-order offerings with fresh ingredients have been the recipe for success for hot restaurant chains like Panera Bread and Subway. Seventy percent of the communities interviewed in the *2003 National Main Street Trends Survey* of the National Trust for Historic Preservation reported record levels of attendance at local festivals. Three-quarters reported increases over years past, a consistent finding since 1999.

The Slow Food movement is a bellwether for the U.S. consumer marketplace, just as Earth Day (started in 1970) and Greenpeace (founded in 1971) were early indicators of an emerging environmental sensibility that would eventually lead to every product conforming to at least a minimum standard of environmental friendliness. As a November 26, 2003 *USA Today* story noted, the biggest concentration of Slow Food USA members is in Northern California and New York where food trends often begin. While many factors, health concerns in particular, are stimulating greater interest in alternative foods and stress-free lifestyles, social movements like Slow Food USA are accelerating these trends by providing thought-leadership and validation for the values of quality, intangibles and time.[3]

SLOW FOOD IN THE FAST LANE

People want the stuff they buy to connect them with the nonmaterial values that now matter most to them. One place to see this combination of tangibles and intangibles is in the pages of *Real Simple* magazine. *Real Simple* is filled with aspirational images of lifestyles that show off these new values in comfortable, even luxurious ways. No sacrifice, frugality or privation. The magazine does not picture simplicity; it shows people who are in control and thus able to enjoy a life filled with more than just things. The success of *Real Simple* magazine, as well as that of the new sub-genre of shelter magazines it has pioneered, is a testament to the fact that people will shop with extra enthusiasm when the marketplace better matches their dreams and aspirations.

Of course, it's not as if quality, intangibles and time have ever been unimportant in consumer marketing. The difference now is that these values have become dominant, to the point that almost nothing else matters. These values are the emerging opportunities in the marketplace and thus the best if not the only vehicle for growth and future expansion.

Yankelovich first alerted clients to this nascent trend in the 1997 MONITOR Management Summary entitled "Resolving the Paradox of Possibility." Recently, several other marketplace observers have noted this change in core consumer values as well. Consultants Joseph Pine and James Gilmore were the first to outline a business model to fit this shift in values in their book, *The Experience Economy: Work Is Theatre & Every Business a Stage* (Harvard Business School Press: 1999). Their now-classic example of birthday cakes illustrates the progression in the marketplace culminating in today's experience economy: from birthday cakes baked from scratch to cakes made from a mix to cakes bought to go to businesses that put on the whole party. The cutting edge of growth lies in providing consumer experiences.

More recently, Michael Silverstein of the Boston Consulting Group (BCG) and Neil Fiske, formerly of BCG and now CEO of Bath & Body Works, have focused on the business implications of consumer expectations of luxury and prosperity. In their book *Trading Up: The New American Luxury* (Portfolio: 2003), Silverstein and Fiske explore the marketing implications of an increasingly affordable and ubiquitous luxury. Brands can no longer leverage quality and indulgence to their advantage because luxury has become a cost of entry in many categories. Instead, marketers must start with luxury and then add a strong emotional edge for differentiation.

In her book *The Substance of Style: How the Rise of Aesthetic Value is Remaking Commerce, Culture and Consciousness* (HarperCollins*Publishers*: 2003), Virginia Postrel, an "Economic Scene" columnist for the *New York Times* and the former editor of *Reason* magazine, zeroes in on design, aesthetics and glamour as the new driving forces in the marketplace and society at large. Aesthetics invest things with the meaning for which people are willing to pay.

Whether it's experiences, emotions or aesthetics and design, what each of these observers has highlighted is one of the many ways in which intangibles have come to dominate the marketplace. Intangibles are nothing new to marketers, but nowadays intangibles are all that matter. In today's marketplace, material characteristics like reliability, comfort, convenience, performance and functionality are taken for granted. Only intangibles can make a difference that matters to consumers. It's not just experiences or emotions or aesthetics. It's intangibles broadly defined, in whatever form or manner they best fit a particular business category. Indeed, a complete list of future opportunities related to intangibles should also include relationships, service and authenticity.

If all of this sounds vaguely familiar, it's probably because marketers have long been enamored of the work of mid-20th Century psychologist Abraham Maslow and his famous Hierarchy of Needs. Maslow was interested in the concept of self-actualization and what it took for people to develop healthy personalities that enabled them to realize their full potential in life. Maslow outlined a pyramid of needs that had to be satisfied in order for people to reach the highest level of personal fulfillment. At the base of the pyramid are basic survival needs. Security and safety needs come next. Then come social needs or people's desires for community and connections with others. Finally, come needs related to ego and esteem. Only after all of these types of needs are satisfied can people focus on self-actualization, the highest level in Maslow's pyramid of needs.

Maslow's work was very popular during the 1960s and 1970s when lots of people, Baby Boomers in particular, were focused on self-fulfillment. This was a time of great expectations about the future, notwithstanding many social and economic problems to be solved along the way. People believed that the future was going to relieve them of worrying about their basic needs, thus freeing them to focus on other things.

What Maslow posited was a framework that demonstrated how intangibles come to dominate people's priorities once all of their basic tangible needs are assured. The interest of marketers in Maslow's Hierarchy of Needs has traditionally been concerned with the level of development in particular product categories. The consensus of current thinking, however, as seen in the work of experts like Pine and Gilmore, Silverstein and Fiske, and Postrel, is that the marketplace as a whole has risen to the highest level in Maslow's Hierarchy. Given the current level of material abundance, intangibles are all that matter for business growth and competitive differentiation.

This is not to suggest that basic survival and safety needs have been secured for everyone, nor to suggest that many people aren't struggling financially. It is only to recognize that the latter half of the 1990s ushered in something that University of Florida English and advertising professor James Twitchell calls the "democratization of luxury" (*Living It Up: Our Love Affair With Luxury:* Columbia University Press, 2002). In a marketplace in which everyone at every income level has expectations of luxury, the tangibles are presumed, so intangible benefits and features dominate people's priorities and aspirations, not to mention what they want and expect from marketers.

THE MAINSTREAMING OF AFFLUENCE

Nobody aspires to be middle class anymore. Everybody expects to live in a place with a view of the water, so to speak, and the character of the marketplace reflects that. Every car should have the look and feel of a luxury car. Every hotel room should be a five-star experience with a high-speed Internet connection and satellite TV. Every home should show off a designer's touch, whether it's Martha Stewart, Katie Brown, B. Smith, Nigella Lawson, Rachel Ashwell or even HGTV. People's heroes, irrespective of the taint of scandal, are celebrity CEOs, hip-hop moguls and bubble billionaires.

This is more than just daydreaming about the lifestyles of the rich and famous. This is the debunking of ordinary tastes. People want to live luxuriously every day. Indeed, they think they deserve it. The only thing worth having or doing is something rich and marvelous. The only way to look or dress or live is in the highest style. Nothing ordinary passes muster anymore. The run-of-the-mill has to be replaced lock, stock and barrel, although only after it's been lampooned for its unsightliness. This is public entertainment à la the Roman Coliseum. Millions tune in to watch as people suffer their humiliations and triumphs on hit TV shows like "Trading Spaces," "Extreme Makeover," "The Swan" and "Queer Eye for the Straight Guy." Some shows allow viewers to give the thumbs up or down. The lesson of such reality TV is that any place or anyone can be renovated or made over in a fabulous way, so it's not surprising that everyone now expects to live like that.

The argot of prosperity has become the vernacular. A sumptuous lifestyle is seen as an entitlement. People expect regular life to be beyond compare. This is the mainstreaming of affluence, the presumption that everyone should be able to enjoy the consummate things that were once the exclusive preserve of the rich and elite. Gourmet coffee, sushi, day spas, overnight delivery, wireless phones, cosmetic surgery, golf vacations, adventure trips, boutiques, antilock brakes and reserve wines—all now within reach of the average Joe. Today's bare minimum is yesterday's extra special. There is a new floor in the consumer marketplace, and it has a penthouse view (Fig. 3.3).

But because affluence has become a mainstream expectation, it is difficult if not impossible to charge a premium for luxury. People expect the very best at the very best price. Luxury is not something extra; it's the cost of entry, and thus certainly not worth a premium price. Cheap no longer means shoddy; it just means a great price on the best stuff.

It has gotten to the point where it's hard to tell what's luxury and what's not. JetBlue offers leather seats and 24-channel private TV's at

Figure 3.3: **Affluent-Speak**

Then		Now
Used cars	▶	Pre-owned automobiles
Old	▶	Vintage
Glasses	▶	Eyewear
Curtains	▶	Window treatments
Stove	▶	Ranges and cooktops
Sales clerk	▶	Sales consultant
Face lift	▶	Cosmetic procedure
Coffee guy	▶	Barista
Lettuce	▶	Field greens
Vitamins	▶	Nutritional supplements
String beans	▶	Haricot verts
Soap	▶	Cleanser / beauty bar
Bartender	▶	Mixologist

economy class fares. Song and Ted hit the market with bright, shiny planes, yet their parent companies, Delta and United, continue to charge higher fares for more threadbare seats. A Mercedes sports coupe costs less than a Pontiac Bonneville or a Toyota Avalon or a Mitsubishi Lancer. Panera Bread serves its casual dining fare on real china with real utensils. No paper plates or plastic forks. Costco sells high-end wines at discount prices.

Curiously enough, however, it turns out that while we want to be pampered as if we were wealthy, we have mixed feelings about actually being wealthy. A 2000 survey sponsored by the American Association of Retired Persons found that 27 percent of men and 40 percent of women had no desire at all to become wealthy.[4] Even those who wanted to become wealthy worried about what wealth might do to them. Three-quarters of all respondents thought wealth would make them insensitive, and 80 percent feared that wealth would make them greedy. People did agree that wealth would mean less stress and the freedom to live as one chooses, yet the majority did not agree that wealth would bring peace of mind.

Nowadays, though, people do not have to risk the compromises of being wealthy. People can get the look and feel of wealth without actually being wealthy. Luxury has become the norm of the middle class even as middle-income households are under mounting, often perilous, financial pressure. A 2002 pictorial piece for the *New York Times Magazine* profiled seven families with household incomes equal to the national median of $54,400.[5] Each of these families had significant financial responsibilities and obligations, yet little savings. Still, each had recently splurged on at least one nonessential, expensive luxury item—a vintage car, a boat, an SUV, a second home, a wide-screen TV and entertainment center, an expensive vacation, a digital camera, or a swimming pool. Material affluence is no longer a "want"; it has become a "need," something everyone expects and that no one feels he or she can or should be forced to live without.

The mainstreaming of affluence has turned the consumer marketplace on its head. The trade-off between price and quality has been done away with, as has the status that used to come with owning the top of the line. Merciless price competition overwhelms even the best efforts at value-added marketing.

Many factors have made this marketplace of luxury parity possible: the rising excellence in design and production from decades of corporate quality initiatives; continual declines in the costs of technology alongside continual increases in power, performance and speed; the shift of manufacturing to cheaper labor markets around the world; and, the unlimited access and information now available to consumers, particularly via the Internet. With nothing to make luxury special, difficult or costly, people have grown accustomed to it.

Most marketers, though, have yet to catch up. With tangible luxuries no longer the acme of aspirations or value, marketers can grow their brands only by investing in the intangibles. The opportunities for snob appeal and premium pricing are no longer to be found in what a product is but in what comes after a product has first measured up to the new expectations arising from the mainstreaming of affluence.

MARKETING PRACTICE AS BRAND BENEFIT

Marketing is affected in two ways by the mainstreaming of affluence in the consumer marketplace. First, marketing practice must change to meet a higher level of expectations. Second, the practice of marketing has the opportunity to be the primary source of differentiation and value delivered by a brand.

People are enveloped by abundance, yet marketers still operate as if people lived in the midst of scarcity. The old models of using hard sell to push things on people without enough don't work for people who are surrounded by too much. People want something more from marketing itself, not just something more from the marketplace.

In a marketplace of luxury parity in which it is increasingly difficult, and often impossible, for brands to maximize their opportunities by selling themselves on nothing but tangible features and benefits, marketing itself has to create the difference that matters. Obviously, the marketing for a brand must emphasize the intangible features and benefits of a brand, but it has to do more than that. The practice of marketing must measure up to the same demands being placed on products and brands.

People have higher expectations of brands. Similarly, people have higher expectations of marketing. People want something better from marketers than more clutter and saturation. Just as a brand must deliver the intangibles that people want, so, too, must the marketing practices associated with a brand. The practice of marketing must also deliver the sort of consumption experience that people want. In this sense, marketing does not simply pitch the value of a brand, it *is* the value of a brand.

The quality of the time that people spend with marketing is just as important to them as the quality of the time that they spend with the product. When marketing practices are intrusive and annoying, the entire consumer experience is diminished. People will think less of a brand because of unpleasant marketing. By the same token, when marketing practices are enjoyable and engaging, the total consumer experience is enhanced. When brands are indistinguishable in other ways, differences in marketing practices can be decisive.

In fact, how marketing is practiced is much more salient to people nowadays. This is not to let any of the other marketing "P's" (product, place, promotion, price) off the hook, but it is to say that a fifth "P," practice, is a source of value that cannot be neglected. People are demanding more from marketing in return for their time and attention. Marketing can no longer promise the value of something else; it must deliver quality, intangibles and time, too. In fact, marketing practice is important these days not only because everything else is at luxury parity but because marketing practice has a unique power to deliver the intangible satisfactions that people value the most.

A brand and the marketing for that brand are not identical, of course. But the perceptions that people have of a brand are dependent upon marketing practice to a greater extent than ever before. It's not a matter of good ads boosting a brand's image or bad ads hurting it; it's a matter of better marketing practice being the very thing that a brand promotes about itself. When Capital One advertises no more telemarketing calls as a reason to apply for its Platinum Card, it is making marketing practice a brand benefit. When Earthlink touts its anti-spam features as a reason to subscribe, it is promoting the experience associated with marketing practices a specific product feature.

Car buying is another example. Few people have ever liked the high-pressure experience of buying a car, but in the past people had no other options, and, besides, the special value of the car more than compensated for the unpleasant buying experience. Nowadays, though, people can choose among many different ways of making a purchase and many more comparable automobile options. To win business, car dealers have had to make a better marketing and sales experience as big a selling point as anything related to the car. The experience of getting a car has become as important to people as the car itself, so people are now making buying decisions on the basis of the marketing and sales experience. Marketing practice can be a brand benefit.

THE PARADOX OF PROSPERITY

American consumers are much better off than ever before. And no better off at the same time. This is the fundamental paradox of super-abundance. Awash in so much stuff, people often feel that they are in up to their necks. The very things with which people are blessed are also their curse.

Super-abundance worsens the experiences people have in the consumer marketplace. Psychologists Sheena Iyengar of Columbia University and Mark Lepper of Stanford University have studied the impact of abundant options on how people make and evaluate choices.[6] In one laboratory experiment, college students were offered a choice of Godiva chocolates. One group was given six choices; the other group, 30 choices. The results of the experiment showed that the students given six choices were more satisfied with their choice and had fewer regrets. In addition, when given a choice of more chocolates or money as remuneration for participating in the experiment, students in the group choosing among six chocolates were four times as likely to choose chocolates over cash.

In another study conducted in a single grocery store, Iyengar and Lepper set up two tasting tables that were rotated hourly. One tasting table was set up to display 24 varieties of a brand-name jam. The other tasting table set up to display 6 varieties of the same jam. Although shoppers were more likely to stop at the table with 24 varieties, those stopping at the table with 6 varieties were 10 times more likely to actually buy a jam—30 percent versus a mere 3 percent.

Additional research has shown the same impact of super-abundance on choice in other areas such as classroom assignments, magazine displays, and mutual fund options in retirement plans. As Iyengar and Lepper have observed, the operative principle is simple. Greater choice is more enticing at first, but limited choice is actually more motivating.[7]

But the saturation impulse is too strong for marketers to resist, particularly in the heat of competitive jockeying for display space and share of voice. More seems better when potential customers are being targeted aggressively by competition. The smart response seems to be to build an overwhelming presence in the marketplace, yet, this winds up creating a marketplace experience that is demonstrably suboptimal in satisfying and motivating consumers.

However, sweeping, indiscriminate cutbacks in product choices and marketing communications are not the answer. The enormous variety of things available for sale is the result of marketers trying to offer something for everyone. While people don't enjoy sorting through a super-abundance of options, they do enjoy getting the one option that is perfectly customized for their tastes and preferences. The smartest way for marketers to engage people is not to take away customization but to provide better navigation tools that move people quickly to a small number of suitable options.

What's important is being relevant. Irrelevant alternatives are not only unwanted, they create a huge stack of things that people have to push out of the way in order to find the one alternative that they really want. This task is a burden that people dislike so much that it taints their eventual satisfaction with the choice they make. The more that people have to dig for a needle in the haystack, the less they will like the needle when they find it. Keeping everything relevant means keeping everything focused. A focused set of choices is necessarily fewer.

This is not to suggest that variety is bad. People like variety. Consumer research consistently finds that variety and a large selection are highly desirable because they enable people to find things that are unique and best suited for them. But it's not variety per se. Variety is a liability when it overwhelms people with a super-abundance of choices. Only good navigation keeps variety from being a burden.

Economists Erik Brynjolfsson and Yu Hu of MIT and Michael Smith of Carnegie-Mellon have studied the value to consumers of the abundantly greater selection available online.[8] Their research examined online book buying and found that nearly half of the titles bought online are hard-to-find books that cannot be easily or affordably obtained in any other way. They made a calculation of the economic value that this variety represents to consumers and found it to be 10 times the value from the cost savings of lower prices online. Abundance has value, but as Brynjolfsson, Hu and Smith point out, only if it can be navigated. It's the search features and personalized recommendation tools offered by online booksellers that unlock the value of variety. Without these navigation tools, online variety is nothing but an overwhelming, unapproachable and ultimately unsatisfying super-abundance of titles.

The paradoxical experience of super-abundance is true for happiness as well. In the midst of more social and personal prosperity than ever before, people are no happier. This puzzle was examined in detail by emeritus Yale University political scientist Robert Lane in his turn-of-the-millennium synthesis, *The Loss of Happiness in Market Democracies* (Yale University Press: 2000). Notwithstanding rising indicators of social and material well-being like growing GDP, equality for women, old-age pensions, a free press, democratic institutions, greater education and more access to media and information, survey measures of self-reported happiness have been declining for decades. Additionally, depression and teen suicides are up. The old saw is true: Money can't buy happiness.

This is not to say that people in abject poverty are the happiest people of all. More money does bring more happiness, but only up to a point. That threshold was calculated from the World Values Survey of 1990–91 by University of Michigan political scientist Ronald Inglehart.[9] He found it to be equal to the per capita GNP of Ireland in 1990. Above that level of prosperity, there is no correlation between the average wealth of a country and its average level of happiness.

There are many reasons why money and happiness are unrelated. Lane concludes that the primary reason for the declining levels of happiness in more prosperous societies is that the pursuit of prosperity takes time away from personal relationships, yet it's relationships with others that make people happy. Making money estranges people from one another, and that leaves people less happy, even depressed.

Structural elements and other characteristics of the consumer economy also play a part. Various researchers have cited things like too many choices, an overemphasis on instant gratification and selfish interests, the overarousal of appetites, spiraling levels of expectations, more stress, less free time, too much focus on the future and too little on the here and now, worries about debt, and the unrelenting pressure to buy. Indeed, it is difficult to envision a market-driven society in which people are perfectly content because the engine of market growth is consumer demand. Marketing plays the central role in stimulating consumer demand by motivating people to want something different or something more than what they have right now.[10] A certain degree of dissatisfaction, if not unhappiness, is essential. But in a marketplace of super-abundance and luxury expectations, the ever-greater time and energy spent on acquisitiveness leaves people with an even more acutely felt need for happiness.

A desire for more meaning and fulfillment began to bubble up as the decade of the nineties drew to a close. The super-abundance of the bubble did not translate into a surplus of happiness. As people moved into the new millennium, they began to ask themselves tough questions. They looked back to take stock of what they had gained and found that being better off and feeling better did not always go hand in hand. In Yankelovich MONITOR tracking, three in four respondents have been saying for the past several years that they are "spending more time these days thinking about what works and what doesn't work" in their lives. There is a more widespread and deeper feeling among people nowadays that, notwithstanding all that they've accumulated and attained, something vital is still missing.

MEANING OVER MATTER

The mainstreaming of affluence enables people to focus on the intangibles in life because they can take the tangibles for granted. The various dissatisfactions inherent in a marketplace of super-abundance intensify this focus on quality, intangibles and time. Tangible things can only take people so far. More stuff gets people no closer to the meaning and fulfillment they really want, and oftentimes it takes them further away. So, as the marketplace continues to move in the direction of more super-abundance and luxury parity, the yearning for quality, intangibles and time will grow stronger.

Some observers credit the 9/11 terrorist attacks as the cause of this value shift. *Real Simple* magazine, for example, was not a success at first. It hit its stride only after 9/11. It is certainly true that September 11, 2001 was an afternoon off in America, when people all over the country sat down and thought about what really mattered to them. What gave people comfort on that awful day was not any of the stuff they owned but their families, friends, communities and spiritual values. People were reminded of what was most important to them. A chord was struck that still resounds today.

But people did not change their values overnight. Quality, intangibles and time were already growing in importance. The Yankelovich MONITOR detected the first signs of this shift in priorities as early as 1996. The events of 9/11 were simply a precipitating event that gave people the permission they needed to follow through on the value changes and lifestyle shifts that they had already been considering.

It was a Jeff Van Gundy phenomenon. Van Gundy was the hardworking, 24/7 head coach of the New York Knicks who put in infamously long, grueling hours throughout his seven-year stretch in New York during the bubble years of the nineties. Van Gundy was the NBA equivalent of a dot-com entrepreneur, sacrificing everything for success in his career. But over the summer of 2001, as he was approaching 40, Van Gundy felt he had lost his focus. He began rethinking the priorities in his life. He talked about quitting with then-president of the Knicks Scott Layden. Yet, despite his change of heart, Van Gundy could not bring himself to leave. Then came 9/11. People very close to Van Gundy were lost that day, something that put his priorities in a new perspective. He found the personal resolve he needed to follow through on what he had already realized that he wanted to do. So, on December 8, 2001, Van Gundy announced his resignation, saying that he was going to "exhale" for the first time in 13 years and that his daughter was looking forward to having lunch with him. He called that "cool."[11]

In the period immediately after 9/11, people all over America found the permission and courage they needed to follow through on changes they had already decided they wanted to make. Few people made changes as dramatic as that made by Van Gundy, but everyone started to do whatever he or she could afford in order to put more balance into his or her life. 9/11 was simply the catalyst that hastened a process of change that was already underway, accomplishing in a day what might otherwise have taken years. This blending of values and priorities into a more balanced fusion of tangibles and intangibles continues to strengthen.

Van Gundy is now back in the NBA as head coach of the Houston

Rockets. He still works hard and wants to win just as much as ever. But the *USA Today* profile on September 25, 2003 described a coach who is trying to leaven his intensity with some balance and perspective. Not to lose his winning edge, but to build a winning tradition without losing himself in the process.

The agenda of values for America as a whole, as it has been for the last four decades, continues to be led in large part by Baby Boomers like Van Gundy. All Baby Boomers are now over 40; most are in their mid- to late forties and fifties. This is a stage of life when people naturally begin to think less about the material obsessions that have consumed them for decades and to think more about nonmaterial priorities like family, friends, community and spirituality. Given the size, wealth and power of Baby Boomers, it's no surprise that the salience and importance of quality, intangibles and time are on the rise. The conjunction of aging Baby Boomers with the mainstreaming of affluence, the super-abundance of the marketplace, and the impact of 9/11 has ignited a value shift of enormous reach and intensity that is forcing marketers to reconsider and re-examine the values that motivate people in the consumer marketplace.

MARKETING RELEVANCE

The marketing challenge is clear. The underlying foundation of desire in the consumer marketplace is no longer a straightforward need to acquire and accumulate. Since the end of World War II, when people were focused first and foremost on filling their pantries and driveways, the marketplace has evolved to a post-materialism stage in which nonmaterial values are the predominant influences on consumption decisions. Needs, aspirations and benefits are now rooted in quality, intangibles and time. The same old messages in the same old ways will ride far behind the breaking wave of tomorrow. Marketers must develop new ways of being relevant to consumers. This is a new frontier for today's generation of marketers.

The consumer marketplace is in transition. In a period of transition, consumer preferences and loyalties are in flux, which provides the best chance for brands to make inroads that could not otherwise be made.

Finding new relevance is not just a product challenge; it's a marketing challenge as well, perhaps even more so. In the post-materialism marketplace it is possible for a brand to gain a sustainable competitive edge as much through its marketing practices as through its product features. Not only do products and marketing messages have to be more relevant, so does marketing practice.

Marketing must mirror what people want both by what it communicates and by how it communicates. If the marketing is bad, so is the message, irrespective of what the message says. If the marketing is good, the message is that much better. In the marketplace of tomorrow, the marketing is the message.

SUMMING UP

- In a marketplace of super-abundance, people have needs that are different from those they had in the less abundant past. Not only are people seeking different benefits from the products they buy, they want something different from marketing, too.

- In today's marketplace, things like reliability, comfort, convenience, performance and functionality are taken for granted. So, people want more than those things. People want brands that can connect them with the intangibles that now matter most to them.

- With the mainstreaming of affluence, marketing practice must meet a higher level of expectations. Even more importantly, the practice of marketing can be the primary source of differentiation and value delivered by a brand.

- Marketing must deliver relevant brand value by enriching the time that people spend with marketing. Marketing must get in tune with the intangibles.

NOTES

1 Ed Kerschner, "The All American Shopping List," UBS Warburg, April 1, 2001. This report and these themes in particular were developed in large part from data and analysis in the Yankelovich MONITOR.

2 "Snapshot: If I Were A Rich Man," *USA Today,* October 24, 1997.

3 As psychologist Robert Cialdini has pointed out, in ambiguous or transitional situations where people are uncertain about what to do, they look to the example of others. If everyone is uncertain and looking to everyone else for clarity about what to do, then no one acts because there is no example offering any guidance. This is why small fringe movements often have an influence disproportionate to their size—they provide the example that offers guidance.

4 Kirsten Gerencher, "Keep Your Lifeline Regis," CBS Marketwatch.com, May 16, 2000.

5 Camille Sweeney, "The Middle of the Middle Class," *New York Times Magazine,* June 9, 2002.

6 S. S. Iyengar & M. Lepper, "When choice is demotivating: Can one desire too much of a good thing?" *Journal of Personality and Social Psychology,* Vol. 76, 2000.

7 There are many reasons why this is true. The best introduction to the psychology of choice is *The Paradox of Choice: Why Less Is More* (Ecco: 2004), by Barry Schwartz.

8 Erik Brynjolfsson, Michael D. Smith and Yu Hu, Consumer Surplus in the Digital Economy: Estimating the Value of Increased Product Variety, *Management Science,* Vol. 49 (2003).

9 Ronald Inglehart, *Modernization and Postmodernization: Cultural, Economic, and Political Change in Societies* (Princeton, NJ: Princeton University Press: 1997).

10 Most marketers don't try to create artificial demand. Rather, they look to solve real problems and meet genuine needs. Even so, the ultimate objective is to create enough dissatisfaction to motivate purchasing by showing people a better way to deal with their problems and needs.

11 ESPN.com, "Van Gundy Quits; Chaney Reportedly Will Finish the Season," December 8, 2001.

Self-Invention

Expectations of self-invention are blurring the lines between consuming and marketing. Increasingly, people expect the act of consuming to include and encompass the ability to be a producer. In a world of self-invention, people want more, if not all, of the power and the control that marketers traditionally presumed was theirs alone.

Nothing is more emblematic of the consumer marketplace to come than Web rings. They are perhaps the clearest example of how new technologies have opened up a whole new world of self-directed personal possibilities for people.

Web rings are linked Web sites organized around a common theme or a specialized topic, frequently some obscure bit of arcane knowledge. Oftentimes, these linked sites are coordinated through a central Web site that provides a forum for interaction and dialogue. However organized, though, these hyperlinked Web sites constitute a virtual community of interest for people with a passion for a particular subject. The pertinent Web ring is the place for single-minded, unadulterated topical immersion.

Yet, the role of building virtual communities by bringing people together online is not the most important impact of Web rings. The impact that matters is how Web rings have changed the ways in which people view their own personal capabilities, competencies and possibilities due to the knowledge and resources offered. Or to put it another way, what Web rings have revolutionized the most is access, not community.

Imagine someone who wakes up one morning and decides for no reason in particular that he or she wants to become an expert on Australian law enforcement insignia. All that he or she needs to do is to go to the Web ring(s) on that subject. A little time there and, voila, the subject is mastered. Then, suppose the next day that same person awakens and decides that he or she wants to become an expert on the town of Almost Heaven, West Virginia. Again, all he or she needs to do is to go to the appropriate Web ring(s). A little study there will instantly make that person an expert on that topic. This can go on day after day, issue after issue, topic after topic. Not that no work is required, but the work required is different than what's been needed before, and this difference changes the whole idea of what it is to have expertise or to be an expert.

No longer is expertise something that comes only through a lifelong commitment to learning or a career in a certain field. No longer is expertise attainable only through intensive research or dedicated study. No longer is expertise an all-consuming matter that defines a person's very essence and identity. Instead, expertise is now simply a matter of whatever someone wants to have or wants to be when he or she wakes up in the morning. In effect, expertise has become a fashion statement.

This is not to suggest that every Web ring is accurate and complete or that demanding topics are any less difficult to comprehend and master. Caution and commitment are required. But it is noteworthy that Web rings have opened up vast new possibilities for people to invent for themselves what and who they want to be. Web rings instantaneously envelop people in specialized parallel universes that accelerate the learning curve and hence the possibilities for self-invention—and for reinvention as often as one likes.

POSSIBILITIES WITHOUT LIMITS

This opening up of individual possibilities is a byproduct of the Internet as a whole, of course, not just of Web rings in particular. The flowering of greater individual empowerment was a big part of the early excitement about the information superhighway, and it is a big part of the value that people see in the Internet today. Seventy-three percent of respondents to the Yankelovich MONITOR survey agree that access to the Internet has helped them do more things on their own that would have necessitated the help of others in the past. The Internet facilitates self-empowerment and self-invention, but the way in which the Internet has empowered people is more than just making things a click away. The real breakthrough of the Internet is that it enables people to wrap themselves in cocoons entirely of their own making.

People's expectations now reflect these greater personal possibilities, not because of Web rings alone but because the entire character of contemporary life encourages people to think in terms of self-invention. People want to participate in the creation of meaning not simply look for meaning in what's made available to them. People want to write their own scripts, not shoehorn themselves into life scripts with foregone conclusions. People want to transcend traditional limits, not resign themselves to living within pre-existing limits and constraints. Self-invention is how people expect to live.

Self-invention is not just another term for self-reliance and self-determination. It is more than self-reliantly choosing among options made available by others. Self-invention is all about having the power and the control necessary to create and produce the very options from which choices are made.

Just as people want to use things like Web rings to reinvent themselves, so, too, do people want to use whatever it takes to reinvent their relationships with marketers. Expectations of self-invention are blurring the lines between consuming and marketing. Increasingly, people expect the act of consuming to include and encompass the ability to be a producer. In a world of self-invention, people want more, if not all, of the power and the control that marketers traditionally presumed was theirs alone. People don't want complete power and control for every product or purchase, of course, but they have come to take it for granted that if or when they want power and control, they are entitled to it.

A CULTURE OF REINVENTION

Belief in the opportunity to reinvent oneself, to become whatever one chooses for oneself, is an integral part of the American psyche. Indeed, self-determination has been central to the American experience and is regarded by every American as a basic entitlement. Throughout American history, impediments to self-determination have been fiercely resisted and, thankfully, progressively removed.

The self-made man is the acme of success. While the consequences of overreaching to reinvent himself proved tragic for Jay Gatsby in F. Scott Fitzgerald's classic novel about the American dream, people have never given up a belief in the transformative power of self-determination. Some social commentators have suggested that this is why Americans are willing to tolerate staggering inequalities in the distribution of wealth. People fear that steps to close the gap would penalize everyone, not just the super-rich, by imposing limits on entrepreneurial success. No one wants to close off the opportunity for the next Bill Gates (or to lose that opportunity for oneself, however remote). The ability to invent oneself has long been the great calming force in American politics as well as the great motivating force in American business.

America has a tradition of self-improvement and of self-help groups. Self-improvement is seen as essential to self-reliance, which in turn is the key ingredient for self-determination. While a pop culture icon like the Lone Ranger embodies the American ideal of self-reliance, the reality has always been more along the lines of a football quarterback. People have been able to determine their own affairs and accomplish things for themselves as part of a bigger team effort, not as isolated free agents. The successful quarterback wins not by doing everything himself but by organizing and directing a team of skilled players. Each team member plays a key role in supporting the success that the quarterback leads. Thus, the American strain of self-reliance has always been a matter of getting the best help and of having the best resources, not of being independent of all ties and connections.

The tension between individualistic ideals and organizational (or bureaucratic) realities exists because the tools and resources that have been available for self-improvement, self-reliance and self-determination have necessarily tied individuals to a team. The chance to be truly independent has been constrained by the limits of the available technologies. But now this is changing.

The new technologies, tools and resources available today are erasing the old limits. As a result, people's expectations are being reshaped. No longer do people believe that their individual options must be limited and constrained. Technological developments are liberating people from dependence on others, particularly from the long-standing ties to authorities and institutions. The American culture of reinvention is being transformed from the old one of mere self-determination to a new one of boundless self-invention.

While Internet technologies like Web rings are a central part of this transformation, other technologies are also playing a role in a wide variety of areas including medicine, food, fashion, home and pop culture. And even apart from technologies, the craving for self-invention is being felt in areas like religion and ethnicity. People's expectations about all aspects of their lives, marketing included, now reflect a belief in the unbounded possibilities of self-invention.

WHATEVER I WANT TO BE

Everywhere people look, self-inventive possibilities are available to them. If not today, then soon to come. Old limits look laughable. The individual is in control, unconstrained by the need to find support or win approval from others.

In Medicine

Modern medical procedures are giving people total and affordable control over their physical appearances.[1] Modern medical procedures do more than save lives; they open up new personal possibilities and encourage new lifestyle expectations. People have learned that they can remake themselves into whatever they want to be. A popular reality TV show, "The Swan," follows women as they receive cosmetic surgery to transform their looks from ordinary to fabulous. After undergoing various procedures, these women reappear with new looks that are spectacular enough for them to compete in a beauty pageant. As it entertains, this show teaches that it is not unreasonable to expect to be able to completely reinvent one's physical appearance, not just as a TV contestant but all on one's own.

No longer do people believe that they must accept and live with the bodies with which they were born. The *Atlanta Journal-Constitution* led with this banner headline underneath the page one masthead on July 11, 2004: "Teens Not Shy About Getting Breast Implants." The story told of young women who have come of age with "Extreme Makeover" and "The

Swan" and who don't see breast implants as "a life-altering experience but as a cosmetic improvement, like teeth whitening or blond highlights."

The American Society for Aesthetic Plastic Surgery reports that cosmetic surgeries are up 87 percent from 1997 to 2003. The top three procedures in 2003 were liposuction, breast augmentation and eyelid surgery. While Baby Boomers account for the largest proportion of these surgeries, nearly one-quarter involve people under the age of 35. Stomach stapling is up ten-fold over the past decade. Nearly 1.5 million people undergo Lasik eye surgery each year.

The completion of the human genome project has ratcheted up the promise of bodily self-invention even more. Many scientists believe that we are on the verge of being able to reprogram or override our genetic make-ups, at which point we will be able to ask ourselves consumer questions about our health that we've never been able to ask before. Like how healthy does one want to be and what is that worth? Is a 5 percent improvement in one's health a good investment? Or even more unusual questions, like what kind of stamina is best to give to oneself—the Winston Churchill kind of stamina, which is the constitution to eat too much, drink too much, smoke too much, lead his country through two World Wars and still live to 90, or the Michael Jordan kind of stamina, which is the fitness to play all out for an entire game but still have enough left at the end to clinch a sixth title with a final shot in the clutch?

New York Times writer James Gorman noted in an essay about the growing use of pharmaceuticals that prescription drugs are now being used to treat physical and psychological conditions that were once thought to be outside the purview of medicine.[2] Gorman noted that the use of drugs for personalized lifestyle enhancement has grown to the point that Dr. Christian Daughton, chief of environmental chemistry for the Environmental Protection Agency's National Exposure Research Laboratory, worries that water supplies are becoming polluted with dangerously high levels of still-potent medications that are introduced through careless disposal and normal human waste.

In Fashion

Computer-enhanced fashions will take bodily self-invention a step further. So-called wearable computers are going to make it possible for people to completely determine the environments within which they spend their time. An IBM TV ad that ran in 2000 offered people an enticing peek into this future. The ad showed a man sitting in a piazza filled with pigeons, but he is in fact in a world of his own making, oblivious to everything but the stock quotes he can see scrolling by on a screen attached to his glasses. As he watches, he shouts orders into a microphone linked to speech-recognition software. This ad resonated so strongly with people's interests and expectations that IBM fielded a flurry of calls from people wanting to buy this nonexistent wearable technology.

Early prototypes of wearable computers are available, though, and FedEx and Bell Canada have outfitted some of their workers with them. Fashion-forward technologies are being developed that will integrate earpieces into earrings, microphones into necklaces, and cameras into eyeglasses. Many observers contend that the handheld wireless devices carried by millions are, in effect, primitive wearable computers.

While some critics scoff that no one will don RoboCop-looking outfits, others point out that lots of people already go through life with headphones plugged into their skulls. *USA Today* writer Kevin Maney argued that it's a mistake to "underestimate how stupid" people are willing to look in order to take advantage of innovative technologies (especially technologies that enable them to invent their own environments and experiences).[3] Besides, these technologies are becoming much more inconspicuous.

In mid-2004, Adidas announced the introduction of a $250 running shoe called "1" that has a sensor in the heel connected to a microprocessor that operates a motor to adjust the cushioning of the shoe. In realtime, this running shoe reshapes itself according to the changing terrain in order to maintain the ideal compression for optimal cushioning. People see that from here it is but a short step to the next generation of computer-enhanced clothing and accessories that, when slipped on, will create self-personalized experiences for the wearer.

At Home

The so-called smart houses under development today utilize sophisticated technology platforms that enable people to live in interior environments that are actively responsive to their individual preferences and tastes. The smart houses to come will do more than simply reflect what someone likes; they will learn and react to someone's wants and needs.

Basic technologies like home entertainment systems and wireless security systems that also control heating, cooling and lighting have already enabled millions to self-invent a small part of the character of life for themselves. The tidal wave of home renovation that swept through suburbia during the post-2001 mortgage refinancing boom accelerated the diffusion of these basic systems by turning home remodelers, in the words of science writer James Gleick, into home "systems integrators."[4]

The next wave of smart houses will wrap people even more tightly in self-personalized physical environments. Computer labs at several leading universities are quickly bringing the necessary cutting-edge systems online: homes that learn the best time to raise the heat and start the coffee based on an individual's morning routine; homes that monitor a person's health and weight and then recommend a menu on a screen in the kitchen or, if needed, contact the doctor or 911; systems that allow people to keep an eye on what's going on at home from a distance, even using graphical displays to show relevant status information; homes that read food labels and make menu suggestions; homes that keep track of kitchen activities and provide reminders and prompts; and homes that study and then enhance sleep patterns and bathroom routines.[5] While it will take a while for smart houses to become pervasive, the word is getting out that people should expect home to be a place where self-invented experiences can be created and enjoyed.

In Society

People have come to expect the ability to be self-inventive in every aspect of their lives whether technology plays a facilitating role or not. Increasingly, religion is being self-invented. People feel free to pick a religion that fits their personal tastes. Dean Hoge, professor of sociology at Catholic University of America, has noted that so-called religion switching is "more common now" than at any point in American history.[6]

Martin Marty, the former dean of the University of Chicago Divinity School, has noted that people's choice of church and even denomination is no longer based solely on religious beliefs. Instead, it has come down to "a choice [about] a way of life."[7] In other words, like everything else in a self-inventive world, people choose their religion to fit their lifestyles rather than live their lifestyles in accordance with their religion.

Similarly, people are defining their race and ethnicity in self-inventive ways. In the 2000 census, 42 percent of all persons choosing Hispanic as their ethnicity chose no racial category at all, marking the box for "some other race" instead. The traditional census categories no longer suffice to reflect the racial identities that many people have defined for themselves.

FACING THE MUSIC

The first business category to feel the full effects of self-invention is the music business. The traditional model of delivering music doesn't accommodate self-invention. Today's listeners want power and control, yet music companies won't give it up. As a result, a bitter fight has ensued.

The music business model is built on the royalties paid on the basis of copyright ownership. The copyright law governing the music business dates back to the heyday of Tin Pan Alley and sheet music during the late 19th and early 20th Centuries. The music business has changed significantly since this era, but the underlying model is still the same. Listeners can buy music for personal use. Copying and sharing are not allowed.

Implicit within the traditional music model are certain roles and expectations for producers and listeners of music. These roles and expectations fit the technologies of the past. But the advent of digital technologies has challenged all of the old assumptions because digital music technologies have completely changed the roles and expectations of listeners. Listeners want to use digital technologies to be more self-inventive, and this subverts the old music business model, both in terms of compensation and control.

The emergence of downloading in the late 1990s completed the development of the new digital culture for music that had been percolating since the appearance of CDs in the early 1980s. The music business was entering a new era. In 1998, *New York Times Magazine* editor Gerald Mazorati published a long lament about the passing of the old kind of rock 'n' roll musical experience, and in doing so, he offered a picture of the self-inventive future ahead.[8]

Mazorati noted that the convenience and plasticity of digital music meant that listeners are no longer obliged to listen to music only in the way in which artists recorded and presented it. Listeners can now scan, skip and reprogram CDs and MP3s and listeners can make their own CDs with the songs they prefer in any order they like. Or to put it another way, Mazorati saw that digital technologies have empowered listeners to be active participants in the creation of their musical experiences. No longer must listeners give themselves over to "somebody else's desires."

Because of listener control, Mazorati was singing a dirge for the concept album, that fully integrated rock LP that revolves around a core concept or theme:[9] Pink Floyd's *Dark Side of the Moon,* The Beatles' *Sgt. Pepper's Lonely Hearts Club Band,* Marvin Gaye's *What's Going On,* to mention but a few. For a concept album to work, the artist must control the listening experience in order to be able to present his or her conceptual vision. When listeners can use technology to do whatever they want—remixing, rematching, sampling, reordering and skipping—instead of what the artist wants, the concept album is no longer viable. What Mazorati put his finger on was the flowering of a new music culture of listener control.

By 1999, the new era had begun, yet the old models of compensation and control continued to hold sway even as listeners young and old were demanding something completely different. The music industry has been slow to adapt its business practices to make peace with this new world, particularly the practice of downloading. Indeed, the response of the music industry has been to close its fist ever more tightly around the reins of power by suing to retain control rather than sharing power and control with consumers who have come to expect it. Resistance to downloading turns a deaf ear to the emergence of self-invention as a marketplace phenomenon rife with opportunities for growth and new revenue streams. With self-invention on the rise because of digital technologies, the legal fight against downloading has enabled others to steal a march on the music industry.

The most innovative responses to the digital music culture have come from outside the music industry. While the music industry was busy fighting downloaders tooth and nail, the future of the industry was being formulated and led by people by people like Steve Jobs of Apple. Instead of devoting all of his time and creativity to devising legal stratagems, Jobs thought about how to structure a business model for downloading that would offer something of mutual value to music providers and listeners.

In late April 2003, Apple announced iTunes, a music downloading service featuring music from all of the major music companies for 99 cents a song. With iTunes, Apple has dictated the starting point for the future of the music industry—structure, pricing, access, experience—all piggybacked on the success and reputation of Apple's popular iPod MP3 player. While services to download songs for a fee have been available for years, they were cumbersome and inconsistent. iTunes has become the visionary exemplar for an industry still focused on suing the very people iTunes is serving. As self-invention grows and as the music industry slowly begins to change, it is a safe bet that iTunes will own a marketplace position that will cost other companies a fortune in profits and shareholder value to match or overcome, if indeed they can catch up at all.

In its first year, iTunes sold 70 million downloads. As it turns the corner on its second year, Apple is on track to more than double that, selling 2.7 million iTunes downloads per week.[10] As of early 2004, Apple claimed 70 percent of the legal downloading market. In fact, music has become a crucial part of Apple's future business strategy. While traditional music companies have been struggling with a long-term decline in CD sales, Apple has created new momentum for itself by accommodating and collaborating with downloaders. In the first quarter of 2004, Apple sold more iPods than computers and the percentage of total corporate sales accounted for by products other than computers was 39 percent, double the percentage two years earlier. Apple's ultimate vision in consumer electronics is broader than music alone, but it is driving that long-term strategy with a solid foundation in music.[11]

Coke, Pepsi and McDonald's have also tapped into this new music culture of self-invention. The highly popular U.S. CokeMusic.com Web site is a place where teens can go to download music as well as create their own mixes of music that's available there. It is the third most popular Web site among teens.[12] In October 2003, Pepsi and Apple announced a promotion to give away 100 million free downloads from the iTunes Web site. Codes were printed underneath bottle caps of Pepsi, Diet Pepsi and Sierra Mist that could be used to download a song. In mid-2004, McDonald's announced a similar promotion that gives buyers of a Big Mac Extra Value Meal a code they can use to download a song of their choice from the Sony Connect Web site. This promotion was launched in the U.S., then rolled out into Britain, France and Germany.[13]

The successes of Apple, Coke, Pepsi and McDonald's show the folly of stiff-arming the shifts in the consumer marketplace being ushered in by self-invention. Surely, by this point in time the music industry would have pioneered a new source of revenue growth for itself if accommodation, not litigation, had been its first instinct.

The music industry believes that its litigation strategy has been successful. By the end of 2003, millions of people had abandoned illegal downloading (although downloading, illegal and legal, continues to grow), and by early 2004, CD sales had started to rebound. But lost opportunities don't get tallied in industry figures, and the question of whether litigation against downloaders has helped boost CD sales yields surprising answers. Initial research suggests that when it comes to downloading and CD sales, one does not affect the other. A study by Felix Oberholzer-Gee of the Harvard Business School and Koleman S. Strumpf of the University of North Carolina at Chapel Hill found that the impact of downloading on music sales was "statistically indistinguishable from zero."[14]

In fighting downloaders, the music industry may well have been focusing on the wrong factor behind its recent sales declines. Industry observers caution that the sales recovery in early 2004 is probably due more to the improving economy and to reductions in the prices of CDs.[15] There has been a highly competitive proliferation of available media and leisure alternatives. Long-term music sales have been hurt by a growing dependence on big, chancy, blockbuster hits, the consolidation of radio stations, and fewer new releases. The CD sales boom of the last twenty years was created to a large degree by Baby Boomers replacing their LPs, and that has now ended.

The music industry is desperately searching for the next breakout opportunity while fighting an exhausting rear-guard action against downloading. The problem is that downloading *is* the next breakout opportunity. Or at least the new culture of self-invention that downloading represents. As in every area of life, people are looking forward to greater control over their musical experiences. While the lure of free music has attracted lots of people to downloading, there is much more to downloading than free music. Downloading is a cultural phenomenon rooted in and reflective of the broader social dynamic of self-invention.

When *New York Times* pop music critic Jon Pareles reflected on what free downloading sites like Napster meant to him, he didn't mention price.[16] Instead, he talked about live cuts, alternate takes, forgeries, parodies, homemade collages, audio snippets, video clips, news outtakes, photos, and more—things he could use to make music more fun for himself, things not offered or sanctioned by the traditional music industry. Indeed, Pareles speculated that when music companies finally get around to offering downloads of their catalogs, their Web sites will look sterile next to the eclectic variety of things available today on free downloading sites. Yet, these are precisely the kinds of things that give Pareles the power and control to invent something for himself that is more gratifying. While Pareles didn't put it in these terms, what he is describing is a self-invented musical experience.

Admittedly, not everyone is a music fan like Pareles, but everyone wants more power and control. Besides, as Pareles notes, the people who do share his (self-inventive) interest are the most active fans who should be coddled by the music industry because they have more potential than most to be strong sources of value, growth and opinion leadership. Alienating those who care the most about music, particularly with banner headline coverage in the national media, shuts off emerging opportunities.

GO MY OWN WAY

The swiftness with which people have taken up the new opportunities for self-invention is evidence of a pent-up interest that was lurking just beneath the surface. When the technological moment finally arrived, people leapt at the chance for self-invention.

Two factors are behind the eagerness to be self-inventive. One is a grave lack of trust in anyone or anything else. The other is an utmost self-confidence in one's own abilities. These two attitudes have been building for many years. New technologies have simply unleashed what people were already primed to do.

Trust in public authorities and institutions has been in decline since the Watergate era, and it has been and continues to be besieged on many fronts. Years of emboldened investigative reporting and a perennial stream of scandals in government, business, sports, the clergy and even the media itself have conditioned people to expect the worst. The public appetite for tabloid headlines, Internet rumors and celebrity paparazzi feeds a frenzy of one-upsmanship to pop the balloons of famous people, thereby reinforcing the perception that nothing is as it seems and that no one can be trusted. Decades of politicking against big government by Democrats and Republicans alike adds to the belief that big institutions can't be trusted (Fig. 4.1).

Trust has suffered some particularly hard body blows since 9/11. The last few years have been rife with revelations about abuses of power and exploitations of trust. Enron. Worldcom. Adelphia. Dynergy. Tyco. HealthSouth. Martha Stewart. Frank Quattrone. Jack Grubman. Henry Blodget. 9/11 intelligence failures. No weapons of mass destruction in Iraq. Sexual abuse involving Catholic clergy. BALCO. Abu Ghraib. Events have dashed people's hopes for a revival of trust and faith following the Monica Lewinsky debacle and the persistent (though, ultimately, baseless) reports and rumors swirling around about Whitewater, Travelgate and Vince Foster.

Current public opinion about business is especially low, in large part because of the recent parade of corporate scandals. A CBS News Poll released in July 2002 found that 67 percent of the general public disagreed that most corporate executives are honest. This was substantially higher than the 55 percent who disagreed in 1985.[17] Thirty-five percent report no confidence in big business, compared to 25 percent in 1992.

Additionally, over the course of the last few decades, American business usurped a large part of the visionary leadership traditionally provided by government and political leaders. Business more than government has been hailed as the builder and guarantor of America's future. So, as trust in general has been undercut in recent years, it is no surprise that business is bearing much of the brunt of the public's disappointment and sense of betrayal.

Results from the Yankelovich MONITOR show that distrust of business is widely felt. The overwhelming majority worry that businesses are too focused on profits to be trusted to take care of their other responsibilities. About two-thirds feel that businesses look for ways to break the rules and that this necessitates government oversight. Even worse, public distrust of business translates into concerns about how businesses treat their customers (Fig. 4.2).

When people don't trust companies to treat them well or to take care

Figure 4.1: **Trust in Institutions and Authorities**

Things have a great deal of confidence in:	1987	1999	2003
Your own abilities	n/a	73%	72%
Doctors	n/a	61	57
Pharmacists	64	47	45
Police and law enforcement	n/a	35	39
Religious leaders	42	40	36
The President	n/a	n/a	30
Public schools	45	27	26
TV news	54	24	21
Newspapers	49	20	19
Judicial system	n/a	18	18
Bankers	n/a	n/a	16
Federal government	18*	12	14
Web sites	n/a	n/a	12
Consumer information provided by major corporations	29	12	12
News in magazines	37	14	9
Advertising	8*	7	7
Stockbrokers	n/a	11	6
CEOs of major corporations	n/a	n/a	5
Auto salesmen	12	5	5

Source: Yankelovich MONITOR (*1991)

of their needs, people look for other ways to ensure that they can get what they want. While ombudsmen and consumer watchdogs provide some help, for the most part, people have turned to themselves. Growing distrust has thus nurtured and intensified the shift towards self-invention.

The traditional business model assumes a large degree of consumer dependency. Companies study consumers, analyze the data, assess the

Figure 4.2: **Distrust of Business**

	Agree
2003	
American business is too concerned about making a profit and not concerned enough about its responsibilities to workers, consumers and the environment	**80**%
2004	
If the opportunity arises, most businesses will take advantage of the public if they feel they are not likely to be found out	**70**
Even well-known, long-established companies cannot be trusted to make safe, durable products without the government setting industry standards	**61**

Source: Yankelovich MONITOR

options and then decide what options to make available to consumers. Presumably, these options are properly configured to satisfy the exact needs of individual consumers, but regardless of the fit, the operative business model is one in which consumers have to trust that their needs will come first when companies decide what to do. But people don't have that trust anymore, so the old business model no longer works. People want a way of participating in the consumer marketplace that does not require that they be in a position of dependency.

Self-invention is the way in which people are looking to protect themselves and ensure their satisfaction in the consumer marketplace. It is a necessity borne of distrust as well as an opportunity created by new technologies. Not only do people feel the need and the permission to be self-inventive, they feel capable, too.

When asked in the Yankelovich MONITOR whether they think that their IQ is above average, 61 percent of respondents agreed. People have a high opinion of their abilities and smarts, so taking charge in the marketplace is not seen as a problem. Other MONITOR findings confirm the high self-regard and self-confidence that people have in themselves. Yet, how often does a person leave an interaction with a company feeling that he or she has been treated like a person of above-average intelligence? If the latest MONITOR ratings of business performance and product quality are any indication, the answer would be not too often (Fig. 4.3).

Figure 4.3: **Perceptions of High Quality**

	2000	2003
Food and grocery products	48%	45%
Household appliances, large	48	46
Prescription drugs	46	43
Household appliances, small	41	38
Domestic cars	39	30
Household cleaning products	38	35
Cosmetics and toiletries	37	30
OTC Medicines	35	32
Local phone service	35	31*
Long distance phone service	34	29*
International air travel	29	27*
Health insurance	28	20*
Investment brokerage firms	22	16*
Food from fast food restaurants	23	15

Source: Yankelovich MONITOR (*2004)

Self-invention is the consequence of both opportunities and necessities. People have been anxious to do more for themselves, and now they are able to do so—not just to get more, but to get something entirely of their own making. People are still learning how to make their way through this new landscape of self-invention. And that is where marketers can make a difference that counts.

CONSUMER POWER

The marketing imperative is unambiguous: Get control by giving up control to consumers. This is the path to success. Fighting to retain control in the face of self-invention will only hurt everyone involved.

Customizing products is pretty much the essence of what marketing is all about. But notwithstanding universal agreement with this fundamental notion, there are better and worse ways of putting it into action. Self-invention is a special challenge because it involves more than customization; it requires a shift of control, too.

Consultants Don Peppers and Martha Rogers popularized one approach to customization in their bestselling book, *The One-to-One Future* (Currency: 1993). Their basic premise was that marketers should deal with people one to one, meaning as individual people instead of as faceless members of a target group of consumers. A one-to-one approach will build relationships, and relationships create stronger, more profitable ties to consumers. This general approach has become widespread in the last decade. Marketers have invested tens of millions in the technologies and databases to support customer relationship management (CRM) marketing systems.

But since Peppers and Rogers first influenced a generation of marketers, the kind of customization that people want has changed. With the emergence of self-invention, marketers must do more than simply customize, marketers must facilitate self-customization. And this requires a different way of doing marketing.

The inherent bias built into the notion of one-to-one is readily apparent in the phrase itself. One-*to*-One describes a marketing approach in which marketing goes from marketers *to* consumers. Just like traditional marketing approaches, one-*to*-one presumes that all power and control resides with marketers who use it to offer highly customized products to consumers. One-*to*-one presumes consumer dependency.

Marketers would object that they do listen to consumers and that consumer preferences dictate everything they do. Marketers would argue that they are as dependent on consumers as consumers are on them. This is true, as far as it goes. But as much as marketers listen to consumers and respond to what they hear, marketers do so from a position of power and control. Marketers study consumers. Marketers interpret what they've learned. Marketers decide how to act on the basis of what they've learned. Marketers devise the products to be made available for sale. Marketers advertise to persuade consumers that what's available is what they want. While marketing is all about consumers, it's marketers who are in control. Consumer input is just part of the process. One-to-one marketing entails more individualized input and response, but marketers are still in control.

At a minimum, self-invention means sharing control. But in many cases, it means relinquishing control. Consumers want power or at least the possibility of power because consumers want to be self-inventive. Finding profitable ways of giving power to consumers is now the only way to succeed at giving consumers what they want.

SUMMING UP

- The American culture of self-determination has been transformed into one of boundless self-invention.
- Self-invention means having the technologies to participate in the creation of meaning and to transcend traditional boundaries and limits. The culture of self-invention is rooted in distrust and self-confidence but was able to flower because of the advent of digital technologies over the last decade.
- The expectations of self-invention are blurring the lines. People see no reason why they should not be involved with marketers as collaborators in design and production. People don't want complete power and control for every product or purchase, but they want the opportunity.
- Traditional marketing models operate on the basis of consumer dependency. This no longer exists. People want to participate and people feel capable of doing so. Marketers must surrender power and control in the new marketplace of self-invention.

NOTES

1 The bumper sticker that reads, "I may be fat but you're ugly and I can diet," will no longer be much of an insult in a world where both size and looks can be readily changed and "perfected."

2 James Gorman, "The Altered Human Is Already Here," *New York Times*, April 6, 2004.

3 Kevin Maney, "Wearable Computers: A Different Kind of Fashion Statement," *USA Today*, April 18, 2001. Maney's report is the source for the prior two paragraphs as well.

4   James Gleick, "The Way We Nest Now: When the House Starts Talking to Itself," *New York Times Magazine*, November 16, 2003.

5   Kelly Greene, "Encore: Inside the Home of the Future," *Wall Street Journal*, February 23, 2004.

6   Stephen Dubner, "Choosing My Religion," *New York Times Magazine*, March 31, 1996.

7   Bill Bishop, "The Great Divide: Church, Political Beliefs Align; People Decide Where to Worship Based on the Congregation's Culture," *Austin (TX) American-Statesman*, July 25, 2004.

8   Gerald Mazorati, "How the Album Got Played Out," *New York Times Magazine*, February 22, 1998.

9   Although Frank Sinatra's *In The Wee Small Hours* (1955) is generally regarded as the first concept album.

10 "70 Million Songs and Counting," MSNBC, April 28, 2004.

11 John Markoff, "Oh Yeah, He Also Sells Computers," *New York Times*, April 25, 2004.

12 Anthony Bianco, "The Vanishing Mass Market," *Business Week*, July 12, 2004.

13 Shelley Emling, "Coke Site A Hit In Europe," *The Atlanta Journal-Constitution*, July 14, 2004.

14 Felix Oberholzer-Gee and Koleman S. Strumpf, "The Effect of File Sharing on Record Sales: An Empirical Analysis," March 2004, see http://www.unc.edu/~cigar/papers/FileSharing_March2004.pdf.

15 In September 2003, Universal Music Group, the world's largest music company, cut retail and wholesale prices by as much as $6 per CD.

16 Jon Pareles, "Critic's Notebook: Envisaging Industry as the Loser On Napster," *New York Times*, February 21, 2001.

17 CBS News Polls, "Poll: Little Faith in Big Biz," July 10, 2002.

Out of Time

The perception of a time famine is the single biggest detriment to the quality of people's otherwise comfortable and productive lives. Timesaving devices have the paradoxical effect of intensifying perceptions of a time famine. Unable to find more time, people have begun to develop new approaches to fit more into the time they have, which makes it harder for marketers to get people to pay attention to marketing. Marketers must do more to compensate people for their time.

Everybody feels like the free time in their lives is running short, so everyone is searching for more. Time has become the most precious resource of all, trumping money and things as the epitome of success. The people who have made it are people with time to waste. Because wasting time is something few people feel they can afford. Most people believe that they have no time to lose.

Yankelovich MONITOR results show that the large percentage of people who say that they never have enough time keeps inching up. In 2001, 73 percent of respondents agreed that they didn't have enough time to do all that they needed to do. In 2002, it was 75 percent; in 2003, 76 percent; in 2004, 77 percent. Year-to-year shifts are unremarkable, but over several years the trend is clear. Ever more people are worried about having too little time.

When it comes to time, art has begun to imitate life. Award-winning

British journalist Allison Pearson says that she was inspired to write her transatlantic best-selling first novel, *I Don't Know How She Does It: The Life of Kate Reddy, Working Mother* (Alfred A. Knopf Anchor Edition: 2002), which is about the time-stressed work-life conflicts of a female hedge fund manager, by a survey of working mothers that appeared in *Good Housekeeping* magazine a few years ago. In that survey, three-quarters reported that they lacked time to do things properly, and half said that their relationships with their husbands were suffering due to a lack of time. What these women wanted most for Mother's Day was time for themselves. Pearson's novel must have struck a chord because it won Newcomer of the Year honors in the 2003 British Book Awards.

Survey after survey finds that people feel more and more pressed for time. This perception of a time famine is the single biggest detriment to the quality of people's otherwise comfortable and productive lives. Nowadays, everyone keeps lawyer's hours.

Notre Dame law professor Cathleen Kaveny contends that a "billable hours mentality" has taken over as the predominant view of time in America today, a view in which time itself has no intrinsic value, only the kind of instrumental value measured by goals accomplished and profits realized.[1] While people could choose not to approach time in this way, Kaveny believes that lifestyle pressures have trapped people in a billable hours mentality that keeps people from feeling at peace. People are unable to forget that time comes with a price tag, and thus they can't help but be aware of how every minute ticks by either as money earned or as money spurned.

Robert Reich, former Secretary of Labor during President Clinton's first term and currently University Professor and Maurice B. Hexter Professor of Social and Economic Policy at Brandeis University, made much the same point as Kaveny but in starker terms. In his book *The Future of Success: Working and Living in the New Economy* (Alfred A. Knopf: 2001), he notes that in the economy of today and tomorrow, predictable work and steady pay are things of the past. This has put people in more precarious positions and demands continuous effort in order to keep up, much less get ahead. Workers are now evaluated by their value to customers not by their value to the organization. Work and life have become indistinguishable since every moment must be available to meet customer needs and demands whenever they arise. Even though every moment is not spent working, every moment is at the mercy of work. Opportunities to "make hay," as Reich colloquially puts it, are getting to be infrequent and episodic, so when they appear, people feel that they have no choice but to drop everything and get busy.

People don't enjoy being harried by money for time, but they put up with it because they don't see a choice. If people had a choice, though, time is what they would choose. In Yankelovich MONITOR research, respondents were asked if they would rather have two more weeks of vacation or two more weeks of pay. More vacation was preferred by nearly a two to one margin. At least when it comes to modest amounts of time versus money, time is overwhelmingly preferred.

John Robinson, a professor of sociology and the past director of the Americans' Use of Time Project at the University of Maryland, has been studying how people use time since 1965. Robinson reports that in his 1998 survey, for the first time ever, more people said they were pressed for time than for money.[2]

It is ironic that the additional time people are putting into managing their lives—both for work and for leisure; both because they have to and because they want to—is keeping people from having the times of their lives. People are determined to make sure that every hour earns its keep in order to justify its passing, whether by bringing in lots of money or lots of fun. Progressively, people have lost touch with the texture and character of activities and celebrations that draw upon a different experience of time. As a result, people have begun to rue the loss of a sense of leisure with which to spend their time. Life has become nothing but a calendar crammed full of places to be and people to see.

Yet, nobody wants to slow down or do less. Indeed, people want more of what it takes time to do. Consequently, people are looking for more time in their lives. This is bad news for marketers, unless marketers stop doing things the old-fashioned way.

WHERE DID THE TIME GO?

Notwithstanding what people report about the loss of time, not every expert agrees that people have less free time today than ever before. In a major longitudinal analysis of time use trends over the past few decades, Robinson and his colleague, Geoffrey Godbey, a professor of leisure studies at the School of Hotel, Restaurant & Recreation Management at The Pennsylvania State University, report in their book *Time for Life: The Surprising Ways Americans Use Their Time* (Pennsylvania State University Press: 1997) that since 1965, Americans have gained an average of approximately one hour of free time a day.[3] What's declined is the gratification people get from time, not the amount of free time itself.

Robinson and Godbey highlight crucial differences in study methodologies to contrast their findings of more free time with findings of less free time reported by other researchers. These differences are not academic. They go to the heart of how people are thinking about time and what that means for marketers.

Robinson and Godbey utilized 24-hour time diaries that they call "An Average Day in America." Over the period of one day, each respondent records every activity he or she does and the time spent on it. This is a real-time measure that focuses on specific and recent time periods. Respondents record what they are doing in their own words rather than try to fit their activities into predefined categories that are often interpreted in different ways by different people.

Telephone surveys are the most common methodology used by other researchers for gauging time use. Telephone surveys ask people to recall the amount of time they have spent on different activities during a given period of time. This approach does not produce reliable results. Recall is difficult and the definitions of different categories of activities can be ambiguous.

However, telephone surveys are a good measure of people's feelings about time. The fact that people are reporting less free time means that they are experiencing time pressures in their lives notwithstanding research showing that they actually have more free time on their hands. The paradox is that the best measure of people's behaviors shows a steady increase in free time while the best measure of people's feelings shows a steady decline in how people perceive the time available to them.

What people are experiencing is a loss of equanimity. Whatever amount of free time people actually have, it is not enough (if it is even the right thing at all) to restore a sense of balance and composure to people's lives, which is why 81 percent of MONITOR respondents say that they are looking for ways of simplifying their lives. People are not literally looking to take up austere, unadorned lifestyles, but they are tiring of always feeling out of control, of always racing against the clock. The interest in simplicity is a desire for control and a longing for a respite.

Everywhere people turn, they are under pressure to respond and perform. Whether working, playing or shopping, it is all just one thing after another. There is more to do and more to choose from than ever before, so people are squeezing in more and more. More free time is not time off; if anything, it is more time available to get on with something else.

TIME'S UP

The extra free time measured by the diary research of Robinson and Godbey is not enough to change people's perceptions of the time pressures in their lives. The extra hour each day is an aggregate amount of time, not an uninterrupted block of time. It consists of short stretches of five minutes here, ten minutes there, that add up to an hour. These small increments are not sufficient to give people a break or to enable them to make any substantive changes in the pace and tempo of their days. Nor is this extra time well timed. The hour per day is an overall average. Most of the additional free time comes on weekdays, not on weekends, so people are limited in what they can do with it.

The free time tracked by Robinson and Godbey is not time spent doing nothing. In fact, it is specifically measured as time spent on certain activities. Free time is the time people spend watching TV, reading, listening to the radio or the stereo, participating in sports or outdoor activities, pursuing hobbies, socializing, attending church, school or cultural events, and volunteering. Many of these activities are done simultaneously. Free time is a busy mix of many things to do. More free time doesn't mean any less pressure on people's time. In fact, it may mean more.

The number of things possible for people to do in their free time has been growing much faster than the amount of extra time that people have for doing them. People have a little bit more time, but an exponentially greater number of things to do. The paradox is that abundance has created scarcity: Too much stuff equals too little time.

Fifty-four percent of MONITOR respondents agree that they always seem to be in rush. Women more so than men; younger people more so than older people. Even with more free time, people aren't able to slow down. The pressure to do things quickly and move on leads to perceptions

Figure 5.1: **Time Famine**

of a time famine because people are always doing everything in a hurry; and, hence, the enjoyment that people get from the things they do is diminished or else quickly forgotten as they dash off to the next thing to do (Fig. 5.1).

Time-saving devices make life more efficient but have the paradoxical effect of intensifying perceptions of a time famine. Time management tools impose a discipline that can make people feel trapped, even oppressed, by their calendars. Every block of time is accounted for, so moving through the course of a day is like a ballet. The synchronized, calculated progression of steps belies the outward appearance of spontaneity and freedom of movement. Surely, it is more than a coincidence that so many people are now wearing digital watches that have a chronometer built right in.

Cell phones, laptops and personal digital assistants enable people to carry on with work outside of the office. Free time is no longer time away from work. Work has come to have a continual presence, giving people the feeling that their time off is more compressed as well as more suffused by the stresses and strains of work.

People are particularly distressed when they think that their free time has been cheapened or depreciated. Leisure has a very high value in American society. People are spending more money on leisure activities like travel and home entertainment systems. The lure of early retirement is the prospect of being able to engage in nothing but leisure activities. With more prosperity, in some cases personal and in all cases societal, comes more interest in being able to indulge oneself and have fun. Leisure has a strong pull on people, not just because of their personal needs for a break from work but also because success is having the time and the autonomy to live at one's leisure.

People want leisure to deliver on its promise of tranquility and fulfillment. Indeed, the mainstreaming of affluence makes people feel entitled to the luxury of leisure. This puts pressure on leisure time. If leisure time can't be enjoyed the way it is depicted in magazines, TV shows and commercials, then people feel it is wasted time. This urgent need for leisure time that measures up to the ideal adds to the impression that time is scarce and that good times are getting harder to find.

The riches of the marketplace are intensifying people's feelings that their time is more congested and clogged up. With so many leisure options available to people, particularly media options, the time people have available for these activities gets overrun with the hustle and bustle of trying to do them all. This makes time off feel overcrowded and overscheduled. This is the psychological phenomenon found by Dale Southerton, a Research Fellow at the Economic and Social Research Council Centre for Research on Innovation and Competition (CRIC) at the University of Manchester in the U.K. and Mark Tomlinson, a Senior Research Associate at CRIC, in their analysis of data collected between 1985 and 1992 by the British Health and Lifestyle Survey.[4] The people most likely to feel harried and pressed for time were people whom Southerton and Tomlinson described as omnivorous, meaning infrequent involvement in lots of cultural activities as opposed to frequent involvement in just a few activities.

Shopping, too, is filled with so many options that it has become an overwhelming chore. MONITOR findings show that the percentage of people who agree with the statement, "Shopping is relaxing and enjoyable; I make time to shop and browse," has dropped from a 56 percent majority in 2000 to a 48 percent minority in 2003.

Demographic trends further exacerbate the concerns that people are expressing about time. More people have fewer of the resources it takes to create time for themselves. In particular, the emergence of single households in place of married households means that more people are in household situations in which they have no people to whom they can turn to for help, assistance and support. Single people have to do everything for themselves, which makes them feel more harried and frazzled. Similarly, the large number of two-income households means that even married households now face the same resource deficits as single households.

Marketers have developed many new products, even whole new product categories like meal solutions, carry-away, home delivery, concierge services and personal shoppers, to give people more expedient ways of getting things done. People find these products to be helpful, yet by the mere act of using them, people are reminded, at least subconsciously, that they have no time to spare in their lives. These products help people with their time, but at the same time never let people forget that time is slipping away from them.

The actual amount of free time that people have, whether it's more or less than in the past, is beside the point when it comes to people's perceptions of time. People feel more pressed for time because they are living more time-pressured lifestyles. Even if people had more free time than they do today, people would still be at wit's end about having enough time in their lives.

Unable to find more time, people have begun to develop new techniques and approaches to fit more into the time they have available to them. Traditional marketing is going to face tougher times ahead as people adopt new ways of managing the time in their lives. Because all of these time management strategies are making it harder for marketers to get people to pay attention to marketing messages and offers.

MULTITASKING

Multitasking is the time management strategy that gets the most attention. And not without reason. People have mastered multitasking as *the* essential life skill for the 21st Century. Seventy-four percent of MONITOR respondents report that they are always doing more than one thing at a time.

Of course, sometimes multitasking can get carried to extremes. A story in *USA Today* a few years ago told of one mother who recalled the day she told her six-year-old daughter not to waste time by just sitting on the potty, but to brush her teeth and her hair at the same time. As soon as she said this, though, this mother said that she caught herself, realizing at that moment that her multitasking had gotten out of control.[5]

Awash in an unprecedented surfeit of pastimes and diversions, people want to do them all. The only way to do them all is to become skilled in the ability to do several at once. Indeed, this is the new conundrum. Nowadays, downtime is not having nothing to do; it's having only one thing to do.

In a national survey commissioned by MTV Networks a few years ago, people reported on the extent to which they juggle several entertainment and media options at once. When everything is added up, it turns out that people are doing 5.8 more hours of activities than there are hours in the day, which means, of course, that a lot of the time people are doing several things at once. The net result of such multitasking is a 24-hour day crammed with 29.8 hours of stuff to do.[6]

A 2003 study of online users completed by BIGresearch quantified the extent of media multitasking.[7] Frequent and occasional usage of two or more types of media at the same time is true of more than half of all online users at any given point in time. This includes all combinations of watching TV, listening to the radio, using the Internet, reading magazines, reading newspapers, and going through the mail. One-third reported that when using media simultaneously, they pay equal attention to each medium instead of to one more than the others.

A 2003 online study of kids completed by MindShare and Arbitron found similar results.[8] Eighty percent of teens regularly use more than one type of media. Sixty percent of pre-teens do so, too. While watching TV, 67 percent of teens go online, 66 percent read a magazine, and 56 percent use instant messaging. While listening to the radio, about 80 percent go online, roughly 75 percent read a magazine and over 60 percent use instant messaging. While online, almost 80 percent listen to music, 75 percent listen to the radio, and over 50 percent watch TV.

Media multitasking is true of many adults as well. A study of online users by eMarketer using data from BIGreserach found that over one-third of adults watch TV while online. Seventeen percent listen to the radio while online, and 8 percent read a magazine or a newspaper.[9]

Multitasking is not just about the simultaneous use of different media. It is often built into the format and functionality of an individual medium. The new trend in media is to present content with a real-time multitasking look of hyperactivity, busy-ness, simultaneity and total interconnectedness. Many TV shows have become a jumble of informational sidebars, programming promos along with news and sports headlines crawling across the bottom of the screen, network logos in the bottom right corner, and Web site addresses for more information. Web sites, too, are teeming with animation, highlighted text, pop-up windows, and ads of every shape and size.

Multitasking is changing how media are consumed, not to mention the way life is lived. While people can attend to more things when multitasking, their abilities to concentrate and process information are reduced; hence, the power of marketing is weakened. Research conducted in the early nineties by Joshua Rubinstein, then at the University of Michigan and now at the Federal Aviation Administration, and David Meyer and Jeffrey Evans of the University of Michigan found that the cumulative time it takes to complete a task is longer when doing so while switching back and forth between tasks.[10] This is because the brain has to take time to decide to switch and then get ready for the next task after making the switch. These few extra seconds add up over the course of a lot of switching, and when doing something like driving a car, even a half-second lost while switching one's concentration from talking on a cell phone to steering away from danger can be fatal.

Lost time and attention due to multitasking affect information processing, too. People's capacities to process and act upon information are diminished by the time and concentration lost when switching back and forth. Brain-imaging studies conducted by Marcel Just of Carnegie Mellon University found that less of the brain is activated for a given task when another task is being performed at the same time. Apparently, there is an upper limit on total brain capacity at any given time.[11] Various other studies have found that multitasking increases stress, makes it harder to concentrate for long periods of time, reduces perceived control and contributes to physical problems like headaches and stomach aches.[12] In short, multitasking diminishes the power and impact of information.

But multitasking is here to stay. Hence, marketing must change. Traditional marketing offers people little in return for their time and attention, so marketing gets relegated to the background to begin with. But it is particularly far removed when people are engaged in media multitasking. Traditional marketing assumes that media usage is done as a single tasking activity, so earning people's attention at the moment of viewing is not an issue. Multitasking means that the message itself must have instantaneous value in order to win the interest of people who have multiple options directly in front of them at every moment.

The foundations of contemporary marketing systems and practices simply do not take account of multitasking. Offering immediate value in exchange for people's time and attention is not a consideration at all. Marketers have never learned or understood that the relationship with consumers must be reciprocal. If the message itself is little more than another marketing come-on, then the message will be ignored in favor of other options immediately at hand.

The authors of the BIGresearch study about media multitasking note that media planning models assume that each medium will be viewed discretely and therefore should be measured in isolation. The brief but excellent research review provided by the authors cites each of the landmark studies conducted during the early 1960s that led to every one of the core tenets underlying the ways in which marketing continues to be executed forty years later.[13] Not a single one of these key assumptions is an accurate reflection of the contemporary multitasking marketplace, yet marketers continue to use systems built on the basis of these ideas. As long as marketing continues to operate in the same old way, marketing productivity cannot recover. The execution itself will be misdirected and the measurement of performance will provide no guidance that is accurate or precise enough to make needed improvements.

TIME MANAGEMENT

Although multitasking is the form of time management that has gotten the most attention in recent years, it is not the only thing that people are doing to cope with the time famine they feel in their lives. Robinson and

Godbey refer to the general practice of trying to do more in a limited amount of time as "time deepening." They identify four sorts of time-deepening of which multitasking is only one.

Speeding up is a common time-deepening practice, which means rushing through an activity in order to get it over with faster. The problem for marketers is that when people rush through activities, like hurrying through a store or fast-forwarding past the trailers at the beginning of a rental videotape or using TiVo to skip commercial breaks in TV shows, people ignore or pay less attention to the marketing. In fact, the marketing is often viewed as a downright hindrance because it keeps people from getting through something faster. Ads have always been evaluated in terms of their "stopping power," or their ability to get people to look closer, pay attention and absorb the message. But as people rush through things, marketing, too, will be passed over and ads that depend on stopping people will suffer.

The substitution of a shorter activity for a longer activity is another time-deepening practice. For example, perusing the headlines online rather than watching network news or comparing cars on the Internet instead of visiting different car lots or using a self-service checkout aisle rather than standing in line for a cashier. People will be less tolerant of advertising in settings where they are trying to hasten their involvement. Plus, shorter activities generally provide fewer opportunities for marketing and selling. For example, in a self-service checkout line, there are fewer opportunities to sell impulse items because people won't be exposed to these items while waiting in line.

The final time-deepening practice mentioned by Robinson and Godbey is tighter scheduling of activities. By eliminating or significantly reducing breaks or transitional periods between activities, more activities can be squeezed into a given period of time. As consumers start to demand that activities follow closer on one another, there will be less tolerance for ads that delay or cover up the loading of Web pages or for extended, if any, commercial breaks or for cross-selling in the middle of a telephone service inquiry.

Besides the four time-deepening strategies mentioned by Robinson and Godbey, there are two other time management strategies, both of which pose problems for traditional marketing practices, too. One is delegation, either by hiring people or using technologies to handle errands, chores and responsibilities. This helps people manage their lives, but it also puts people at least one step away from marketing. For example, Internet shopping bots ignore marketing entirely in a determined, single-minded online search for the lowest price.

Another strategy is to prioritize. Unfortunately, marketing is near the bottom of the list of things with which people want to spend time. So, when people prioritize, they often look for ways to take marketing out of the equation. The traditional marketing model is actually built to deal with this reluctance to spend time with marketing. The heart and soul of traditional marketing is saturation and intrusiveness—a big enough presence to get in front of people whether they like it or not. But this doesn't work very productively anymore.

People are not going to allow marketers to monopolize their time anymore. Time has become too precious to give it away for free or to spend it on anything that isn't worth their while. To engage people's interest and to motivate their purchasing, marketers are going to have to earn the right to be heard. People are demanding value not only from the products being promoted but also from the promotions themselves. Marketing can no longer stop with nothing but a promise about the value of something to buy; marketing itself must deliver value. Otherwise, people will ignore marketing in favor of all of the other activities possible for them to do, activities that offer a higher and immediate return on the time spent doing them.

CONSUMER RECIPROCITY

People feel so pressed for time that they are willing to give up almost anything to find more time in their lives. Thirty-seven percent of MONITOR respondents agree that they regularly give up sleep to save time. In April 2000, *Vogue* magazine declared that the ability to sleep in had become the new measure of luxury, status and privilege because nowadays eight hours of sleep is harder to come by than a luxury car or a big house. Today's look of success is the fresh face of a good night's rest.

If people are willing to give up sleep because they feel pressed for time, then marketing is in big trouble. Marketers are an easy target in this battle for time. The easiest way for someone to get 10 minutes back in his or her day is to throw all of the junk mail in the trash without opening any of it. The easiest way for someone to get an hour back every night is to use TiVo to skip all the ads in prime time. At 18 minutes of commercial breaks an hour, 3 hours of prime time can be viewed in roughly 2 hours. The easiest way for someone to avoid time-consuming interruptions is to put his or her home telephone number on the Federal Do-Not-Call Registry.

What people want most is time. Yet, that's what marketers ask people to give them and to give it to them for free. Even though people feel that they have less time to spare than ever before, marketers ask people to view the ad, read the letter and browse the store. So, what marketers are asking of people is exactly the wrong thing to ask, which, in turn, adds to people's annoyance with and resistance to marketing.

Marketing saturation and intrusiveness make people's experience of time more hassled. It takes up valuable time for people to get past marketing intrusions in order to do what they want to do or to see what they want to see. People want a more leisurely experience of time, yet marketing interferes with that. Sorting through clutter not only takes more time, it offers nothing fun or informative in return.

Clutter aside, the bedrock foundation of the traditional information models that have guided marketing systems in the past involve elements that take time—browsing, searching, comparing, researching, reading, clipping, remembering, organizing. All of these tasks are time-consuming. But the time pressures people feel today make them uncomfortable spending time browsing a magazine from cover to cover or searching every relevant Web site for a full download of information or reading long copy filled with lots of product information. People want quick, easy take-aways, and then they want to move on.

More importantly, when people spend time with marketing, they want something in return right then and there—not in the future, but immediately. People want more than the promise of a reward later on from something they could buy. They want value for the time spent watching or reading the marketing itself. They want direct mail that delivers value for the time spent reading it as they're reading it, not letters that only describe value people could get later if they buy the product being promoted. The value people get from what they buy is not to be dismissed, but it is not enough to make the time people spend with marketing worth it, at least not when people have so many other interesting options about what to do, yet so little time available to do them.

Marketing must become reciprocal. People's time used to be a free resource for marketers. No longer. The marketing relationship must now be characterized by reciprocity. Marketers have to give something back to people if they are going to ask people for their time. Marketing must earn the time and attention it demands. Marketing must deliver instantaneous value, not simply promote the value of something else. Marketing must respect people's time, reward people's time, enrich people's time and give people time back. People feel that their time is far too precious not to be well spent every moment of every day.

This is not about time-saving products. The issue at hand is about marketing that is respectful of people's time. It's about marketing that saves time, not products that save time. It's about marketing that provides value in return for time, not products that provide value. It's about marketing that makes time better, not products that make time better. Marketing practices have to measure up to the value that people place on their time.

It is not too far out of realm of possibility to suppose that in the very near future marketers will have to start paying people to watch their ads or read their direct mail. Not that this hasn't been done on a small scale in the past. Marketers have long offered various kinds of merchandise and contests to get people to respond, but more is needed today. Not just trash and trinkets with throwaway value or points to accumulate for something out of a catalog, but cash money. In fact, marketing researchers have already learned that the only way to offset severely declining survey response rates is to pay people for the time it takes to complete an interview. Marketers, too, will have to learn this same lesson very soon.

Ravi Dhar, a marketing professor at the Yale School of Management, has recommended the creation of a telemarketing "do call" list that would provide people with coupons and other incentives to agree to hear a certain number of telemarketing pitches each month.[14] Matt Cain, a senior vice president with technology consulting firm META Group, expects that some companies are going to begin offering cash and bonus points to get people to watch their pop-up ads. KMGI.com, an Internet advertising production firm, already offers people free anti-spam software in exchange for viewing a 30-second TV-style ad online.[15] BrandPort launched a marketing service in early 2004 that pays college students to watch ads online.[16] Marowin.Freeservers.com and Itsvery.net are Web sites that serve as clearinghouses for a variety of different online services that will pay people to view online ads.

But even if marketers don't reciprocate by paying people money for the time people spend with marketing, marketers must do more to compensate people. Truly engaging entertainment, not just jingles. Truly meaningful information, not product pitches. Truly helpful tools, not more selling. Consumers will be more receptive to marketing if they are rewarded in real-time for their attention and effort. With time at more of a premium than ever before, reciprocity must become central to the practice of marketing.

Making reciprocity a central part of marketing not only addresses the concerns people have with the ways in which marketing impinges on their time, it makes a proven and powerful element of persuasion paramount to the practice of marketing. Simply put, people are more likely to believe something or to do something if they have first been given something of value. The reason for this is that people want to reciprocate the value they have received from others, even if they didn't ask for it in the first place. While people may start out by feeling like marketers owe them something for the time they spend reading or viewing marketing, a well-chosen, high-value, authentic reward will not only give people what they think they are due, it has the potential to create a feeling among people that they should repay marketers in return.

Reciprocity must stop being an afterthought to marketing or something delivered only by the products being marketed. Reciprocity must become a basic norm of marketing practice itself.

SUMMING UP

- People feel under enormous time pressure. Changes in work styles, lifestyles, demographics and leisure are all major contributors to perceptions of a time famine. As a result, time is now viewed as more precious than money.
- Time use studies suggest that people have more leisure time these days. But the number of things to do, including leisure

and media activities, outstrips the amount of time to do them. As people look to get more time back in their lives, marketing is being squeezed out.

- Time-saving strategies like multitasking mean that marketing gets a smaller audience and less attention.
- People must come to feel that marketing is worth the time they spend with it. Marketers must incorporate much more reciprocity into marketing practices.

NOTES

1 Peter Steinfels, "Beliefs: How should time be lived? A professor sees a billable-hours culture, and religious antidotes," *New York Times*, December 29, 2001, p. A10, national edition.

2 John Robinson, "The Irrelevance of Time," *College Park: The University of Maryland Magazine*, Fall 1999.

3 The 1997 first edition of this book examined time use trends through the mid-1980s. The 1999 second edition of this book included additional data and confirmed the continuing growth of free time during the 1990s.

4 Dale Southerton and Mark Tomlinson, "'Pressed for Time' Mechanisms, Contexts and Multiple Experiences of Temporalities," Presented at International Association of Time Use Research Annual Conference, October 15–18, 2002, Institute of Economics and Business Administration, Technical University of Lisbon, Portugal.

5 Maria Puente, "Multi-tasking to the Max: The Only Thing You Can't Do At the Same Time Is Smell the Roses," *USA Today*, April 25, 2000, p. D1.

6 Stephen Battaglio, "TV, Napster, and the 29.8-Hour Day," at www.inside.com, June 27, 2000.

7 Joseph J. Pilotta, Don E. Schultz and Gary Drenik, "'Simultaneous Media Usage: A Critical Consumer Orientation to Media Planning," *Journal of Consumer Behavior*, Pre-Publication Release, March 3, 2004.

8 David Leonard, "Nightmare on Madison Avenue, *Fortune*, June 28, 2004, and Kevin Downey, "Our Very Media Multitasking Teens," *Media Life*, September 25, 2003.

9 Downey, op cit.

10 Porter Anderson, "Study: Multitasking Is Counterproductive," CNN.com, December 6, 2001.

11 Renee Montagne, "Problems Associated With Multitasking," NPR Morning Edition, August 6, 2001.

12 Larry Rosen and Michelle Weil, "Inner Game of Work: Multitasking Madness," *Context Magazine*, Fall 1998.

13 These are: (1) audience duplication calculations based on separate and discrete exposures at different times; (2) audience accumulation estimates calculated as audiences building over time for a particular medium, not instantaneously or via multimedia forms; (3) audience reach calculations of unduplicated audiences based on separate people receiving unique media exposures; (4) the number of message exposures required for an ad to have an effect based upon repetition in a single medium; and (5) opportunities to see an ad calculated on households not on individuals as the basis for measuring media performance.

14 Matt Richtel, "Feelings Mixed, Millions Enroll to Block Calls," *New York Times*, July 10, 2003.

15 Jon Swartz, "Marketers Hunt for Ways to Score Attention Online," *USA Today*, November 25, 2003.

16 Kate Kaye, "Web 101: Company Pays College Students to Watch Ads," *Media Post's Media Daily News*, February 24, 2004.

SECTION II
The Concurrence Marketing Imperative

The Crisis of Marketing Productivity

Consumer resistance is the norm today, not the exception. Most of the time, most people are actively avoiding marketing. As a direct result, marketing productivity is hurt. Although many factors have combined to create today's crisis of marketing productivity, until marketers find a smarter approach than marketing saturation, marketing productivity will remain a crisis because consumer resistance will frustrate efforts at a turnaround.

Marketing is at a turning point. A new direction is certain. The only question is whether marketers will be at the wheel or simply be along for the ride.

If nothing else, the seriousness of the challenge facing marketers can be seen in the headlines. In its June 28, 2004 issue, a *Fortune* article screamed, "Nightmare on Madison Avenue." In its June 24, 2004 issue, *The Economist* warned, "The Future of Advertising: The Harder Hard Sell." The *Business Week* cover story of July 12, 2004 announced, "The Vanishing Mass Market: New technology. Product proliferation. Fragmented media. Get ready: It's a whole new world."

Marketers are saying the same things to themselves. On May 31, 2004, *Advertising Age* published a long article entitled, "Fight for the Streets," that was simultaneously posted on AdAge.com, its online edition, as, "Battle for the Streets: Marketers vs. Ad-Weary Consumers."

In August 2004, Jagdish Sheth, the Charles H. Kellstadt Professor of Marketing at the Goizueta Business School at Emory University, and Rajendra Sisodia, the Trustee Professor of Marketing at Bentley College, organized a one-day meeting in Boston of well-known marketing academics to consider the question, "Does Marketing Need Reform?"[1] The mere act of posing that question answered it in the affirmative, of course. The only issue up for debate was how to go about it.

THE ISSUE AT HAND

At every turn, marketers are being confronted with an urgent need for change. Yet, misunderstandings abound about the true nature of the problem. One extreme, a fanatical view, argues that marketing is beyond redemption and now kaput. Another extreme, a delusional view, argues that there is nothing wrong with marketing that a few great TV ads couldn't solve overnight. And another extreme, a suicidal view, argues that consumer resistance just points to the need for an even bigger blitz of more aggressive marketing.

Sales growth pardons a lot of sins, so marketers have stepped up the amount and intensity of their marketing efforts to boost sales. Marketers figure that if marketing saturates every nook and cranny of people's lives, then their marketing messages will break through the background noise of clutter and competition. The Catch-22 is that by spending more to be heard above the clutter and competition, marketers wind up worsening the clutter. And the worse the clutter, the more that people resist. In short, the more money spent today, the more money that will have to be spent tomorrow.

Although many factors have combined to create today's crisis of marketing productivity, until marketers find a smarter approach than marketing saturation, marketing productivity will remain a crisis because consumer resistance will frustrate efforts at a turnaround. Force-feeding marketing messages to an unwilling audience simply won't work.

Many marketers have turned to more specialized, narrowly focused micro-media in hopes of reversing declines in marketing productivity by establishing a closer connection with people. By attracting people who share a preference for certain content or shopping channels, specialized media provide opportunities for more tailored ads and offerings.

The aggregate cable TV audience, though spread across many niche channels, now has a 52 percent share of prime time viewing, compared to only 44 percent for network TV. Twenty years ago, 30 percent of consumer magazines were general-interest titles. Today, it's only 10 percent. The investment research firm Sanford Bernstein & Co. estimates that ad revenues for so-called narrow-cast media will grow 13.5 percent annually from 2003 to 2010 while ad revenues for mass media will grow 3.5 percent annually, well below the projected 5.7 percent projected annual growth in GDP. Bernstein forecasts 2010 ad revenues of $27 billion for cable TV and $22.5 billion for the Internet, and only $19.1 billion for network TV and $17.4 billion for magazines.[2]

Of course, by definition, these specialized media can't offer the same cost efficiencies as the mass media they are replacing because the audiences are smaller. Plus, the growing interest in and use of specialized media changes the productivity equation as the resulting scarcity of time and space in these media drives up costs. So, the response generated by specialized media must be proportionately greater to offset the reduced cost efficiencies. If not, marketing productivity is not improved. Unfortunately, by and large, response rates across all types of media, mass and micro, have been declining as costs have been rising.

The crisis of marketing productivity is not a crisis of failure; it's a crisis of performance. Marketing still works, just not as productively, which hurts the entire corporate enterprise. Every dollar that marketing subtracts from the bottom line affects shareholder value. Every extra dollar spent on marketing is a dollar less for capital expenditures, R&D, customer service, product design or any of the dozens of other investments that could be made to grow a business.

Similarly, every consumer turned off by marketing saturation is a person more likely to switch, to complain or to buy on price. It is a person whose complaints are more likely to hurt employee morale and perhaps even attract regulatory attention.

When bad marketing happens to good brands, the last bit of consumer goodwill is often lost. In today's marketplace, marketing practices matter more than ever because these are often the only differences between brands that matter to people.

MARKETING RESPONSE

Jagdish Sheth of Emory University and Rajendra Sisodia of Bentley College have estimated that marketing costs, including selling, distribution, advertising, sales promotion and customer service, account on average for half of total corporate costs.[3] Since World War II, manufacturing costs have dropped from 50 percent to 30 percent of total corporate costs because of significant improvements in efficiency and productivity. For similar reasons, management costs have dropped from 30 percent to 20 percent over the same period of time. But marketing costs have not seen comparable improvements and thus account for a substantially greater proportion of the costs of doing business, rising from 20 percent to 50 percent. This puts the productivity of marketing on the firing line. CEOs are paying attention, and what they see is not always reassuring.

In 1999, three leading marketing research firms completed an industry-wide study called AdWorks2 for which they pooled data and analytic resources to assess the sales response of 800 heavily advertised brands to TV advertising. [4] Results showed a disappointing return of only 32 cents for every dollar invested in TV advertising.

A 2004 report by Deutsche Bank also concluded that TV advertising is more miss than hit nowadays.[5] In an analysis of IRI data for 23 brands, it found that TV advertising generated a positive short-term ROI just 18 percent of the time. Even over the long term, a positive ROI was realized only 45 percent of the time. New brands were the most likely to enjoy a positive ROI from TV advertising, leading Deutsche Bank to conclude that for many brands, new items and better distribution are more effective at increasing sales than TV advertising.

Media costs for TV, radio and magazines have been growing in recent years at rates exceeding the rate of growth in the Consumer Price Index. An analysis by the Boston Consulting Group completed in 2003 calculated that the overall cost of reaching people between the ages of 25 and 54 has skyrocketed 300 percent since 1995.[6]

From 1977 to 2003, prime time ratings for network TV dropped 41.5 percent. Daily newspaper readership fell from 81 percent of U.S. households in 1964 to 55 percent in 2002. The number of consumer magazines is off by one-third since 1999, and total circulation is down by 6.9 percent. Despite these audience declines, rising ad rates have driven significant revenue growth for these media over the same period of time. For example, the Television Advertising Bureau reports that the advertising cost per thousand-viewers was $1.96 in 1972. Today, it's $16.79. So, despite the fact that the network prime time audience declined by nearly half from 1977 to 2003, network TV ad revenues grew 500 percent over that same period of time.[7]

The pre-season buying of network TV advertising time, known as the upfronts, set a record of $9.3 billion for the 2003 fall season, up 13 percent over 2002, even though the network television audience is continuing to splinter and shrink. For the fall 2004 upfronts, price increases averaging 7 percent enabled the networks to stay almost even with upfront commitments from advertisers in the neighborhood of $9 billion, according to initial reports in the TV trade press. The TV networks remain essential because notwithstanding audience declines, the networks continue to deliver bigger audiences than cable TV or other media alternatives. Just not as productively.

Across all media, the combination of rising prices (in a period of no inflation) and declining audiences means that marketing productivity is decreasing. Marketers are getting much less bang for their buck.

And when TV reaches an audience, its impact is not guaranteed. People are paying less attention to TV. Various surveys tracking the percentage of people saying they watch TV with their full attention show a significant drop over the past 40 years. It used to be seventy-some percent. In a 2004 Yankelovich MONITOR OmniPlus survey, it was only 36 percent. Seventy-nine percent flip the channels during TV commercials compared to 51 percent in 1986. Fifty-three percent turn the sound down during TV commercials compared to 25 percent in 1986.

Even if consumers wanted to pay more attention, the TV advertising environment works against it. Industry leaders at the American Association of Advertising Agencies have long cautioned against crowding too many ads into a TV show. Longer commercial breaks and shorter ads worsen clutter, thus affecting the power of the ads that are shown as well as the overall value of TV as an advertising medium. Or to put it another way, the more marketing there is, the less effective it is. Yet, more ads and shorter ads continue to get squeezed into TV shows at every time of day including prime time.

Marketing response is declining across all vehicles, including telemarketing, email, banner ads, pop-up ads, catalogs, and direct mail. For example, *DIRECT* magazine has tracked a decline in direct mail response rates for both house lists (internal customer lists) and outside lists (purchased lists).[8] Average response rates for house lists dropped from 13.6 percent in 1997 to 8.5 percent in 1998 and have not recovered. Average response rates for outside lists improved from 1997 to 1999, but are now less than 2.5 percent compared to 4.5 percent in 1997. While the overall productivity of direct marketing has been helped by reductions in costs, particularly lower telemarketing costs and a shift to online direct marketing, those costs savings will soon bottom out, so the productivity of direct marketing is going to depend upon reversing declining response rates.

This is not to suggest that every marketing campaign is unproductive. It is only to point out that the typical performance is below par. Individual marketers hope for breakthroughs notwithstanding the general underperformance of marketing as a whole. And breakthroughs still happen, although these are only exceptions that prove the rule.

Developing systems to figure out what works has gotten a lot of attention in recent years. The Marketing Science Institute (MSI) affirmed the importance of addressing the challenge of measuring marketing productivity in its 2002–2004 research priorities. MSI brings together top-tier practitioners and academics to investigate important marketing issues. The number one priority of MSI in its 2002–2004 research priorities was assessing marketing productivity and the return on marketing. In other words, the area that marketing practitioners said they would most like for marketing academics to devote more study was the broad area of marketing productivity.

The main focus of MSI, though, like that of most practitioners and academics, is on measurement and performance metrics. The objective in MSI's study of marketing productivity is to quantify the impact of advertising and promotion and then use that information to make better decisions about allocating marketing spending across various initiatives. The interest in marketing mix models and marketing dashboards reflects this emphasis on measurement.

While measurement is important, a focus on measurement alone overlooks the most important part of the productivity issue: That of declining performance and the barrier put up by consumer resistance to better performance. Measuring the relative impact of different marketing activities ensures the optimal allocation of marketing spending but sheds little light on the central issue of re-engaging resistant consumers. It's a lot like having the biggest market share in a rapidly declining category—even winning is losing.

RESISTANT CONSUMERS

On May 5, 2004, the Columbia TriStar Group announced a promotional event to publicize the opening of "Spider-Man 2" a little over a month away. A webbed film logo would appear on the bases and the on-deck circles in the 15 stadiums hosting interleague games over the second weekend in June. The logo would also be placed on home plate and the rubber on the pitcher's mound before the game although not during the game.

This was something new. Columbia planned to do all of the typical introductory promotions, but it wanted to make a bigger splash, so it agreed to pay a total of over $3 million to Major League Baseball and the individual teams to get the film logo on the bases.

Marketing and promotional deals have always been a part of sporting events, to the point that companies pay naming rights for the privilege of having their names on the very arenas where games are played. But, lately, marketers have been pushing the envelope even further. Brand logos appeared on players' uniforms and helmets during the season-opening series held in Japan in 2000 between the Chicago Cubs and the New York Mets and in 2004 between the New York Yankees and the Tampa Bay Devil Rays. National Hockey League rinks have ads on the dasherboards around the ice, and some teams have embedded advertising in the ice itself. Gatorade cups, coolers and towels appear on National Football League sidelines. Two days before the running of the 2004 Kentucky Derby, the jockeys won a lawsuit overturning a racetrack rule prohibiting them from wearing advertising or brand logos during the race.

It has seemed as if no blank space in sports is off limits to advertising and brand promotions. But the Columbia "Spider-Man 2" promotion proved to be too much: Immediately following the announcement of the promotion, a fan revolt erupted.

The announcement was disseminated on the Internet, and afternoon talk radio turned this news into an angry buzz of discontent. Fan Web sites and Internet bulletin boards filled up with denouncements and incomprehension. Petitions rapidly collected signatures. Television announcer Bob Costas and baseball commissioner Bud Selig both weighed in against the promotion.

Major League Baseball and Columbia were caught by surprise, so they put their ears to the ground and listened. In particular, Columbia began watching the online polls that had been opened by ESPN.com and AOL. In massive numbers, people were voting overwhelmingly against the promotion. After conferring overnight, Major League Baseball and the Columbia TriStar Group announced the very next day, May 6, 2004, that they were canceling the promotion.

Score one for the fans.

Of course, Columbia still promoted "Spider-Man 2" in those 15 baseball stadiums that weekend, but it used more time-honored things like foam fingers with the film logo and trailers on video scoreboards between innings. But Major League Baseball and Columbia got first-hand experience with the power of consumer resistance. Armed with technology and willing to get assertive—even belligerent—when pushed too far, consumers can shut down a marketing campaign. And every little success, like this flap about baseball bases, teaches people that resistance can get them results like nothing else.

Unfortunately for marketers, consumer resistance is not limited to marketers who meddle with the national pastime. It is directed at marketing of all sorts. Indeed, the fervor with which the vast majority of consumers are resisting marketing shows a clear and sizable impact on marketing productivity.

Marketing resistance to unwanted marketing practices affects buying decisions. In the 2004 Yankelovich study, 54 percent said that they avoid buying products that overwhelm them with marketing and advertising. The strongest marketing resistance is not found among people who want to shop less but among marketers' best customers. Yankelovich MONITOR OmniPlus research conducted in 2002 for *DIRECT* magazine found that people who had purchased something through a direct channel in the past six months were much more likely to be engaged in marketing

Figure 6.1: **Resisters Are Best Customers**

Actions Have Ever Taken:	Direct Marketing Non-Responders*	Direct Marketing Purchasers*
Name removed from list	31%	45%
Number removed from list	27	36
Complained	32	44
Refused to buy	20	31

* Within past 6 months
Source: DIRECT Magazine and Yankelovich MONITOR OmniPlus 2002

Figure 6.2: **Resisters Are Shopping Enthusiasts**

	Those who believe it is . . .	
	Important to their happiness to shop and spend freely	Not important to their happiness to shop and spend freely
Thinking about shopping and spending less than I have in the past	63%	56%
Wish for quiet, simpler life even if it means less stuff	54	40
Feel overwhelmed by all the stuff I own	36	27

Source: Yankelovich MONITOR OmniPlus 2003

resistance than people who had not responded to a direct marketing offer at all (Fig. 6.1).

Similarly, results from the Yankelovich MONITOR show that people who espouse the greatest interest in changing the ways in which they respond to marketers are those who say that being able to shop and spend freely is important to their happiness. Marketers want more customers who say that spending freely makes them happy (Fig. 6.2). But to win the loyalty of these kinds of people, it's going to take a different kind of marketing.

Intrusive marketing affects the trust that people have for brands. Too much marketing breeds dissatisfaction, which in turn undermines the trust people feel for a brand. This worsens marketing productivity even further. A special Yankelovich MONITOR study on trust found a substantial financial impact from a loss of trust.[9] Forty-five percent of respondents said that there is at least one retail business they no longer trust. The impact of that lost trust is substantial. Ninety-four percent reported that they spend an average of 87 percent less money with companies they don't trust. Or to put it another way, when people lose trust in a company, they pretty much quit doing business with it. They probably still spend as much or more in the marketplace as a whole, but none with that company.

Consumer resistance goes further than not doing business with a company. In the 2004 Yankelovich study on marketing resistance, 65 percent said that there should be more limits and regulations on marketing and advertising. Of those in favor of more limits, 43 percent preferred limits on times and places, 42 percent preferred limits on total amount, and 14 percent wanted a complete ban on any marketing that they did not agree to see ahead of time.

When asked where they would like to see advertising eliminated entirely, only email (58 percent), public schools (55 percent), and mail (51 percent) were mentioned by at least a majority of respondents. However, large numbers mentioned other heavily used media and marketing vehicles. Rounding out the top ten were faxes (43 percent), cable TV (40 percent), movie previews (39 percent), Web sites (38 percent), public TV (36 percent), network TV (34 percent), and concerts (30 percent).

People understand that changes in marketing entail trade-offs. People don't want an end to marketing, but if that's the only possible alternative, then many people are willing to live with the trade-offs. In exchange for no advertising or commercials, 61 percent of people are willing to do more research themselves to find out what's on sale, 41 percent are willing to pay for traditionally free media like network TV or radio, 33 percent are willing to accept a slightly lower standard of living, and 28 percent are willing to pay a significantly greater amount for magazines.

Perhaps the most intriguing take-away from these particular findings is that there are large numbers of people ready and willing to do business in a completely different way. These people are open to alternatives that enable them to live and shop marketing-free. So, why keep trying to force marketing down the throats of these people? Devising a new business model seems more far more sensible than continuing to saturate these people with marketing.

The growth of digital video recorders (DVRs) like TiVo and ReplayTV shows that people are willing to pay for the ability to control their television viewing, especially the power to skip over ads. Technology consulting firm Forrester Research forecasts that in five years, over 30 million households will have DVRs, which is more than 25 percent of U.S. households, compared to 3 million today. But that number could be much higher five years from now if cable companies like Comcast and Time Warner offer DVRs in their set-top boxes. Thirty million households is the key threshold, however. Forrester found in a survey that 75 percent of advertisers will cut their spending on TV advertising once the penetration of DVRs crosses that threshold.[10] The reason why is obvious. Research into the usage patterns of DVRs shows that 60 to 80 percent of the ads in the shows that people watch are skipped and Forrester predicts that because of DVRs, viewing of TV ads will drop 15 percent by 2007.[11]

Consumer resistance is the norm today, not the exception. No matter how well media and marketing are bought, allocated and measured, marketing productivity will not improve until marketers are able to re-engage people in a productive and profitable way.

BETTER, NOT CHEAPER

The impact of higher marketing costs has ruinous potential. That's why changes in marketing economics are being investigated as a solution to spam. Spam is not particularly effective marketing. Response rates to spam are extraordinarily low, but it is a productive and profitable form of marketing because the fractional response rates are offset by infinitesimally low marketing costs. While spammers are constantly being forced to update their tactics to outwit innovations in spam-blocking software, the costs of keeping one step ahead are minimal. The servers, programmers and lists required are cheap, relatively speaking, so even very low response rates provide a very high return on investment.

Probably the best way to stop spam is to change the cost structure of spamming. If costs go up even moderately, spammers won't be able to earn a profit from the extremely low response rates that generate their sales revenue. In which case, spammers would shut down voluntarily.

Email postage is perhaps the best way to increase the costs of spamming. Microsoft chairman Bill Gates introduced this idea to a wider audience at the annual World Economic Forum in Davos, Switzerland in January 2004. Gates noted that even a penny postage for each email would be more than sufficient to put spammers in the red.

The notion of an email stamp has not been met with rousing support. For postage to work, a central clearinghouse would be needed to handle collections, and such an intermediary would quash the fundamental strength and essence of the decentralized, server-to-server nature of the Internet. A postage system would also require authenticating identities. Microsoft's Passport is one of the biggest Internet authentication systems, so with his postage idea, Gates has been accused of putting his own interests ahead of the public interest.

Whatever his stake in the outcome, though, Gates has a more perceptive understanding of the economics involved than his critics. The advanced technology solutions being considered to stop spam like Domain Keys or SPF will work only if spammers can't figure out how to beat them. The track record of spammers to date certainly suggests otherwise.

Ultimately, when Gates talks about postage, he is not really talking about cash. The "penny" that Gates is referring to is the cost from added computer time to send an email. It's an idea first proposed in 1992 by Cynthia Dwork, then at IBM and now at Microsoft, and Moni Naor of the Weizman Institute of Science in Israel. It's known today as hashcash, and many organizations are developing hashcash systems, including Microsoft whose hashcash initiative is called Penny Black.

In a hashcash arrangement, email from an unfamiliar source would be sent back to the sender with a computational puzzle attached. The sender's computer would have to solve the puzzle and re-send the email. The recipient's computer would then accept the email. Added up over tens of millions of emails, the costs of the extra few seconds needed to solve the puzzle quickly become significant. The expense of more servers and of more processing time to perform the calculations would be too much for spammers to afford, given the low response rates to spam.

The practical challenge is figuring out how to devise a computational puzzle that is complicated enough to be a costly burden on the high-speed computers and the hijacked networks of personal computers at the disposal of spammers, yet not so complicated that it overtaxes the less elaborate computer systems of private individuals and small businesses. While this is not an easy problem to solve, cryptographers and systems managers are teaming up to work it out because the best way—indeed, probably the only way—to eliminate spam is to change the microeconomics of spamming.

The economic impact of email postage on spamming is a clear illustration of what's at stake for legitimate marketers struggling with rising costs and declining response rates. When response rates aren't high enough to support the costs, the business can't survive. This is what makes the growing resistance to marketing the biggest factor affecting marketing productivity.

Keeping costs in line is imperative, of course, so cheaper ways of doing marketing are of constant interest to marketers. But ultimately, cost reductions are not the way to reverse the ongoing declines in marketing productivity. There is a limit to what can be saved through cost reductions, not to mention the fact that the organizational impact of a cost-savings mentality usually smothers the innovation and creativity needed to produce effective marketing. Furthermore, the ongoing changes in the marketplace that are driving up marketing costs are beyond the control of marketers. The explosion of new media, the diversity of demographics, and the self-inventive attitudes of consumers will sustain the upward pressure on marketing costs no matter what marketers do. To reverse the declines in marketing productivity, marketers must find ways to boost response rates. The answer is better marketing, not cheaper marketing.

One of the promises of the Internet during the heyday of the dot-com boom was that marketing costs would be significantly reduced because Internet access was so inexpensive. It was thought, too, that electronic interactions between marketers and customers would be better informed and thus more profitable as a result. The reality of the Internet, though, is not that sort of panacea. For the Internet no less than for any other marketing vehicle, marketers face limits on the productivity improvements that can be realized through cost savings alone. There is only so much to save and then no more. After that, productivity gains will have to come from higher response rates. And that means better marketing.

Unfortunately, spam aside, Internet marketing is viewed as no less annoying and intrusive than other forms of marketing. A survey conducted by the technology consulting firm GartnerG2 found that pop-up and pop-under ads are rated as highly annoying by over three-quarters of Internet users, and other types of Internet advertising like banner ads or interstitial ads by close to half.[12] Another study by BURST! Media found that Internet users regard more than two ads on a Web site as clutter.[13] Half of Internet users have a lower opinion of a brand when its ads appear in Web sites that look cluttered, and three-quarters pay less attention to ads in cluttered-looking Web sites.

Marketers have begun to investigate alternative ways of communicating with people. For example, many marketers are looking more at product placements within TV shows as a means of getting a product in front of people who are skipping over or not paying attention to TV commercials. It's referred to as embedded advertising, and it's nothing new. For years, almost all of the branded products that have been seen on TV shows have been placed there pursuant to an embedded advertising deal. Product placements are so common that there are marketing services firms in the business of evaluating and tracking product placements. In the last few years, though, embedded advertising has been getting a lot more attention.

Reality TV shows sparked the recent craze over product placements. Breakout hits like "American Idol" and "Survivor" gave branded products star billing; Coke, Ford and AT&T Wireless, among others, on "American Idol"; Visa, Target and Reebok, among others, on "Survivor." Every reality TV show since then has done likewise.

Other shows have begun to feature more embedded advertising, too. Beer company signs are part of the set for "The Best Damn Sports Show Period." "Trading Spaces" gets its remodeling supplies from Home Depot. Bill Gates made a guest appearance on the 200th episode of "Frasier," which coincided with the launch of Window XP. Microsoft Windows Media Center Edition 2004 was featured on "CSI," "The Wire" and "24."

Ford sponsored the entire first episode of the second season of "24" in the fall of 2002. A Ford ad was shown at the beginning and at the end of the show, but the rest of the show was shown without any commercial breaks. During the show, Kiefer Sutherland, the show's star, drove a Ford Expedition.

The interest in embedded advertising shows every sign of strengthening. Marketers are talking about it as a defense against DVRs. In a complaint filed in late 2003 with the Federal Communication Commission asking for more disclosure of paid product placements in TV shows, Commercial Alert, an advertising and marketing watchdog group co-founded by Ralph Nader, cited a survey conducted among media planners about embedded advertising.[14] Eighteen percent had negotiated at least one product placement in the previous six months, and 26 percent—nearly a 45 percent increase—expected to do so in the next six months.

Embedded advertising offers a better guarantee that viewers won't be able to avoid seeing brands. This guaranteed exposure gets the attention of marketers, but the need for good marketing is not obviated by the assurance of good exposure. Solving the problem of exposure could easily lull marketers into a false sense of security about marketing productivity.

TV was in its infancy during the halcyon days of old when sponsorship and embedded advertising were in vogue. TV was a novelty and people were less annoyed by the wiles of marketers. Not so anymore. So, as this old approach is revived, adjustments will have to be made for today's consumer.

People will get out of product placements exactly what marketers put into them. If product placements are pursued because they facilitate the continuation of saturation marketing, then it is certain that in no time at all product placements will be executed in a highly intrusive way. Imagine the placement-saturated show of the future in which every single item in every single scene is branded and vying for more notice and attention with every other branded product placement. This could quickly become an advertising nightmare—far more cluttered and pushy than today's commercial breaks. At which point, the openness of people to product placements will sour. In other words, if marketers pour their creative juices into designing innovative product placements in order to force people to watch a sort of proto-ad whether people want to or not, then product placements will degenerate into the kind of marketing that people are determined to resist.

In an interview about the rejuvenated interest in product placements, Frank Zazza, founder and CEO of iTVX, a research and consulting firm specializing in product placements, cautioned that a lot more than mere placement is required for embedded advertising to work.[15] In addition to the product placement itself, marketers have to remind people of the placement and tell people a brand story that gives the placement context and meaning. Otherwise, the appearance of the product in the TV show goes unremembered because the placement is little more than a fleeting billboard with a brand name.

To date, the up-tick in embedded advertising has primarily involved well-known brands that have been advertising their stories for years. Seeing them in a TV show reminds people of what they know already. Product placements work if good marketing and good and appropriate programming surround them. Product placements don't eliminate the need to re-engage consumers with better marketing practices. No matter how good the product placement, the need for good marketing will never go away.

The challenges facing product placements are true as well for all the new media that people are turning to these days. Video games, DVDs, iPods, cell phones, Blackberries, video on demand, and the like have all come of age as advertising-free media. When marketers start to push ads into these media, consumer backlash is a real possibility. Marketers have had success with products placed in video games, but to date, only a few marketers have used this medium. Video games are not yet super-saturated with intrusive marketing. As marketers begin to use new media, it will be imperative to do so with greater precision and relevance, otherwise the new media will become just as tired and overworked as the old media.

EVERYBODY'S TALKING

The imperative to do better marketing, not just more marketing, applies to everything in marketing, old and new. In fact, if marketing itself is not good, then it is a bad idea to do more of it. Yankelovich MONITOR results show that people tell a greater number of other people about things they don't like than things they do like—7.9 versus 5.4, respectively. Marketers are upside down with this word-of-mouth multiplier if every marketing interaction is just another cluttered and intrusive experience.

Some marketers are trying to take direct control of word-of-mouth through marketing initiatives to influence opinion leaders and so-called early adopters. Word-of-mouth is not new. Marketers have long understood the importance of the opinions that people share with each other, particularly the negative opinions that can diminish people's interests or start false rumors.

Bubble Yum's struggle with false rumors about spider eggs in its gum is the classic example of a brand battling a persistent urban legend. The LifeSavers Company introduced Bubble Yum in 1976. It was the first soft bubble gum, ready to blow bubbles after only a few chews. It was an instant success, but a year later sales plummeted suddenly in New York. A little digging around revealed that about half the kids in New York had been told by friends that spider eggs (or spider legs or spider webs) was the secret ingredient that made Bubble Yum soft. Negative word-of-mouth was killing the brand, and the rumor mill was spreading the word fast. So, Bubble Yum responded with full-page ads in 50 different newspapers under the headline, "Somebody is telling very bad lies about a very good product." Confidence in the brand was restored, although people remember the rumor to this day.

It wasn't until the Internet exploded onto the scene that marketers began to think about word-of-mouth as something positive to be exploited rather than as something negative to be watched. It became known as viral marketing based on the metaphor of an epidemic. The electronic, instantaneous interconnection of people all over the world made the Internet into a web of chitchat and conversation. While marketers worried that information could now turn into misinformation at the speed of light, marketers also began to realize that persuasive marketing communications could be disseminated just as quickly. Interest in word-of-mouth grew and decades-old social science research into the flow and exchange of information was dug out of the vaults.

Social psychologist Stanley Milgram, best known for his electric shock experiments about people's obedience to authority, introduced his so-called small world hypothesis in an article he wrote for the inaugural issue of *Psychology Today* in May 1967. In this article, Milgram provided a general description of two studies he had conducted in which he gave randomly selected people in Kansas and Nebraska a packet and asked them to help get the packet to a target person in the Boston area. Milgram instructed each person to forward the packet to a first-name acquaintance who might know the target person or who might know someone else who might know the target person. A log was kept to keep track of the number of people it took to complete the delivery. When the packets were finally received and cataloged, Milgram found that the median number of people between the person at the start and the target person was five. From this comes Milgram's notion of the six degrees of separation (i.e., there are six spaces between seven people lined up in sequential order).

Milgram's work has been at the center of much debate in the last few years. Judith Kleinfeld, a professor of psychology and Director of the Northern Studies Program at the University of Alaska at Fairbanks, reviewed Milgram's original research notes at Yale and discovered that only five to 30 percent of the letters Milgram gave out were actually delivered, suggesting that far more often than not people are not connected at all. Her literature review of other small world studies turned up almost no other replication of Milgram's findings.[16]

On the other hand, a 1998 landmark paper in *Nature* written by mathematicians Duncan Watts, then at Cornell University and now at Columbia University, and Steven Strogatz of Cornell University identified a mathematical basis to support Milgram's small world hypothesis. Their paper stimulated new interest in small world studies in fields ranging from epidemiology to neurophysiology to biochemistry to economics to engineering. Watts himself recently published findings confirming Milgram's six degrees of separation. In this research, 18 target people in 13 countries were identified and study participants were asked to get an email to them by sending emails to acquaintances. More than 60,000 people visited Watts' Web site to participate. On average, it took people three to five steps to reach a target person.[17]

Notwithstanding the ongoing scientific debate, Milgram's small world hypothesis has enjoyed a strong revival among a popular audience, especially marketers.[18] Marketing author Seth Godin of *Permission Marketing* (Simon & Shuster: 1999) fame urged readers to turn "ideas into epidemics" in his book, *Unleashing The Ideavirus* (Hyperion: 2001). *New Yorker* staff writer Malcolm Gladwell wrote about mavens, connectors, salesmen and stickiness in his book, *The Tipping Point: How Little Things Can Make A Big Difference* (Little, Brown and Company: 2001). And in his book, *The Anatomy of Buzz: How To Create Word-of-Mouth Marketing* (Currency: 2000), ex-software marketer Emanual

Rosen reviewed the science and numerous case studies to distill a how-to guide for creating buzz.

Most of the marketing interest stirred up by popular theories of word-of-mouth has centered on the opinion leaders who supposedly influence the attitudes and behaviors of others. This is how Godin, Gladwell and Rosen are referenced most often. Social science research has clearly demonstrated the persuasive impact of others on how people behave. Arizona State University psychology professor Robert Cialdini has outlined all of these various interpersonal influences in his primer on persuasion, *Influence: Science and Practice* (Allyn and Bacon: 2001), including such factors as reciprocation, commitment, social proof, liking and authority. Where the research falls short is in proving that there are a limited number of people who influence everybody else in all circumstances. The influence of others is a recognized and well-researched phenomenon, but much of that research identifies the importance of social influence or the power of the group, not of an opinion leader. The idea that a core group of universal opinion leaders exists and has disproportionate power is up for a lot of debate.[19]

Despite the uncertain scientific evidence about opinion leaders, more and more marketers have begun initiatives to locate these sorts of influential people in order to blanket them with marketing communications. In doing so, marketers are looking for ways to ensure that their messages get in front of people notwithstanding consumer resistance to marketing. These efforts are to be applauded for the attempt to reach people in a more personal way. But these efforts ignore the single most important element that makes word-of-mouth successful and that often makes it unnecessary to spend a lot of time looking for opinion leaders: Something worth talking about.

A bad marketing idea—an idea that is executed with imprecision and irrelevance and that offers people no power or reciprocity—won't get passed along just because it's delivered to a so-called opinion leader or influential. People don't tell other people about everything they hear, only about the most interesting things they hear. It's much easier to get a message in front of someone than to get that person to pass it along. The hardest job is doing marketing that warrants word-of-mouth.

Godin refers to this as an idea that is "worth it." Gladwell talks about it as "stickiness." Rosen lists the six characteristics of "contagious products."

In her review of Milgram's original research, Kleinfeld observed that the experiment generating the highest delivery rate utilized packets that had a much more impressive appearance—royal blue cardboard bearing a gold logo and the name Harvard University in gold letters, along with a list of signatures, each in a different color ink. These packets had the look of materials that warranted passing along.

For the most part, the fundamental necessity to start with good marketing is the aspect of effective word-of-mouth that has been ignored by marketers looking to do viral marketing. The shift to word-of-mouth is being pursued because it offers a way to keep doing saturation marketing. Only the delivery is different. The character of the marketing itself is the same. If marketers undertake word-of-mouth with the same approach to marketing that is true today, then opinion leaders will be overwhelmed with products and pitches. Word-of-mouth will be no less cluttered and intrusive than TV or direct mail. Pretty soon, every conversation people have will be about marketing, and that will smother the spontaneity and sincerity that makes word-of-mouth so effective.

Of course, the availability of word-of-mouth as a viable marketing vehicle will probably disappear before clutter and intrusiveness become overwhelming. Word-of-mouth is heavily dependent on trust and credibility. Too much marketing-speak and soft sell from opinion leaders will quickly undermine their believability. In all likelihood, though, these opinion leaders will recognize this threat to their standing in time to be more critical and less tractable. At which point, the problem of diminishing marketing productivity will have a new dimension to it.

Some marketing to opinion leaders is not about word-of-mouth. It is only about getting influential people to buy or use a brand so that others will be persuaded by example. But this still involves the challenge of communicating effectively and persuasively to opinion leaders in the first place. In fact, personal involvement and interest in a particular product category usually makes people more demanding, not less. Opinion leaders push back the most.

The first step for reversing the ongoing declines in marketing productivity is to do better marketing. This means taking a different approach to marketing—in particular, abandoning marketing saturation. Once this is done, marketers can begin to find new media and fresh ways of delivering marketing communications. But until this is done, new marketing vehicles will have little impact on the crisis of marketing productivity. Because consumers will still be resistant to marketing however it gets delivered.

SUMMING UP

- Marketing productivity is in decline. Rising costs, shrinking audiences and declining response rates have combined to give marketers less bang for the buck. This problem is compounded by the growing consumer resistance to marketing.
- Until the problem of consumer resistance is addressed, efforts to improve marketing productivity will be piecemeal. Efforts to develop better measurement systems will only ensure the optimal allocation of spending but won't point to ways of re-engaging resistant consumers
- Marketing resistance affects buying decisions. People buy less from brands that contribute to clutter, saturation and intrusiveness. In fact, the biggest resisters are often a brand's best customers. Large numbers of consumers are interested in alternative business models that entail different kinds of marketing.
- Alternative media and new marketing approaches don't address the central issue of how marketing is practiced. If new approaches are undertaken with the same kind of intrusiveness, they will quickly become just as tired and overworked as old approaches, and consumer resistance will continue to be a problem.
- What's needed is better marketing, which means moving away from the model of marketing domination, saturation and intrusiveness.

NOTES

1 J. Walker Smith, president of Yankelovich Partners, gave the opening presentation at that meeting entitled, "Concurrence Marketing: Re-engaging Resistant Consumers." The presentations from this meeting have been collected in a book edited by the meeting organizers.

2 All figures in this paragraph came from Anthony Bianco, "The Vanishing Mass Market," *Business Week,* July 12, 2004.

3 Jagdish N. Sheth and Rajendra S. Sisodia, "Marketing Productivity: Issues and Analysis," *Journal of Business Research,* Vol. 55, 2002.

4 MMA and IRI, *AdWorks2,* 1999.

5 "The Harder Hard Sell: The Future of Advertising," *The Economist,* June 26, 2004.

6 The Boston Consulting Group, *Darwin Pays A Visit to Advertising,* 2003.

7 All figures in this paragraph came from Bianco, op cit.

8 From *DIRECT* annual forecast studies.

9 This study was a 22-minute Internet survey from April 6 to April 13, 2004, among a nationally representation sample of 2,606 respondents, ages 18+, conducted in partnership with the FGI SmartPanel® of MindBase-coded Internet panelists.

10 Stefanie Olsen, "Advertisers Face Up To TiVo Reality," CNET News.com, April 26, 2004.

11 "A Farewell to Ads?" *The Economist,* April 17, 2000, and Gary Arlen, "Cache and Cachet, But With a Catch," *Broadband Week,* June 3, 2002.

12 Pamela Parker, "When Is A Pop-Up Not a Pop-Up?" ClickZ Network, January 17, 2003.

13 "Online Clutter Drives Traffic Away," iMedia Connection, May 27, 2004.

14 Patricia Odell, "Watchdog Group Files Complaints With Feds Over Product Placements," *PROMO,* October 2, 2003.

15 Ben Grill, "Valuing Product Placements: iTVX," *TVSpy,* February 24, 2003.

16 Judith Kleinfeld, "Could It Be A Big World After All? The 'Six Degrees of Separation' Myth," *Society,* April 2002.

17 Stefan Lovgren, "Six Degrees of E-mail Separate Wired World?" National Geographic News, August 7, 2003. However, despite the fact that 24,000 different messages chains were created, only 400 actually reached the target person. Watts believes that this failure rate is deceptive because many more people could have completed the chain had they not forgotten or lost interest.

18 Not to mention John Guare's play "Six Degrees of Separation," that was made into a 1993 movie starring Will Smith, and the trivia fad in which people try to link movie actors to actor Kevin Bacon in six steps or less based on the movies in which these actors have appeared together.

19 See, for example, Patricia Cohen's scathing yet insightful criticism of the research behind *The Influentials* by marketing researchers Ed Keller and Jon Berry in the January 31, 2003 *New York Times* book review entitled, "They May Be Yakkers But a Lot of People Are Listening."

Concurrence Marketing

Concurrence Marketing is a set of principles and tools for meeting the challenges of the marketplace ahead—a marketplace in which marketers must learn more about the nuances of permission than the techniques of persuasion, in which the intangibles of experiences and emotions matter more than product features and attributes, and in which value must be created jointly by companies and their customers through the commitments one makes to the other.

Marketers have a different opinion about the state of marketing than consumers. There is little concurrence, so it is no surprise that they continue to engage in the practices that people are resisting. People see a need for change, but marketers only see a need to be persistent and unwavering. So, consumer resistance worsens. There is a big opportunity for marketers, though. Consumer resistance is not so much a problem as an opportunity, as are all problems when scrutinized from a marketing perspective. That is not yet the perspective of most marketers, however.

WHAT MARKETERS THINK

In conjunction with the 2004 Yankelovich MONITOR OmniPlus study on consumer resistance to marketing, Yankelovich interviewed senior marketing directors to assess their take on the current state of marketing.[1] Many of the same questions asked of consumers were asked of these marketing directors.

Marketing directors agreed that there are serious challenges ahead. More clutter, higher costs and increasing competition topped their list of concerns. These are the very elements making for declining marketing productivity. Yet, only 43 percent of these marketing directors agreed that the productivity of marketing spending is declining, far fewer than those agreeing that clutter, costs and competition are growing problems.

Marketers understand the importance of demonstrating a financial return on marketing spending. Eighty-two percent agreed that better financial performance is a top priority. Forty-nine percent agreed that top management cares only about measurable financial returns and not about intangibles like positioning, branding or creativity. Of course, the other 51 percent thought differently, but financial performance is no less of a priority just because other things are important, too. Only a little more than half of marketing directors, 54 percent, agreed that the tools available to measure the impact of marketing programs are better than rudimentary.

Hamstrung by the tools available to them, marketers can't always see the impact of clutter, costs and competition on marketing productivity, which means that there is no assurance that marketers will address these problems in ways that boost productivity. If productivity is difficult to measure and quantify, more saturation to try and boost sales, which are easier to measure, is a more likely response than better marketing to re-engage resistant consumers.

Marketing directors look at the challenges they face in a way that is process-centric, not consumer-centric (Fig. 7.1). Clutter, costs and competition are seen as marketing execution issues related to tactical processes. Marketers express less concern about the increasing fragmentation of consumer tastes and preferences and the growing consumer resistance to marketing. Most marketers do not believe that they are facing any serious problems with consumers.

There is a sizable gap between the attitudes of consumers about marketing and the attitudes of marketing directors. While the majority of people agree that there is too much marketing and that most of it is not relevant to them, a comparably sized majority of marketing directors feels otherwise. Almost no marketing directors believe there should be

Figure 7.1: **Marketing Challenges**

Being heard or noticed through the sheer volume of marketing communications consumers are exposed to on a daily basis	**83**%
Rising advertising and production costs	**77**
Increasing levels of competitive response	**76**
Recruiting and training people who can deliver high quality service to customers	**64**
The need to invest in information technology	**62**
The fragmentation of the media market	**53**
The fragmentation of consumer tastes and preferences into smaller and smaller sub-groups	**52**
Increased difficulty of introducing new products	**46**
The impact of mergers and acquisitions	**42**
Technology that allows consumers to block or avoid marketing and advertising	**35**
Consumer hostility towards marketing and advertising	**27**

Source: Yankelovich MONITOR Survey of Marketing Directors 2004

less marketing or advertising than there is today, compared to a majority of consumers. The vast majority of marketing directors believe that consumers hold all the cards; most consumers believe the opposite is true. (Fig. 7.2).

Similar percentages of marketing directors and consumers recognize the growing clout of consumers in the marketplace. Seventy-five percent of marketing directors and 81 percent of consumers agreed that consumers feel more powerful and comfortable about what they buy and where they shop than ever before. And 78 percent of marketing directors and 73 percent of consumers agreed that consumers feel more in charge as shoppers than before. However, consumers still don't believe that they have sufficient clout; hence, people want to increase their clout by forcing changes in marketing practices. On the other hand, marketing directors think that the clout that consumers have now is plenty.

Figure 7.2: **State of Marketing**

Today's communications environment is packed with more clutter and competition than ever before	**91%**
Better financial performance of marketing programs is the top priority facing marketers	**83**
Consumers feel more in charge as shoppers than they used to	**78**
Consumers feel more powerful and comfortable about what they buy and where they shop than ever before	**75**
In today's marketplace, consumers have more power than marketers	**75**
New product failure rates have increased during the past two decades	**57**
Top management only cares about the measurable return on marketing spending and not positioning, creative or branding	**51**
Marketing today is more effective than marketing in the 80's and 90's	**50**
The quality of the advertising today is superior to advertising in the 80's and 90's	**48**
The tools available to measure the impact of marketing programs are still rudimentary at best	**46**
Most marketing programs produce a reasonable ROI	**44**
The productivity of marketing spending is declining	**43**
The amount of marketing and advertising today is out of control	**35**
Most marketing today is not genuinely relevant to consumers	**33**
There should be less marketing than there is today	**17**

Source: Yankelovich MONITOR Survey of Marketing Directors 2004

Marketing directors misgauge the depth and breadth of consumer antipathy toward current marketing practices. Sixty-eight percent of marketing directors agreed that consumers have taken steps to reduce the amount of marketing to which they are exposed. But only 55 percent agreed that consumers actually pay less attention to marketing than they used to. Contrast this with the 70 percent of consumers who reported in the 2004 Yankelovich MONITOR OmniPlus study on marketing resistance that they pay less attention than before (Fig. 7.3).

Figure 7.3: **Interaction With Consumers**

Many consumers have taken steps to reduce the amount of marketing and advertising they are exposed to	**68**%
Consumers pay less attention to marketing and advertising than they used to	**55**
Most targeting is far less precise than it needs to be	**50**
Consumers should have more control over the timing and content of the marketing directed at them	**38**
It would be a good idea to compensate consumers in some way for the time and attention they give to marketing and advertising	**27**

Source: Yankelovich MONITOR Survey of Marketing Directors 2004

Just a small percentage of marketing directors think that consumers should be compensated for the time and attention they give to marketing. Only slightly more believe that consumers should have more control over the timing and content of the marketing to which they are exposed. Half believe that their targeting efforts are as precise as needed. Consumers feel differently. People want marketers to be more precise and more relevant. People want marketers to give them more power and reciprocity.

It's not that marketers are trying to ignore people's problems and needs. It's just that they have a particular understanding of how problems and needs are to be identified and addressed. Marketers follow a model, either explicitly or implicitly, that gives them guidance and direction. There are many variations, but the core assumption is that marketers have to dominate the time and attention of consumers in order to stay ahead of clutter, costs and competition. Marketing saturation is presumed to be the best way to do business not only because that is the traditional approach but also because popular new marketing theories recommend more saturation as the answer to the challenges that marketers face today.

THEORIES OF MORE

The challenges of the contemporary marketplace have given rise to a variety of trendy marketing ideas, but stripped down to essentials, each idea is just another theory of more, another justification for greater marketing saturation.

For example, ambient advertising is the new name for guerilla marketing, which is a strategy of placing ads and brand logos in unusual places. The impact of ambient ads comes from the novelty of where and how people run across them. But because ambient ads depend on surprise to attract notice, once something novel is done for the first time, it steadily loses impact thereafter. Because it's not novel anymore. So, marketers have to keep doing new things and expanding into new locations. Nowadays, few places have been left uncovered with ads and brand logos. The very novelty that makes ambient advertising work becomes harder to create the more that marketers engage in it. At best, people become indifferent to the advertising that greets them at every turn. At worst, people become exasperated with it and start to actively resist it.

The same dilemma is true of 360-degree marketing, an envelopment contact strategy of communicating with people across all touch points, both traditional and nontraditional. Every point at which a person is available to receive a message is a point at which a message should be delivered. The impact of 360-degree marketing comes from repetition, reinforcement and continuous presence.

The omnipresence of 360-degree marketing can make it feel intrusive and overbearing. In fact, the more inescapable it becomes, the more it saturates people's public and private spaces. Ultimately, the better that marketers get at delivering messages at every point, the less effective any particular message will be. After awhile, the marketing onslaught becomes a blur, which people either ignore or resent—or both.

Marketing strategies like ambient advertising and 360-degree marketing give people no choice. People are forced to view ads whether they want to or not because the ads are everywhere. Permission marketing has been proposed as the alternative.

Permission marketing, or opt-in as it's sometimes called, is the new mantra for many marketers. It is all about getting the okay from people to market to them. Opt-in is said to be better because marketers have to ask for permission instead of people having to ask for relief.

Permission is a necessary step in the right direction. A general permission framework must be part of marketing in the future. However, mere permission is not enough. What people often discover when they opt in is that permission spam is the result—because granting permission doesn't mean that the marketing that follows will be any less pushy or invasive or that their names won't be shared with other marketers. Permission is just a gate, and once opened, marketers can still employ the same old hard sell, the same old saturation, and the same old intrusiveness, just now with permission. Indeed, permission marketers talk about permission as a corporate asset to be leveraged, grown and monetized, and that means permission marketing saturation.

In fact, permission marketing is often little more than a Trojan horse for marketing as usual. Once permission is granted, people find that the marketing directed at them is no different in any way whatsoever from what it was before. Having given permission, people wind up back in the same opt-out position as before. After opting in, the only way to stop or limit marketing is to go through the effort of opting out.

Disaffection with marketing goes much deeper than not being asked first. Permission alone doesn't make marketing any more relevant or any less overwhelming. And once more and more people have the dawning realization that giving permission has changed very little about their overall experience in the marketplace, they will feel betrayed and marketing resistance will be a bigger problem than it is today. Permission raises the bar for marketing. People expect permission marketing to be better marketing.

Many marketers realize that they must establish deeper, more satisfying connections with people. The concept of customer relationship management, or CRM, is rooted in the basic idea that, with or without permission, people prefer marketing that caters to their individual tastes and interests.

In order to deliver personalized marketing, CRM marketers have to accumulate detailed knowledge about individual customers, so databases containing lots of information must be built and maintained. One consequence of this is that in recent years alarms have been sounded about real or imagined breaches of privacy. Despite reassurances, people are suspicious and skeptical that confidentiality and security can be provided. CRM marketers are in a bind: Building a relationship takes lots of information, but collecting that information might spoil any chance of having a relationship.

Encroachments stoke mistrust, wariness and resistance. People tend to lump all marketing encroachments together. Digging into one's private information is no less intrusive than plastering ads all over the place. Both are cut from the same cloth, each just one more way in which everyday life is saturated with the things that marketers do.

So far, marketers have been able to allay privacy concerns by promising a personalized shopping experience in return. Unfortunately, this is the great broken promise of marketing. Only a handful of marketers have actually kept this promise. Too often, the information collected has been used for marketing that is nothing but addressable mass marketing; i.e., the same direct mail piece is sent to every address, which is to say, marketing saturation on a first-name basis.

The personalization that does occur is usually not delivered as part of a mutually satisfying relationship. This happened to a friend of one of the authors who was hurrying to the airport one day to make a flight. Earlier, his plans had changed at the last minute. As he was racing to catch his new flight, he called the toll-free number for his hotel. The operator quickly processed his change and then proceeded to read him a sales pitch for a related service. It was something that fit his tastes so he was interested, but not while he was making a hurried, mad dash to the airport in a rental car. From the hotel's point of view, the relationship was only about triggering cross-sell opportunities, not about looking for the most convenient time to talk. A good service interaction turned into a bad marketing experience. CRM systems are very good at triggering cross-selling and not so good at knowing when to say goodbye.

Marketing saturation is a difficult habit to break. It is a holdover from a bygone era when people were more enamored of shopping and when ads in unusual places were eye-catching curiosities. It is how mass marketing has always operated, and it is true of the new forms of micromarketing, too. Even when marketing saturation is eschewed by a particular marketing concept or theory, it often reappears when marketers put that theory into practice. More marketing saturation is the knee-jerk response to a highly competitive and overcrowded marketplace. The instinct is to add more weight, more frequency, more presence and more saturation. But the result is diminished marketing performance.

GRIDLOCK ON A ONE-WAY STREET

Marketing today is about dominion—two sorts of dominion: control and saturation. Marketers run a business, so, quite naturally, they expect to be in control. And the best way that marketers see to be in control is to have a dominating presence that saturates the marketplace, not necessarily the entire marketplace but at least the attention span of the target audience.

Control is enforced by practicing and policing marketing as a one-way street. Marketers control the process and make all of the decisions. Consumers take their cues from marketers. Marketers produce. Consumers buy. Marketers listen and observe. Consumers view and react. Everything starts with marketers and then goes in one direction—from marketers *to* consumers.

Certainly, marketers pay attention to consumers. Indeed, marketers are so hungry for ways to be more attentive to consumers that books about customer-centricity, like the business classic *In Search of Excellence* (HarperCollins: 1982) by management gurus Tom Peters and Robert Waterman, remain bestsellers for decades. But marketers are customer-centric within the framework of control that defines how they think about and practice marketing. Marketers get consumer feedback at every step along the way, but marketers direct the process and make all the decisions about how to interpret and respond to that feedback. In short, marketers are the starting point for everything that happens.

In a marketplace in which people have less knowledge and information than marketers and in which change is infrequent and slow moving, people don't object to marketers being in control and providing a foundation of structure and support. But that marketplace no longer exists. Yet, marketers continue to dawdle about changing their marketing practices to match the changes in the marketplace. The continuation of traditional marketing approaches in the face of a marketplace that has been turned on its head has spawned marketing resistance.

Marketing saturation is in marketers' genes. The classic hierarchy of effects model begins with brand awareness. Nothing else can happen until consumers know of the brand. Awareness is built by presence and more awareness is achieved by greater presence. Competition can diminish presence and awareness, so competitive presence must be overpowered. The standard measure of media presence is share of voice. The bigger the share of voice the bigger the presence and awareness.

When only a few marketers were competing for attention, this kind of marketplace supersaturation was not a problem. But with so many more—and more aggressive—competitors today, the classic model no longer works as productively as before. Bombarding consumers with additional marketing only further alienates them. More marketing is not the answer to rebuilding marketing productivity in an era of marketing supersaturation. The one-way street of marketing is now bumper to bumper. More traffic is not going to speed things up.

CONCURRENCE MARKETING

Marketing saturation is all about bulk and muscle, but people don't want to be pushed around anymore. Concurrence Marketing is all synchrony and collaboration. It is all about the smarts and the dexterity to make marketing fit the ways in which people shop, live and work today. People want something other than saturation—more specifically, something that reduces clutter and enhances value.

Concurrence is meant in both senses of the word—joining together by synchronizing and by collaborating. Concurrence means getting in sync with customers. Without agreement, there is no concurrence. Concurrence means collaborating with customers. Customers get to be the boss, not merely the respondents or the targets. Without customers having at least an equal say, there is no concurrence.

This is more than just a fancy way of saying the customer is king (Fig. 7.4). Today, marketers put customers first yet keep control through saturation marketing. Concurrence means making customers co-equal with marketers.

Control and dominion from the top down can't work when the marketplace is in continual flux. Too many things are changing at too fast a rate for a hierarchy of control to be in command of the situation. The marketplace today is so dynamic that it is more than merely evolving; it is protean, which is to say that it is constantly assuming new shapes and forms. As soon as something seems to be in place, it changes yet again or is supplanted by something entirely different. All aspects of the marketplace are caught up in this—the brisk cycling of new products, the fickle

Figure 7.4: **The Meaning of Concurrence**

Dominion			Concurrence
Static	◀	MARKETPLACE ▶	Protean
Control	◀	MARKETING PHILOSOPHY ▶	Collaboration
Company to customer	◀	FINAL ARBITER ▶	Customer to company
4P's/CRM	◀	MARKETING PRINCIPLES ▶	P&R-Squared
Push	◀	DIRECTION OF DEMAND ▶	Pull
Products	◀	OFFERINGS ▶	Experiences
Persuasion	◀	CUSTOMER INTERACTION ▶	Permission
Lecture	◀	MARKETING VOICE ▶	Conversation
Muscle	◀	MARKETING TECHNIQUE ▶	Dexterity
Transactions	◀	SOURCE OF VALUE ▶	Commitments
Data	◀	KEY RESOURCE ▶	Insights
Saturation	◀	TACTICS ▶	Specification
Demographics & Needs	◀	CUSTOMER ARCHETYPE ▶	Lifestyles
Segments	◀	CUSTOMER VIEW ▶	People
Positioning	◀	BRAND IDENTITY ▶	Charisma

nature of consumer preferences, the shifting boundaries of personal and demographic identities, the shooting stars of popular culture, the nonstop deluge of technological upgrades and innovations, and more. The character of the marketplace demands an approach that is more collaborative and in which the final arbiter of demand is the customer, not the company. Pull not push must grease the wheels of commerce.

Concurrence Marketing is a set of principles and tools for meeting the challenges of the marketplace ahead, a marketplace in which marketers must learn more about the nuances of permission than the techniques of persuasion, in which the intangibles of experiences and emotions matter more than product features and attributes, and in which value must be created jointly by companies and their customers through the commitments one makes to the other.

Specification must replace saturation. People should come to see that whenever they encounter marketing, they can expect it to be on target and meaningful. The way to stand out in a super-saturated marketplace is to operate in a distinctive way, a way that invites notice rather than demands center stage. When prospects and customers learn that the things they hear from a company are always directly pertinent to their interests, they will pay more attention to the company's marketing messages instead of figuring that it's nothing but more clutter. The expectation of clutter must be replaced by an expectation of pertinence.

When control is the guiding philosophy of marketing, the voice of communications is a lecture about what to buy. Control marshals people into segments in order to regiment their needs in keeping with the logistics of command. This works well in a static marketplace, but provokes resistance in a dynamic, protean marketplace.

Brands must develop charisma by offering a vision of leadership and authenticity that stirs people's passions and motivates them to seek out brands. Marketing is more productive when people are seeking out brands than when brands are seeking out people. Brands must become lightning rods for emotions and excitement. The easiest way to do that is for a brand to show that it cares more about its customers than itself. Brands must be advocates for customers, not rivals for their time and attention. Brands must show they care enough to make a sacrifice if that's the best thing for customers. Being in sync and being collaborative do that. Concurrence Marketing makes brands magnetic in their appeal and allure.

THE ORGANIZATIONAL IMPERATIVE

All marketing organizations are centered on customers. That's what marketing is all about. That said, there are different ways of being customer-centric, some of which are better than others. Concurrence Marketing is directly rooted in what people want from marketing today.

A good way to understand Concurrence Marketing is to visualize the implications of different organizing principles for marketing organizations. The classic marketing organization is the Marketing & Sales Organization (MSO). An MSO is built around the processes of executing and managing the marketing function (Fig. 7.5). Customer knowledge covers

Figure 7.5: **Marketing and Sales Organization**

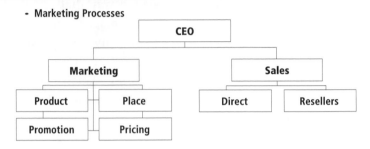

ORGANIZATIONAL FOCUS

- Marketing Processes

CUSTOMER KNOWLEDGE

- Demographic (Who)
- Geodemographic (Where)
- Attitudes/Needs/Motivations (Why)

MARKETING COMMUNICATION

- Mass Media
- Some Micro-media
- Untargeted Direct Marketing

DATABASE STRUCTURE

- Disparate Silo Databases

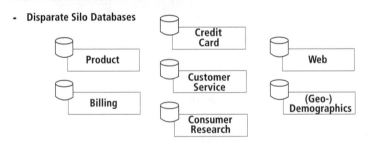

all the basics and marketing communications are directed at mass audiences. There is no need to integrate databases because marketing systems are designed to aggregate, not differentiate, audiences. The key to success is a mass presence in the marketplace, like a bigger share of voice or more shelf space. The sales function is focused on channel dominance and promotional incentives to take advantage of the brand salience created by advertising.

In an MSO, the job of marketers is to keep the marketing process firing on all cylinders. Customers are locked into a highly structured marketplace and have few options to affect the ways in which things operate, so marketers can put more of their focus on products and processes and operate unchallenged in a one-way relationship with customers.

The MSO, of course, is now largely a thing of the past, having been replaced by the Customer Relationship Organization (CRO). The primary focus of a CRO is not on marketing processes but on customer relationships (Fig. 7.6). A CRO is looking to build loyalty and long-term relationships, so the lifetime value of a customer is the key measure of success. To create enduring relationships, a CRO creates a massive database of information about its customers and then uses that data to segment customers into groups of different value and potential. Marketing segment managers in a CRO replace the brand and advertising managers of an MSO.

An integrated database is the indispensable building block of a CRO. Thus, one of the central preoccupations of a CRO is integrating databases by pulling together disparate bits of information about individual customers into a seamless whole. For a CRO, data integration precedes every other function.

Databases must be pieced together and then processed and analyzed to deliver products and communications that fit the profiles of people within each customer segment. Marketers must be skilled technologists who understand how to run a business within the operating framework of database systems. Data mining for a CRO is as important as creative briefs for an MSO.

Attitudinal data is not a part of the database used by a CRO, however. For an MSO, mass aggregation does not require that every bit of data be matched with individual names and addresses. So, aggregate data about attitudes is sufficient. For a CRO, the database is built to interact with individual customers, so every piece of data must be matched to individual names and addresses. Historically, this could be done with demographics and behaviors, but not with attitudes. Hence, attitudinal data gets de-emphasized in a CRO. Attitudes are still available in the aggregate, but it is only marginally useful because the individual-level data that drives marketing for a CRO does not include attitudinal data. Customer relationships are managed on the basis of past behaviors and customer demographics. Attitudes play little part.

A CRO manages customer relationships on the basis of transactional and behavioral data. Past behavior is modeled for predictions of future

Figure 7.6: **Customer Relationship Organization**

ORGANIZATIONAL FOCUS

- **Customer Relationships**

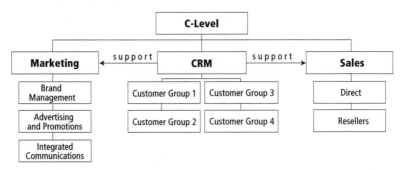

CUSTOMER KNOWLEDGE

- **Demographic (Who)**
- **Geodemographic (Where)**
- **Attitudes/Needs/Motivations (Why)**
- **Transactions/Behavior (What & When)**

MARKETING COMMUNICATION

- **Mass Media**
- **Micro-media**
- **Targeted Direct Marketing**
- **Database Marketing**
- **CRM Activities**
- **Permission Marketing**

DATABASE STRUCTURE

- **Integrated CRM Transactional Database (sans Attitudes)**

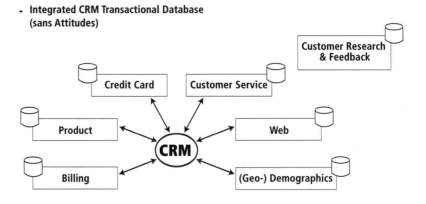

behavior. Customer value is calculated from transactional histories. Segments are defined on the basis of behavioral patterns and similarities. The software tools of CRM are used to keep track of trigger events and to run marketing campaigns.

Even though the limitations of data and analytics sometimes force a CRO to engage in micro-segment marketing instead of one-to-one marketing, a CRO operates much closer to individual customers than an MSO. This puts privacy and permission issues on the front burner for a CRO, so relationship marketing programs have to be designed around strict policies and explicit guarantees that take these concerns into account.

Though very different, both a CRO and an MSO pursue marketing dominion. An MSO is built on a top-down approach, so the one-way flow of communication and development is at the core. A CRO is driven by data, which only marketers are in a position to manage. In an MSO, marketers query people and make decisions based upon their interpretation of the answers. In a CRO, campaign management systems tabulate and rank order the results of alternative offers and messages.

While both an MSO and a CRO interact directly with customers, marketers retain ultimate authority and complete control. Both an MSO and a CRO want to saturate the marketplace in order to dominate the time and attention of customers. An MSO dominates through mass media. A CRO dominates through micro-media and direct marketing. Neither makes customer insights the top priority. But if they did, they would see that customers want something other than dominion and saturation from marketers.

INSIGHT-CENTRIC ORGANIZATION

The primary focus of an Insight-Centric Organization (ICO) is customer insights (Fig. 7.7). Everything follows from insights. Processes and databases have no standing or value apart from insights. An ICO puts customer insights at the center of everything it does. The explicit philosophy is that customers should have at least an equal say in deciding what gets done. Marketers should interact with customers as collaborators, not as marketing targets.

Marketplace trends have led to the need to put insights at the center of a marketing organization. The breakdown of demographic homogeneity

Figure 7.7: **Insight-Centric Organization**

ORGANIZATIONAL FOCUS

- Customer Insights

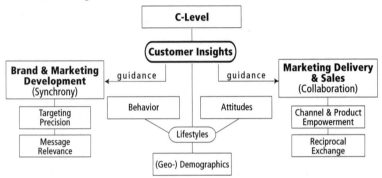

CUSTOMER KNOWLEDGE

- Demographic (Who)

- Geodemographic (Where)

- Attittudes/Needs/Motivations (Why)

- Transactions/Behavior (What & When)

- Addressable Attitudes (All 5 W's together)

MARKETING COMMUNICATION

- Overall Permission Framework

- Mass media

- Micro-media

- Targeted Direct Marketing

- Database Marketing

- CRM Activities

- Personal Media

DATABASE STRUCTURE

- Insights-Driven Marketing Execution Database

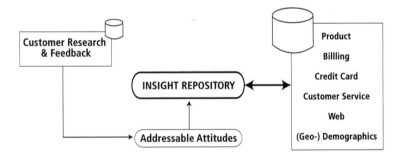

and the emergence of post-accumulation values have undermined the basic, essential foundations of the old approach to marketing, and the demands people are making for power and reciprocity have redefined the terms on which people are willing to form relationships with marketers. Marketers can take nothing for granted any longer, so customer information can't be just another part of the marketing process. Customer insights must be the central component of marketing if marketers are to keep up and sustain their legitimacy and viability in the face of a protean marketplace.

Customer insights don't come from databases or the 4P's. They come from putting the data in perspective and from understanding people's lifestyles. Insights are interpretations, distillations, forecasts and stories, and the only source of breakthrough competitive advantage. Data are good for extrapolating the past. In a protean marketplace, though, the past is not a reliable guide to the future. It takes smarts to make sense of the underlying dynamics of what is observed in the data and then figure out what that means for tomorrow.

For example here are a few insights (shown here only in headline fashion) that Yankelovich MONITOR consultants have reported to clients in recent years:

- Convenience used to mean "easy to get to." Now, it means "wherever I'm at."
- Literacy used to involve "reading and writing." Now, it involves "looking and listening."
- The outdoors used to be about the sublime—"bear tracks," if you will. Now, it involves extremes—"tire tracks," instead.
- Indulgence used to come from "special rewards." Now, it's found in "everyday life."
- Fun was once "escaping the ordinary." Now, it's "enjoying the ordinary."
- Children are no longer "trophies." They're "treasures" now.
- Peers used to "go out together." Now, they "band together."
- Practicality once entailed the "basics." Now, it entails "smarts."

Figure 7.8: **Marketing Organizations**

	Marketing & Sales Organization	Customer Relationship Organization	Insight-Centric Organization
IMPLEMENTATION DATA ▶	Geo-demographics	Transactions/Behaviors	Addressable Attitudes
BUSINESS FOCUS ▶	Products	Behaviors	Lifestyles
PRODUCTIVITY MEASURE ▶	GRPs; CPM	Response rates; Lifetime value	ROMI
SYSTEMS ▶	Mass aggregation	Data integration	Insights Integration
DELIVERY ▶	Undifferentiated	Customized	Self-Customized
FEEDBACK LOOPS ▶	Query and reporting	Campaign management	Customer-initiated
TIMING ▶	Media schedules	Event triggers	Customer preferences
INTERACTION ▶	Top-down	Data-directed	Co-equal
DATA MANAGEMENT ▶	Batch	Real-time	Expert systems
PROFESSIONALS ▶	Marketers	Technologists	Consultants

These kinds of insights provide a more powerful way of understanding market opportunities (Fig. 7.8). Every aspect of an ICO is centered on insights. Marketing is both developed and executed with guidance from insights. Selling is organized around insights into the ways in which channels can meet customer needs rather than the mere availability of channels. Marketing is organized around insights into the ways in which people want to encounter marketing rather than the mere availability of ways to reach people.

Insights are what make the difference. For example, in the early seventies, rising gas prices made big cars uneconomical, so demand for small cars grew. But Detroit figured that once the spike in gas prices was over, demand for big cars would recover. An analysis of past buying patterns would certainly have confirmed this belief. Yankelovich made a different forecast, though. In the 1974 MONITOR report, Yankelovich made this prediction:

- Growth of demand for imports.
- Growth of demand for small cars.
- Trade-up within small cars.

The Yankelovich forecast of trading up within small cars went against all of the received wisdom of the industry at that time. People might start with a small car, the industry experts used to believe, but as soon as they could afford it, they would trade up to a bigger, more prestigious car. That was true for many years. Then people's lifestyles changed.

The consultants at Yankelovich didn't have any data pointing specifically to an interest in trading up within small cars, but they did see a confluence of trends that were changing what people wanted out of their lifestyles—more interest in function and feel over sparkle and glitter, rising concern for the environment, a growing desire for youthful fun over mature status, and more. Looking at these trends, Yankelovich consultants came to the insight that people would no longer switch away from small cars. But Detroit kept making big cars, so Volkswagen, Toyota, Nissan (née Datsun) and Honda captured the momentum in the U.S. automobile market during the seventies and eighties.

This insight into the automobile market was informed by data, but it came from seeing the pattern beyond any particular data point. More importantly, this insight came from understanding the broad pattern of attitudinal data, not just automobile attitudes but lifestyle attitudes. Demographic and behavioral data can't speak for themselves. Attitudinal data are the only way to gain any perspective on what things mean and where things are headed.

Unlike an MSO or a CRO, an ICO is able to practice Concurrence Marketing. By centering itself on the insights provided by a study of attitudes, the organizational structure of an ICO embodies the essence of Concurrence Marketing—making the company subordinate to customers. The organization isn't set up to dominate customers; it's set up to let customers run the show. When customers are in charge, they take only what's pertinent and meaningful to them, and marketers are obliged to provide whatever power and reciprocity that customers demand. An ICO can't help but practice Concurrence Marketing.

Three elements have to be in place for an organization to be insight-centric. First, the organization has to have creative thinkers. Marketers must be more than technologists proficient with data. They must be consultants skilled at interpreting data.

Second, marketing must be centered on attitudes and lifestyles. Insights don't come from observing behavior but from understanding how people are thinking about what they do. Insights don't come from looking at people as category customers but from understanding customers as people who live flourishing lifestyles and who shop and buy to fulfill the aspirations and ambitions of their lifestyles.

Looking at lifestyles is one of the hardest things for marketers to do. Traditional research methods screen people for category or brand usage and then interview people about product purchasing and consumption. The connection with lifestyles is rarely seen. For example, marketers know that many people buy computers for educational reasons. But education is a multifaceted notion. It is tied up with people's views of home, family, children, culture, status, self-image and travel, all of which are part of the richer context within which computers could be marketed more effectively.

Lifestyles are all that matter to people nowadays. People have come to take quality products for granted. So, people are looking at products less in terms of how they perform and more in terms of how they feel. Even a good product can feel wrong if it doesn't communicate or deliver the right lifestyle fit. Marketers must quit thinking in terms of efficient selling relationships and start thinking in terms of meaningful lifestyle satisfactions.

Finally, an organization must have the tools and the ability to integrate insights into marketing systems. Since insights are rooted in attitudinal data, this means getting attitudes overlaid onto and merged into marketing execution systems. This is the way in which insights make an impact.

The problem is that, historically, attitudes and attitudinally-based insights have not been database-compatible. An ICO needs the tools it takes to make attitudes and insights usable by marketers relying on databases and quantitative metrics.

To make attitudes central to marketing, Yankelovich pioneered Addressable Attitudes as the tool for integrating insights into marketing execution systems. Addressable Attitudes enable a marketing organization to function as an ICO. Marketers couldn't organize around insights in the past because they had no way of integrating insights into their marketing practices. Addressable Attitudes make it possible.

ADDRESSABLE ATTITUDES

Addressable Attitudes are attitudes that can be linked to individual names and addresses. They can be included in all of the databases and systems used for marketing execution, ranging from media buying databases to third-party lists to internal transaction files. The attitudes that provide perspective and context for behaviors and demographics can then do so at the level of individual customers. The attitudes that speak for behaviors and demographics can have a voice at the individual level.

Despite all of the information contained in marketing and media databases, there has been a complete lack of any data on attitudes. This is the biggest gap in marketing, which forces marketers to live with certain unavoidable levels of imprecision and irrelevance that cap the potential for improvements in marketing productivity. Direct marketers have focused only on addressability and thus have tried to get by without insights into motivations. Brand marketers have always known a lot about motivations but have lacked the means of pinpointing people with the appropriate attitudes. What has been needed is a solution that provides marketers with Addressable Attitudes.

Addressable Attitudes bring the best of direct marketing and brand marketing together by combining the addressability of direct marketing with the attitudinal insights of brand marketing. The productivity of brand marketing is improved through addressability. The productivity of direct marketing is improved through attitudes. Marketing as a whole comes together as one because Addressable Attitudes provide a universal platform that works across every aspect of marketing. No longer must different types of marketing work with different tools and information. Addressable Attitudes put all types of marketing on a common footing, thus enabling marketing organizations to become insight-centric.

With Addressable Attitudes, marketers can re-engage resistant consumers. Marketing can be targeted to people who are interested in a particular product instead of people with a certain demographic profile, only some of whom are interested. Marketing can be formulated and delivered in a way that is directly relevant to the attitudes, needs and motivations of specific people. Addressable Attitudes re-center marketers around insights into what people think and want. What people want is power and reciprocity, so integrating these insights into marketing systems will significantly improve the overall tenor of marketplace relationships.

Addressable Attitudes make Concurrence Marketing possible. Precision and Relevance are attitudinally based, even if sometimes they are executed on the basis of demographics. Power and Reciprocity are insights that come directly from studying people's attitudes.

Even without demographic and behavioral data, as long as marketers have Addressable Attitudes, they can practice concurrence. The best databases, of course, should include demographics, behaviors and attitudes, but the necessary and sufficient element for Concurrence Marketing is Addressable Attitudes.

People want an end to clutter so they are demanding synchrony—precision and relevance. People want an end to one-way interactions so they are demanding collaboration—power and reciprocity. In other words, people are demanding concurrence from marketers, not as a threat, but as a willingness to do business with marketers who concur with people's opinions about what constitutes better marketing. Marketing practices can create enduring competitive advantage for concurrent marketers.

P&R²

Concurrence Marketing entails two things marketers were taught to do in business school—provide marketing precision and marketing relevance—and two things marketers were taught not to do—provide consumer power and consumer reciprocity. Precision and Relevance are the fundamentals of good marketing. Consumer Power and Reciprocity run counter to traditional ideas of good marketing, but these old ideas must change. Precision and Relevance reduce clutter. Power and reciprocity create cooperation and co-equality. Concurrence Marketing means going back to basics and doing them better as well as going back to the future by adding what's missing.

Precision

Precise targeting is the essential first step. Without it, marketing is nothing but clutter for everyone lacking the pertinent needs and interests. With it, marketing is free of the inefficiencies of communicating with people who will never buy.

Feedback from consumers in the 2004 Yankelovich MONITOR study on consumer resistance to marketing suggests that despite marketer's best efforts, marketing targeting remains so imprecise that it contributes to clutter. Fifty-two percent wish for less marketing and advertising than today; only 7 percent wish for more.

Relevance

Marketers must say something that matters. Speaking loudly and often is not the same as speaking meaningfully. The meaning that people want from marketers nowadays is rooted in a new set of values and priorities that are without precedent in the post-World War II consumer marketplace.

Again, consumer feedback suggests that Relevance is often lacking. Fifty-nine percent say that most marketing and advertising has very little Relevance to them.

Power

People want Power. Marketers have to master the paradox of getting control over their success by giving up control to consumers. People now expect to be able to dictate the terms of every transactional relationship. In the meantime, people are devising homemade solutions to take control, including the ultimate control of resistance. Fifty-three percent complain that nothing has changed because consumers are still at the mercy of marketers and advertisers.

Reciprocity

People don't have time to waste. They want marketing that delivers immediate value rather than promoting the value of something else. They want Reciprocity. This value can be information, entertainment or compensation, but something to demonstrate appreciation and respect. Sixty-one percent say that marketers and advertisers don't treat consumers with respect.

Marketing abounds with creativity, inspiration and invention. But the most common way of putting marketing genius to work today rides roughshod over the fundamentals of precise targeting and relevant positioning and, in doing so, gives no thought to sharing power or to rewarding people for paying attention. Concurrence Marketing is the best way of putting marketing talent to work.

Concurrent marketers are made not born. Above all else, concurrence takes the tools of Addressable Attitudes and Insights Integration. And then it takes using those tools to apply the principles of P&R². Some forward-thinking companies, like Pfaltzgraff, are using the tools and principles of Concurrence Marketing to keep themselves on the cutting edge of marketing productivity.

PFALTZGRAFF: AN INSIGHT-CENTRIC ORGANIZATION TAKES SHAPE

Pfaltzgraff, America's oldest pottery maker, is the premier manufacturer and marketer of casual dinnerware and accessories for the home, including stoneware, glass beverage-ware, stainless steel flatware, dinnerware, kitchenware, and serving and table accessories. The company's continuing success is rooted in one thing: Its resolute, two century-long dedication to excellence for its customers.

The company was begun in 1811 by German immigrants in York, Pennsylvania, as a maker of earthenware and crockery-ware for farming families. As the country grew, the company evolved by adding new product lines to meet the needs of a growing, more urbanized population. As the 19th Century gave way to the 20th Century, Pfaltzgraff adopted modern production methods for the latest and the best in quality and consistency. Its commitment to innovation and modernization to better serve its customers enabled it to thrive even as other local potters were closing up shop during the World War I era.

Throughout the 20th century, responsiveness to customer needs continued to be the key ingredient in Pfaltzgraff's recipe for success. From art pottery in the 1930s to its *Gourmet* bake-ware for the burgeoning interest in French cooking in the 1940s to its lines of popular kitchenware over the next several decades, Pfaltzgraff has maintained an unwavering focus on serving the ever-changing lifestyle needs of its customers.

By the late 1960s, Pfaltzgraff had expanded its retail presence so that customers could find its products in a wide variety of retail outlets. In recent years, Pfaltzgraff has used its strong channel presence to strengthen customer relationships, not just to make products available for sale. This has been particularly true of its direct marketing programs, from catalogs to direct mail to the Internet.

The strategic growth of Pfaltzgraff since the end of World War II reflects its evolution from a classic Marketing & Sales Organization to a modern Customer Relationship Organization. As technologies and channels have improved and expanded, Pfaltzgraff has steadily upgraded the depth and specificity of its customer programs. The focus on serving customers by pushing high-quality products out to mass customer groups through retail stores has grown to include customizing products and managing relationships through databases, direct feedback systems, and direct marketing programs.

Pfaltzgraff did not have a big direct marketing presence until the late 1970s and early 1980s, when it decided to focus on business opportunities beyond traditional retail that would help it to better connect with customers. The company's initial catalogs were developed to make it easy for customers to find replacement pieces. As its direct marketing expanded, with such things as the "Pfaltzgraff Collector's Newsletter," its direct customers became a fan base eagerly anticipating each new catalog.

Pfaltzgraff's commitment to customers also includes its "Direct to Consumer" program offering patterns and items no longer available at retail, which the company sells online, by catalog or through its factory stores. Its "By Request" program offers special made-to-order pieces for retired patterns that are selected for inclusion in an annual December catalog by customer voting during the year. Additionally, the "Connections" page on the company Web site includes stories about "Friends & Family," message boards to share ideas, schedules of events, opportunities to connect with other collectors, recipes, tips and tidbits, and chances to chat with Pfaltzgraff management, including the President and CEO Marsha Everton.

The connection with customers has been championed even more strongly since Ms. Everton took the helm in 2002. This is reflected in its ad campaign, "From Me To You," which takes customers behind the scenes with profiles of Pfaltzgraff designers, as well as in its program called "The Potter's Pledge," which promises customer satisfaction and service "above and beyond" expectations.

In recent years, Pfaltzgraff has taken steps to raise its customer focus to the next level by more thoroughly imbuing a customer-centric orientation throughout the company. This is especially important given today's fast-moving changes in the lifestyles and needs of its customers.

Pfaltzgraff is not short on consumer research or detailed database information, but management recently saw a need for richer insights about its customers. Databases with demographics and purchasing have been at the center of the company's relationships with its customers, tracking things like how much an individual customer spends on what types of patterns through which types of channels. This information is invaluable for anticipating product needs and calculating customer value. But it only goes so far. It helps Pfaltzgraff see the "who" and the "what," but not the "why." To stay ahead in an increasingly competitive and volatile marketplace, management wanted the context and perspective of customer insights to help it better utilize its customer data to manage its customer relationships.

In particular, management wanted to know the core values defining its customers, whatever their demographics and purchasing behavior— the "mindset" of its customers, something about how they think, not more about what they buy and who they are. In other words, Pfaltzgraff wanted to move from integrating customer databases to integrating customer insights. But Pfaltzgraff didn't want to know the customer mindset in general terms; it wanted to know the mindsets of individual customers so that it could do a better job of servicing and satisfying particular people.

Pfaltzgraff turned to Addressable Attitudes. By overlaying its database with Yankelovich MindBase, Pfaltzgraff was able to see the face and personality of its customers based on attitudinal information about values and lifestyles. By gaining this perspective on its customers, Pfaltzgraff learned that there was a strong correlation of customer attitudes with the fundamental elements of the company's brand promise. In total, the entire process of overlaying Addressable Attitudes and profiling Pfaltzgraff customers took less than six weeks.

With attitudes and behaviors in the same database, Pfaltzgraff could look at the attitudes of each of its most profitable customers. In doing so, it found that customers who were most drawn to the values of the brand are demographically indistinguishable from those who are not, yet their attitudes are quite different. The Pfaltzgraff brand is rooted in the values of tradition, quality and selection, and these are values with special resonance for its most interested customers. Buying behaviors differed, too.

Pfaltzgraff's most interested customers used a variety of channels and bought bold patterns (over floral patterns).

Integrating attitudes with demographics and behaviors provided deeper insights as well. For example, Pfaltzgraff could see that selection is about control, not just style, because it relates to the entire customer experience and the chance to select from a variety of options as well as from a variety of channels. Also, tradition and quality don't have to be understated. Bold patterns, perhaps even brash and brassy, offer a sense of classic timelessness and value. Finally, being in many different channels doesn't dilute the brand's image with consumers; instead, it builds the familiarity.

In just a few months, Pfaltzgraff had put the Addressable Attitudes of MindBase in place and integrated the resulting new insights into its marketing systems. This foundation of attitudinal and behavioral data set a solid foundation for Pfaltzgraff to get to work. Three organizational goals were established in order to further solidify the intimate connection with customers that has always been the core strength of its business. First, the company decided to reach out to individual customers through their preferred channel with products and messages tailored to their values and interests. With attitudinal data matched against behavioral data, marketers could see whether each individual customer's preferred channel was being utilized to the proper degree. Pfaltzgraff could also determine which channels to use to win greater patronage and loyalty from the high-prospect new customers who had the same attitudinal mindset as its best customers.

Second, Pfaltzgraff set out to improve its overall marketing communications by speaking directly to the key values and lifestyles of its most interested customers. From product descriptions to catalog copy to Web site design, the company made sure to emphasize its fit with relevant hot buttons.

Product design now reflects these attitudinal insights, too. Varieties that match the tastes and preferences of Pfaltzgraff's most interested customers are emphasized and featured, and different versions of catalogs include different mixes of styles and patterns to match what different individuals most prefer.

Third, Pfaltzgraff decided to create a uniform language for the entire organization to use in describing and understanding its most interested customers. From management to design to merchandising to finance to operations to store employees to its ad agencies, the company wanted to create a common view—not just of the behavioral and demographic data available to every competitor, but of its customers as they live their lives, down to the minutest details, like how they think about family, work or spirituality and whether they eat dinner in front of the TV or at the kitchen table.

Pfaltzgraff fleshed out a day in the life of three imaginary people, each of a different lifestage, based on the detailed data about values and lifestyles available from MindBase. At its annual strategic planning meeting, company employees got their first introduction to their customers as people, including a soundtrack of each imaginary customer's favorite songs. Referring to each person by name, the management team spent time discussing how she lives, what she believes, what she aspires to, what she needs and how Pfaltzgraff could address her wants and needs. In particular, the Pfaltzgraff team brainstormed new ways of reaching these customers such as new media and new retail outlets to offer greater degrees of Power and Reciprocity. Because one of the other key lifestyle values of Pfaltzgraff's most interested customers is marketing resistance.

Pfaltzgraff has now made insights, not databases, the central part of how it approaches its customers. Insights have become the key to building its business. And the results are proving out.

Pfaltzgraff has become an Insight-Centric Organization. The first step was to ask itself how it could deepen its understanding of its customers beyond what it already knew from demographics and behaviors. Addressable Attitudes were the unique answer for gaining context and perspective, which generated a more profound set of insights that were then integrated into all of Pfaltzgraff's information and marketing systems. Pfaltzgraff made these insights the center of its organizational focus and its customers suddenly came alive as real people. Pfaltzgraff can now focus on lifestyle solutions that connect with people in more profound ways and that give people a reason to invite Pfaltzgraff into more and more of their lives.

Pfaltzgraff's assurance of marketing productivity is its commitment to practicing the kind of marketing that people want and that will engage people's attention and loyalty.

SUMMING UP

- Marketing saturation and intrusiveness are inherent to a philosophy of marketing that is rooted in the presumption of marketplace dominion. The emphasis is on doing more marketing. Most new marketing theories and approaches rest on the same ideas of dominion, saturation and intrusiveness.
- Concurrence Marketing establishes a new set of principles rooted in synchrony and collaboration. The essential elements are Precision, Relevance, Power and Reciproicity—the four components of P&R^2. The essential tools are Insight Integration and Addressable Attitudes, or attitudes linked to an individual name and address.
- To practice Concurrence Marketing, companies must reshape themselves into an Insight-Centric Organizations (ICO). Attitudes become central to the organization. Addressable Attitudes are the key tool.
- Addressable Attitudes make it possible to execute marketing on the basis of insights. These insights ensure greater Precision and Relevance because people with the right attitudes will be targeted in the right way. And the focus on attitudes means that marketers will understand the importance of offering Power and Reciprocity to customers.

NOTES

1 This study was a telephone survey from March 19 to April 19, 2004, among senior marketing directors at 153 consumer marketing companies across the full range of company sizes and business categories.

SECTION III
P&R^2

Addressable Attitudes for Marketing Precision

Dealing directly with attitudes is the only way to make marketing as precise as it needs to be. With Addressable Attitudes, marketing can be directed against people who actually have the relevant interests, needs and preferences, which is to say, people who count and only the people who count.

In 2001, a Yankelovich company known as The Segmentation Company® completed an Addressable Attitudes project for a Fortune 500 consumer bank.[1] A segmentation was used to build an Addressable Attitudes marketing system. The segmentation was based upon in-depth interviews with 4,000 respondents chosen at random from the bank's internal customer database. The final solution identified 25 well-defined and robust segments for its check card business group. These results generated detailed profiles that provided the bank with new in-depth information about its customers. But for all of these research successes, the segmentation information was not the most valuable outcome of this project.

This project was not undertaken as a research study but as the essential first step in a broader exercise to build an innovative marketing system for the bank. The specific purpose was to link attitudes to the names and addresses of each person in the bank's internal customer file. The quality of the solution was essential for this objective because segments with tightly clustered mindsets provided the means by which attitudes were merged into a company's database of customers. Models were developed to assign a segment ID to every name and address in the bank's database. To put it simply, attitudes were matched to names and addresses.

With Addressable Attitudes in hand, the bank was able to significantly improve the precision of its direct marketing initiatives by zeroing in on people with exactly the right attitudes. Targeting could be focused only on people with certain key motivations, and communications and offers could be customized to fit people's preferences and interests. The result of this boost in precision due to the inclusion of Addressable Attitudes in the bank's database was a significant improvement in the bank's marketing productivity. The bank estimates that in the three years this system has been in place, it has saved over $30 million in marketing expenses while realizing $100 million in revenue because of strong market response.

Marketing precision matters. Imprecision depresses performance and misses opportunities. Attitudes that can be linked to names and addresses make marketing more precise. In this case, Addressable Attitudes boosted the bank's marketing productivity.

THE LIMITS OF DESCRIPTIVE DATA

A Fortune 500 publishing company that manages the subscription renewals for magazine companies was faced with a marketing productivity problem. Many people become subscribers through incentives and rewards programs. Since they are not paying initially, these subscribers naturally have a lower attachment or psychological commitment to a magazine, which makes them difficult to convert and retain as subscribers paying full price when their first renewal comes due.

The publishing company was looking for ways to improve its conversion of trial subscribers into full-price subscribers. In particular, the publishing company wanted to find better ways of predicting which trial subscribers had the greatest likelihood of renewing so that it could stop marketing to trial subscribers unlikely to renew and direct more efforts against trial subscribers with enough potential to be worth the investment. In particular, the company frequently uses merchandise offers as an inducement for converting to a full-price subscription. These merchandise offers are costly, so the publishing company was interested in a system that could identify which trial subscribers should and should not receive them.

Over the years, the company had accumulated lots of research on the demographic and behavioral characteristics that identified trial subscribers most likely to convert to full-price subscribers. It had used this knowledge in its marketing programs, but despite analyses of these descriptive characteristics, it had been unable to generate any further improvements in its ability predict which trial subscribers would renew at full price. The precision of the publishing company's marketing activities was low to begin with and had reached an unacceptably low plateau. Indeed, the publishing company had never generated a positive ROI through its marketing efforts to convert trial subscribers into full-price subscribers. Without something new to push past the limits of its existing information, conversion rates were not going to get any better.

The publishing company manages its marketing by means of an extensive database of subscribers containing millions of names and addresses along with the demographic and household information provided by subscribers or available from other outside lists and databases. The information in the publishing company's database is descriptive information that can be passively measured, which is to say, information that can be extracted from records that are generated in the ordinary course of completing certain activities and purchases. These include things like using a credit card to buy a TV or taking out a loan to buy a car or filling out a warranty card when registering a new stereo with the manufacturer. The very nature of borrowing money or registering a warranty entails the creation of an electronic paper trail that is stored in a database for future use and reference. Credit card companies keep records for billing purposes, loan companies to track credit history, manufacturers to service products, and so on.

What is not stored on any database are the attitudes that people have about products such as needs, interests, ambitions, preferences or values. Unlike demographics and many behaviors, attitudes cannot be passively measured because attitudes are not a necessary element in the completion of an activity or a purchase.

Attitudes are frequently measured, though. Survey researchers and pollsters conduct thousands of interviews every day by telephone or Internet about dozens of topics ranging from politics to products to pop culture. But attitudes measured through survey samples project the results to groups of people. Well-drawn samples of 600 to 1,000 respondents, for example, are sufficiently large to accurately estimate the overall opinions of a group of any size, including Americans at large.[2]

Surveys do not ask the attitudes of everyone in a group, only of a sample. Surveying an entire group is far too difficult and expensive. Only the Census Bureau undertakes such an endeavor, and only because the U.S. Constitution requires it.[3] In short, attitudinal survey data, unlike demographics and many behaviors, does not link back to individual names and addresses.

To put a finer edge on this point, attitude surveys measure characteristics of groups, like voters or men between the ages of 18 and 34 or African-Americans living in South Carolina or magazine subscribers. The percentage of people who hold a certain opinion is a characteristic of a group. An individual person will either have an opinion or not, so the notion of a percentage does not apply. The percentage of people holding an opinion is a group characteristic. Individual people are interviewed, of course, but the data collected from the individual interviews are used to generalize to the group represented by the sample. While an attitude survey may find that 57 percent of magazine subscribers enjoy self-help articles, it is not possible from the survey alone to know which particular individuals have that attitude.

Since attitudes have not been available by name and address, marketers have had to make do without attitudes in their lists and databases. Demographics and other descriptive data have been used as proxies for attitudes. Sometimes these proxies have worked well, other times not so well. But marketers have never had direct marketing lists or media buying databases containing attitudinal information matched to individual names and addresses. Despite the fact that they appeal to people on the basis of their needs, preferences, motivations, aspirations, tastes and desires, marketers have had to execute and deliver marketing appeals on the basis of people's ages, genders, incomes and races.

This was the difficulty facing the publishing company client of Yankelovich. The descriptive data in its subscriber database were unable to predict which trial subscribers would renew as full-price subscribers. And even if certain attitudes were related to renewal, people with these attitudes could not be identified by name and address. So, the company was unable to make its solicitation and renewal efforts any more precise, relevant or productive.

The publishing company realized that the imprecision in its targeting was hampering its ability to convert trial subscribers. It was unsure about whom to target with more marketing and how to tailor its offers and communications. As a result, a lot of subscribers were receiving marketing offers that, to them, were nothing but clutter.

Yankelovich recommended a solution that would boost the marketing productivity of the company's renewal efforts: The use of Addressable Attitudes. This solution was proposed so that the publishing company could incorporate attitudinal insights into its marketing programs. Addressable Attitudes offered the best, and only, solution to this productivity impasse. To fully appreciate what this approach was able to do for this company, a more in-depth understanding of Addressable Attitudes is needed first.

ADDRESSABLE ATTITUDES

A marketer's best customers are not always easy to spot. The attitudes that predispose people towards a brand are not an external trait recognizable at a glance. A person may look like a likely buyer but that may mask an underlying attitude of reluctance and hesitation towards a brand. The people who look like they should be interested customers may be harboring attitudes that, ultimately, lead them to act differently. The only way to know for sure whether someone is an interested buyer is to get inside his or her head.

Observable characteristics such as gender and age are relied upon by marketers because groups of people with such characteristics often include people with particular needs and interests. But marketers understand that these external characteristics are not valuable in and of themselves, but only because they help pinpoint people with the right attitudes. The challenge marketers face is that many people with the same external characteristics as interested buyers don't have the right attitudes. And the motivations that lead people to buy a brand are often shared by many different kinds of people.

Addressable Attitudes eliminate this guesswork. Since observable descriptive data are really only proxies for finding people with the right attitudes, Addressable Attitudes finesse the difficulty of always being one step removed from the attitudes that really matter. For a direct marketing list, Addressable Attitudes are attitudes matched to the individual people in the list in the same way that matches are made with other descriptive information like gender, age, race, marital status, place of residence, credit rating, number and types of cars owned, and so forth. For a media buying database, Addressable Attitudes are attitudes matched to specific media (such as TV, magazines or the Internet), media content (such as a TV show, a particular magazine or a Web site) or media elements (such as a TV daypart, a magazine section or a page on a Web site) in the same way that matches are made to other descriptive information like the percent of the audience that is of a certain age, gender, race or marital status or that owns or buys certain products.

When attitudes can be addressed in the same manner as other descriptive information, attitudes can be used directly, not indirectly through demographics, in the execution of targeting and media buying. Lists can be drawn and media can be bought on the basis of people with the right attitudes rather than on the basis of people with characteristics that might be associated with the right attitudes.

If a marketer promoting an exotic travel destination wants to advertise to people who think of themselves as adventuresome, then Addressable Attitudes can be used to buy commercial time in TV shows that attract people who think of themselves as adventuresome. Not just people with demographic characteristics that are often associated exotic travel, but people who have adventuresome attitudes.

Similarly, if a direct marketer selling a high-risk, high-return financial product wants to send mail solicitations (or email solicitations) to people willing to take financial risks, then Addressable Attitudes can be used to identify the individual names and addresses of people in a direct marketing list or database who have those kinds of attitudes—not just people who have bought such high-risk products in the past but every individual who is interested in those kinds of financial opportunities, some of whom may not have bought such products in the past because of practical or momentary constraints that no are longer a barrier.

The precision of Addressable Attitudes extends to all types of motivations, needs and values. For example, marketers are always looking for ways to identify people with an interest in being the first to buy new products. The Yankelovich MONITOR includes a battery of questions that identifies these early adopters. Such people constitute a mere 10 percent of the population at large, but are three times as likely to be men as women—15 percent of men compared to 5 percent of women. Smart use of other demographics like age, income and educational level can increase the odds of finding early adopters, but demographics will not identify the names and addresses of people with these attitudes. Demographics can only identify a broad group of people. A broad group will always include some people who lack the appropriate attitudes and will fail include other people who have the right attitudes.

Addressable Attitudes, though, can identify the names and addresses of the individual people who have the mindset of early adopters. One service to provide Addressable Attitudes is known as Lists With Attitude™.4 One of these lists provides the names and addresses of the 13.1 million people who have the attitudes of early adopters (called Early Embracers). Rather than make calculated demographic guesses about who holds the attitudes of being an early adopter, an Addressable Attitudes product like Lists With Attitude can precisely identify these people by name and address.

Marketers know that existing marketing systems operate with built-in imprecision because the proxies for attitudes are only approximate ways of finding people with the right attitudes. Marketers have learned to live with this because Addressable Attitudes have not been available. But now that people can be targeted on the basis of their attitudes, marketers can do a better job of fine-tuning their efforts by focusing only on people with an interest in and a receptivity to their marketing efforts. This has the added advantage of keeping everyone else from getting saturated with irrelevant and annoying clutter.

ATTITUDES PLUS

The importance of Addressable Attitudes is not about making marketing work. Marketing based on demographic and behavioral data works— and has worked for decades. Instead, Addressable Attitudes are about making marketing work more productively. Marketing based solely on demographics and behaviors is not as efficient or as effective as it needs to be. The most productive marketing takes advantage of attitudes along with demographics and behaviors.

Addressable Attitudes bring descriptive data to life. Demographic and behavioral information can be better utilized when augmented by attitudinal information. All marketers realize that this is true when compiling background research about category trends or target groups of customers. However, it is just as true for marketing execution systems such as list selection and media buying.

Marketers know that past buying behavior is a strong predictor of future buying behavior. Add in demographic information that pinpoints people in the lifestages for which a particular product has special relevance and the predictive model is stronger. Then, add in Addressable Attitudes that indicate a keen interest in the sorts of benefits delivered by a particular product and the predictive model is even stronger.

A financial services company had developed a sophisticated model to predict likely response to its marketing solicitations. The model developed by the financial services company is known as a "look-alike" model because it selects people for future solicitations who most resemble the demographic, financial and lifestage characteristics of people who have bought such financial services products in the past. The financial services company was satisfied with its model because it was able to identify prospective customers who responded and purchased at rates that were at industry norms.

Yankelovich recommended that the financial services company assess the incremental value of adding Addressable Attitudes to its model. Using the Yankelovich MindBase system, attitudinal information was added to a file containing the names and addresses of people who had received past solicitations.

The analysis showed that by adding Addressable Attitudes to the demographic and behavioral data already being modeled, several attitudinal groups could be identified with response rates much higher than average. Conversely, several attitudinal groups had response rates much lower than average (Fig. 8.1).

The financial services company calculated that it could significantly improve the productivity of its marketing programs by not sending solicitations to people whose attitudes gave them a below average interest in

Figure 8.1: **Marketing Response By Lifestyle Attitudes**

MindBase Segment	Indexed Response Rate	MindBase Segment	Indexed Response Rate
1	53	9	117
2	74	10	123
3	120	11	144
4	68	12	125
5	80	13	125
6	108	14	63
7	105	15	119
8	120	16	118

Source: Yankelovich MindBase

its financial services product. The response rates for these people did not generate a favorable ROI, something that could not be seen in the absence of the attitudinal information because the marketing program as a whole generated a positive ROI. But the overall ROI would be better still by not marketing to people who look alike yet think very differently.

Additionally, the financial services company expects that it will be able to improve its response rates even further by customizing the content and offerings in its marketing solicitations to fit the needs and interests of people in high-prospect attitudinal segments. Addressable Attitudes enable marketers to get more value from the demographic and behavioral information already being used not only because the targeting models are better but also because an understanding of attitudes puts meat on the bare bones of demographics and behaviors.

For example, upon turning fifty, a man might suddenly show up at a car dealership to buy his first sports car. Marketers know that the demographic event is the trigger, so they develop marketing programs based upon age. But not all men turning fifty will buy a sports car, only those with the right attitudes. Thus, the best prediction of the likelihood of buying a sports car is a combination of demographics and attitudes. And it takes attitudes linked to names and addresses to make this combination of demographics and attitudes work.

Addressable Attitudes also provide an understanding of people that is simply not available from demographics and behaviors. Interest in a sports car strong enough to cause somebody to buy involves a complex of lifestyle attitudes, not just a simplistic statement of interest in sports cars. Other things like a sense of youthfulness, a need for excitement, a willingness to take risks, an interest in novelty and fun, and an appreciation for styling, design and power are relevant, too. With this breadth of information, marketers can profile specific people and develop better marketing for each person. In other words, insight has to be distilled from the full scope of relevant attitudes in order to understand lifestyles in a way that can make marketing more productive.

NEITHER GEODEMOGRAPHICS NOR PSYCHOGRAPHICS

Addressable Attitudes probably sound familiar. There are over five dozen commercially available syndicated segmentations for use in conjunction with direct marketing lists, customer databases and media buying systems. These other segmentations seem to provide attitudes that can be linked to names and addresses. Many of these are geodemographic segmentations that profile the aggregate (not the individual) demographic and behavioral information about people living in a certain geographic area, such as a Zip+4 postal area. Others are lifestage segmentations that categorize people on the basis of demographic data centered on age.

These segmentations are useful products, but they do not offer a solution to the marketing productivity problems facing marketers. Without exception, all of these segmentations are smart, sophisticated ways of re-analyzing and recombining demographic and behavioral data. But they do not provide Addressable Attitudes.

Sometimes, for profiling purposes, these segmentations obtain attitudinal data from other sources. But the segmentations themselves are created on the basis of non-attitudinal data. The variables used to generate the segmentation are demographic and behavioral. Most typically, these segmentations are some version of a lifestage segmentation that gets covered with an attitudinal patina after the fact. No attitudinal data are used to derive the segmentation scheme itself.

Segmentations that do not make use of attitudes in deriving the segments are no different than current marketing systems: All identify groups to target on the basis of demographic and behavioral data. Whatever the attitudinal information used for profiling purposes, demographics still define the basis on which the marketing is being done. The attitudes simply describe the characteristics of groups, not the attitudes of individuals.

A segmentation provides marketers with Addressable Attitudes only when attitudes are part of the derivation of the segmentation itself—when the segmentation is built from the attitudes themselves. When attitudes are used after the fact to profile the demographically or behaviorally defined segments, no Addressable Attitudes are made available to marketers.

In repeated side-by-side comparisons with marketing solutions that use Addressable Attitudes, these other syndicated segmentations have failed to measure up in terms of target group discrimination or improved response rates. The reason is simple. These segmentations are just applications of demographic and behavioral data. These segmentations can perform no better than the data on which they are based. They lack Addressable Attitudes.

A SYSTEM FOR ADDRESSABLE ATTITUDES

A system for Addressable Attitudes has three broad components:

- A source of robust attitudinal data that is pertinent, current and constantly refreshed.
- The consulting talent and historical baselines to provide meaningful interpretations and to distill relevant insights.
- Linkage models to merge Addressable Attitudes into lists and databases.

The attitudinal data behind Addressable Attitudes should include at least three kinds of information:

- Attitudes about the product category of interest: needs and dissatisfactions, things preferred and things liked, and intentions about future behavior.
- Attitudes about lifestyles that relate to the relevant category: ambitions, aspirations, values and desires.

- Attitudes about shopping and marketing: preferences for certain media channels, interest in various retail outlets and promotions, desire for the power to control exposure and experience, and interest in certain kinds of value as reciprocity.

A full range of attitudes is needed in order to distill insights from the data. Category data about product features and usage occasions is very helpful, but understanding it in the context of lifestyle needs is required for insights. A snack food company may know that people are pressed for time, so time-efficient packaging, portions and sizes are essential. But learning that people are putting greater pressure on themselves to avoid family sacrifices suggests that time pressures are building up more because of a stronger interest in family than because of anything else. Time-efficient snacks are good, but they may not be the only, or even the best, product to offer. People might be willing to take the time for a product that enables them to do something for their families, even if that product is not as time-efficient.

The second component of a system for Addressable Attitudes is the ability to find insights in the data, not just report the data. Marketers need to see how the data fit together to reveal the underlying dynamic giving rise to all of the diverse phenomena being observed. With Addressable Attitudes comes the opportunity to act upon these insights on a name and address basis.

There are many different types of attitudes and lots of disputes about how different mental states fit together. For marketing purposes, arguments about definitions and semantics is a dead-end debate. The attitudes that matter, however they are defined, are the mental states that motivate behavior. Depending upon the category or brand, the attitudes that motivate behavior could be needs, perceptions, beliefs, values, ambitions, aspirations, preferences or intentions. That is why these terms are used interchangeably in this book. Addressable Attitudes enable marketers to focus on the specific types of attitudes, whatever they are, that matter for a particular category or brand.

The third component for a system of Addressable Attitudes are models to link specific attitudes to specific individuals. These models are new to the practice of marketing, which is why Addressable Attitudes are only just now possible.

The modeling process for attitudes turns out to be no different than the modeling process for demographics and other descriptive information. The attitudes are known and available from a separate attitudinal source, typically survey research. The independent information in a marketing list or database is used to transfer the attitudes to that list or database. The models identify the relevant variables and profiles of individual people in a list or database that correspond to the variables and profiles of people interviewed in the survey research who hold particular attitudes. Individuals in the list or database are scored with the attitudes of people in the survey research who have the same profiles or characteristics on key variables. This is a complicated modeling process, but when it is carried out with the statistical methods and data resources now available, an extremely high level of individual assignment accuracy can be achieved.

Linkage models for Addressable Attitudes can be built on either a proprietary or a syndicated basis. Proprietary models are built to link attitudes to the names and addresses in a client's internal customer file. Syndicated models are built to link attitudes to the names and addresses in commercially available third-party compiled lists. Typically, the proprietary systems involve more category- and brand-specific data than the syndicated systems. However, the improvements in marketing productivity are significant for both types of systems.

An example from a proprietary modeling assignment illustrates the high level of accuracy that can be achieved matching attitudes to names and addresses (Fig. 8.2). This example shows the actual attitude segment for survey respondents compared to the predicted attitude segment based on linkage models built for the client's internal customer file. The main diagonal in the matrix shows the percent of people in a particular segment who are accurately re-assigned to that segment by the linkage models. The overall accuracy was 72 percent, ranging from 57 percent to 98 percent for individual segments.

High accuracy rates give marketers confidence in relying upon Addressable Attitudes. However, the positive impact of Addressable Attitudes on marketing productivity is *not* necessarily hindered in any way whatsoever by lower accuracy rates. This is a common misunderstanding. The only rates that matter are improvements in response rates, and

Figure 8.2: **Addressable Attitudes Classification Accuracy**

Overall Classification Accuracy: 72%

Predicted Group Membership	Actual Group Membership: Basic Personal Callers	Mobile Managers	Constrained Social Callers	Cost Sensitivity Connectors	Power Personal Callers	Affluent Convenient Callers	Active Business Callers	Safety Minded Seniors	Power Business Callers	Road Warriors
Basic Personal Callers	76%	6	13	8	3	9	0	5	0	2
Mobile Managers	0	64%	1	1	0	1	0	0	0	1
Constrained Social Callers	7	1	73%	2	4	0	1	4	0	0
Cost Sensitivity Connectors	9	11	6	73%	4	1	1	8	0	6
Power Personal Callers	2	27	0	0	64%	0	24	0	0	22
Affluent Convenient Callers	5	0	5	0	3	87%	0	4	0	2
Active Business Callers	0	10	0	0	11	0	68%	0	0	10
Safety Minded Seniors	1	4	2	14	1	2	1	78%	2	0
Power Business Callers	0	0	0	0	0	0	2	0	98%	1
Road Warriors	0	5	0	0	9	0	4	0	0	57%

Source: The Segmentation Company
*Scoring a 20 million record customer file for segment membership using database variables

these improvements are often realized even with low assignment accuracy rates.

The objective is to improve the odds that the right message will get through to the right person. Low accuracy may mean that the odds of doing so are lower, but even these lower odds can still be an incremental and noticeable improvement over current systems. Accuracy rates as low as 20 percent have yielded 60 percent improvements in marketing productivity. This is not an anomaly. It reflects the huge jump in response that occurs when people get the message or offer that is precisely right for them. When just a few more people get precisely the right marketing, the overall impact on the bottom line can be substantial. Or to put it another way, even small improvements in the information available to marketers can lead to considerable improvements in marketing productivity.

As a statistical aside, it is worth noting that assignment statistics about accuracy rates are misleading anyway. Incorrect assignments are not random. A person may be linked to the wrong attitude, but it is almost always an attitude that is close to the correct one. So, when a person receives a mis-addressed marketing message or offer, it is often the case that it will not seem so alien that it will completely fail to resonate.

The best systems for Addressable Attitudes are self-correcting over repeated projects and applications so that low accuracy rates can be improved quickly. Contacts and interactions with customers can be set up to ask a few key attitudinal questions, like a couple of questions on a Web site or at the end of service call or on a direct mail response card. These questions can then be used to assess whether a person has been correctly assigned and, if not, to diagnose how to correctly reassign this person.

Two approaches can be taken in developing Addressable Attitudes. [5] One is to develop an attitudinal segmentation that identifies distinct groups of people with similar and tightly bunched clusters of attitudes. Knowing the segment to which a person belongs establishes that person's attitudes. Linkage models are used to score every person in a list or a database with a code designating segment membership.

The other approach is to look at particular attitudes instead of clusters of attitudes that define segments. Each specific attitude, like risk-taking or simplicity, is constructed as a multiquestion scale so that all nuances and dimensions are included. Linkage models are used to score every person in a list or a database with a code indicating whether or not a particular person has a scale value on that attitude that is high enough to code that person as holding that attitude.

MINDBASE

MindBase provided the Addressable Attitudes that enabled the Fortune 500 publishing company mentioned earlier in this chapter to substantially improve its conversion of trial subscribers into full-price subscribers. MindBase pioneered Addressable Attitudes. A closer look at how MindBase works shows the range of marketing solutions provided by Addressable Attitudes.

MindBase was developed from the Yankelovich MONITOR as the culmination of a decade-long developmental project. The R&D for MindBase analyzed several years of MONITOR data to create attitudinal clusters or segments that are stable over time because they are derived on the basis of the core values and lifestyles that provide the foundation upon which the attitudes that affect purchasing are formed.

MindBase was updated and refreshed in another major R&D project during 2004. The original framework was reconfirmed and revalidated with refinements of specific segment structures and an expansion of the range of measured attitudes in order to be more predictive and more category-specific.

Every person in the U.S. population fits into one of the distinct MindBase segments. Each segment consists of a group of like-minded people who share a number of core values and who approach the marketplace with similar purposes and preferences. People in one segment tend to view the world in ways that are similar, yet very different from people in other segments. Knowing the MindBase segment to which a person belongs greatly improves the ability of marketers to build strong relationships through more relevant communications and better customized products and services. As an illustration, Figure 8.3 shows one set of MindBase segments.

Although MindBase consists of an attitudinally based values segmentation, it is not intended to be used only, or even mostly, as a segmentation tool. It is a statistical device that provides the means of achieving the end of linking attitudes to names and addresses.

It can also be used as an enhancement to an existing proprietary segmentation. Many clients have used it for this purpose and have discovered that within a proprietary segment there are further ways to boost marketing productivity based upon the unique insights provided.

MindBase can also be used as a tool for bringing different internal databases together. For example, a media company with different properties will have multiple databases, such as a subscriber database for its magazines and a registration database for its Web site. By scoring each of these databases with MindBase, the media company can sidestep the logistical and budgetary nightmares of merging them. To understand the

Figure 8.3: **Up & Comer Sub-segments**

New Visionaries

Idealistic and focused, innovative and daring, New Visionaries carry an aura of confidence, even entitlement. They want to bring out the best.

Median age	Median income	Married	Parents	Don't have credit card	Online
23	$50.8K	10%	10%	42%	59%

Nouveau Nesters

Carpe diem! Nouveau Nesters eat, breathe, and spend for today. They want to grab what they see missing from their lives and let the future take care of itself.

Median age	Median income	Married	Parents	Don't have credit card	Online
26	$44.7K	53%	4%	31%	59%

Go Getters

Older, settled, and somewhat more spiritual, Go Getters are not chasing after the latest fads and crazes. But they aren't stodgy either. Go Getters want to be in control and be financially involved, but still have fun.

Median age	Median income	Married	Parents	Don't have credit card	Online
36	$50.9K	19%	23%	33%	58%

Wired Ones

Wired Ones have trouble comprehending how life was possible without tech products. Outspoken and savvy, they thrive in a subculture of independence and iconoclasm. Less likely to be planners and are not worried about debt.

Median age	Median income	Married	Parents	Don't have credit card	Online
22	$56.8K	0%	8%	42%	67%

Source: Yankelovich MindBase

Internet behaviors of magazine subscribers, the media company can simply look at the Internet behaviors of all of the MindBase segments represented among magazine subscribers. Since MindBase can be common to both internal databases, it can provide a unifying view of all aspects of the media company's business.

Information about individual attitudes does not require attitudinal information from individuals, so privacy is not breached. All that's required is knowledge of the MindBase segment to which a person belongs. No private or confidential information is needed.

Because it is rooted in MONITOR, MindBase provides lifestyle insights as well as profiles that can flag attitudes that are in sync with the cutting edge trends forecast by MONITOR. MindBase facilitates the integration of high-think consulting insights into a tactical marketing execution system.

For example, a clothing company that sells cutting-edge, one-of-a-kind fashions for young adults will advertise in print media, sustain an active online presence, and maintain a database of past customers (compiled from previous catalog purchases or retail credit card purchases). This business category is facing increased competition from a growing number of companies offering similar kinds of high-end specialty items. Many clothing manufacturers want to strengthen their positions by developing highly targeted lines of unusual fashions with strong appeal to narrow target groups. The best way to accomplish this is to offer products that reflect a particular group's sensibility about what makes something unique.

MindBase could score a clothing company's database of past customers with Addressable Attitudes. Then it would profile past customers to identify the different ways in which people think about uniqueness. An example profile (Fig. 8.4) shows the kinds of distinctive attitudinal patterns that can be uncovered. Knowing which customers think of uniqueness in which ways, a clothing manufacturer could then appeal to

Figure 8.4: **Perception of Uniqueness**

48% of people under 35 years of age like to buy products that few people have and that are not easy to get (compared to 35% of people 35-49)

Up & Comers (39% of those under 35)	**Aspiring Achievers** (22% of those under 35)	**Realists** (16% of those under 35)
Definition: A **stylish** find "You'll look great."	Definition: A **trendy** find "Just off the runway!"	Definition: The look for **less** "Why spend more?"
They are: "Smart shoppers" so showcase quality at a smart price.	They like: "Entertaining shopping" so put the hottest front & center.	They shop for: "Leisure and bargain" so flag the discounts.
Best Media: Balanced across online, print and TV.	Best Media: Edgy media to grab short attention spans.	Best Media: TV and magazines. No Internet.
TV from ESPN to MTV to NBC. Magazines from Glamour to Men's Health to People.	TV from Comedy Central to the WB to BET to MTV. Magazines from Sports Illustrated to Teen People to PC World to Allure.	TV is a must, from BET to Lifetime to the Cartoon Network, Fox Family. Magazines from InStyle to Ebony to Cosmo to Parents.
Message Style: A unified, upscale message everywhere.	Message Style: Quick cuts, Pump up the music.	Message Style: Honest, practical and helpful.

Source: Yankelovich MindBase

each individual customer with more personalized offerings and communications through special catalogs, targeted media buying or geographically differentiated retail store designs.

An attitudinal analysis like this is noteworthy for two things. First, the attitudinal analysis is not simply an examination of questions about uniqueness. It comes from a complete study of all data on relevant attitudes and values.

Second, these insights are not simply reported; they are deployed on a name and address basis. Each concept of uniqueness can be linked to a specific person in a list or a database. With Addressable Attitudes, a company is able to do more than integrate data, it can integrate insights right down to tactical execution by name and address.

THE IMPACT OF ADDRESSABLE ATTITUDES

As described earlier, the publishing company decided to test Addressable Attitudes as a marketing productivity solution for boosting the conversion rates of trial subscribers to full-price subscribers. Specifically, the company elected to use MindBase. Trial subscribers were profiled and analyzed attitudinally. Attitudinal segments not characterized by strong conversion in the past could be omitted from future marketing. And the attitudinal segments targeted by future marketing could receive offers and communications that better reflect their attitudes.

The scoring of MindBase on the publishing company's database was accomplished through the use of a third-party list company that had employed a series of linkage models to assign every person in the U.S. to one of the MindBase attitudinal segments. The publishing company sent the names and addresses of each subscriber to the third-party list company, which then located these people in its list and matched each name and address to the corresponding MindBase segment. A file with the names, addresses and MindBase scores was returned to the publishing company.

In addition to coding trial subscribers with MindBase, the publishing company also coded trial subscribers who had converted to full-price subscribers in the past. With Addressable Attitudes in hand for these two groups of subscribers, the publishing company was able to define its target groups with greater precision.

The MindBase profile of trial subscribers who had converted to full-price subscribers in the past revealed that this group consisted of only a small number of attitudinal segments. In other words, certain specific attitudes characterized trial subscribers who were likely to convert. Trial subscribers in other attitudinal segments were not good prospects and thus poor marketing targets.

Additionally, the MindBase profiles provided detailed insights into the lifestyle interests of trial subscribers likely to become full-price subscribers. These people had above average interests in travel, spirituality, fun, environmentalism and socializing, and below average interests in trendiness, adventure, romance, materialism, luxury, novelty, sports and nature.

With this information in hand, the publishing company executed a test program to assess the productivity impact of Addressable Attitudes. Trial subscribers who matched the attitudinal profiles of past converters received communications and offers customized to their interests. Trial subscribers who did not match the profiles of past converters received no marketing at all. A control group received the standard marketing with no differentiation of targets or messages.

Compared to the control group of trial subscribers who were targeted as before, the greater precision of the MindBase approach yielded a 25 percent incremental boost in renewal rates. This improvement in response was high enough to generate a positive ROI for the first time ever, even when marketing to fewer people.

Prior to merging MindBase into its subscriber database, the publishing company had been unable to push its conversion rates any higher. It had reached the limits of what its existing data and information could do. The new precision provided by the Addressable Attitudes of MindBase was the answer.

This is a microcosm of marketing as a whole. The limits of existing systems and information have been reached. The next breakthrough requires a new way of thinking about marketing and the tools to carry it out. Addressable Attitudes are the way to take marketing precision to the next level.

SUMMING UP

- Addressable Attitudes make marketing more precise by enabling marketers to target people with specific attitudes. The productivity gains are substantial.
- Addressable Attitudes can be created on the basis of individual attitudes or on the basis of a cluster of attitudes in a market segment. Geodemographic or lifestage segmentations are merely different ways of doing demographic targeting. If attitudes are not a part of the segmentation, then Addressable Attitudes cannot be created, notwithstanding the fact that attitudes might be used to profile these non-attitudinal segments.
- A system for Addressable Attitudes has three broad components:
  - —A source of robust attitudinal data that is pertinent, current and constantly refreshed.
  - —The historical perspective and consulting acumen needed to generate relevant insights.
  - —Statistical models to overlay attitudes onto lists and databases.
- Assignment accuracy is important but is not the most important consideration for improving marketing productivity. Oftentimes, low rates of assignment accuracy can yield substantial gains in marketing productivity.
- The best systems for Addressable Attitudes are self-correcting over time. Improvements can be quickly realized through interaction with consumers over repeated projects or communications.
- Yankelovich has developed an extensive suite of products and services to provide Addressable Attitudes, all of which link attitudes to individual names and addresses in lists and databases.

NOTES

1 Proprietary systems for Addressable Attitudes are developed by a company called The Segmentation Company, which is a specialized unit within the overall Yankelovich family of independent businesses that provides high-end analytics for Concurrence Marketing solutions.

2 Sampling theory is an old and well-established branch of statistics. Many people have the misconception that it takes extremely large numbers of people to accurately measure the overall opinions of very large groups. This is simply not true. Larger samples are needed when the variability of opinions is large but the size of the group itself is not a factor in determining the size of the sample needed to get an accurate estimate of the overall opinions of that group. (Of course, strictly speaking, the size of the group is part of the formula to figure out the best sample size, but the impact of that element of the sample size formula is so infinitesimally small that it is almost always left out of the calculation.)

3 The Census is mentioned in Article 1, Section 2 and in the 14th Amendment.

4 Lists With Attitude is a Yankelovich direct marketing list product selling 29 types of Addressable Attitudes through a partnership with KnowlegeBase Marketing.

5 Yankelovich provides Addressable Attitudes for individual attitudes through Lists With Attitude as well as through an integration of the MONITOR attitudinal database with the KnowledgeBase Marketing AmeriLINK list. This database links all data to individual names and addresses, which facilitates rich consumer profiles and highly predictive consumer models. The MONITOR database of attitudinal data has been enhanced with AmeriLINK consumer data, which provides a unique source of data on the attitudes, behaviors, demographics and lifestyles of individuals. Yankelovich provides Addressable Attitudes on the basis of attitudinal segmentations on a custom proprietary basis through The Segmentation Company as well as on a syndicated basis through a series of category-specific MONITOR panels and through MindBase. The panels provide a source of attitudes for individual categories, such as retail, financial services, health care and pharmaceuticals. Category-specific segmentations can be overlaid onto client lists and databases. MindBase is a source of attitudes based on MONITOR that makes MONITOR insights available for tactical marketing execution.

Addressable Attitudes for Marketing Relevance

In the midst of changing lifestyles, marketing must work harder to ensure its relevance. New insights are needed. It is no longer possible to stay relevant just by keeping current with trends. Now, staying relevant means keeping current at an individual level of specificity.

Addressable Attitudes are the key to better marketing relevance just as they are the key to greater marketing precision. Matching attitudes by name and address is no less essential for knowing what to say than it is for knowing whom to target.

PERSONALLY RELEVANT AND PRODUCTIVE

Productivity is usually measured as a characteristic of target selection. But once a good mailing list or a media plan is chosen, a superior message can generate even more lift or response. In fact, marketing productivity gets a second shot in the arm when the message resounds with a more attitudinally-based relevance. Message relevance is an independent and additive source of performance.

Too often, marketers put a lot of time and energy into picking the target only to deliver a message of marginal relevance. Not only does that exacerbate the problem of clutter, it fails to get the maximum possible return on the investment made in picking the target. And even with a poor mailing list or media plan, a highly relevant message can salvage the marketing ROI.

Addressable Attitudes facilitate the delivery of messages with personal relevance—not just the right product, but the right message to position that product, too. Traditional marketing can only deliver messages that have relevance to the entire group. Yet, marketers have long known that the single best predictor of whether someone will buy a product is whether or not he or she agrees that it is a product for someone "like me." When attitudes can be linked to individual names and addresses, personal relevance is assured.

ATTITUDES IN ACTION

A Fortune 500 regional bank client of Yankelovich MindBase was preparing to launch a direct mail campaign to cross-sell a premium checking account service to existing checking account customers. The bank had identified the people to receive the mailing on the basis of its typical criteria of lifestage, profitability and financial portfolio. The prospects for this mailing were people who were of an age to have the need for this premium checking account service and whose value to the bank in the past made them attractive customers for other bank services.

The bank is a sophisticated direct marketer, mailing millions of pieces of direct mail each year and maintaining an extensive database of information about each customer, including detailed profitability calculations showing the relative value of each customer. The bank does extensive analysis of this information, giving it a detailed understanding of what its customers do and what these activities mean to its bottom line. Yet, even with all of this information, the bank was leaving money on the table.

The bank's database did not include any attitudinal information, so the marketing productivity improvements that Addressable Attitudes could bring through better precision and relevance were not being realized. Yankelovich proposed a simple descriptive analysis. that would quantify these missed opportunities.

From a demographic and behavioral standpoint, the target group for the direct mail offer looked homogeneous to the bank. Every person in the target group met the selection criteria that the bank had used, so to the bank, every person looked the same.

Yankelovich hypothesized that the demographically and behaviorally homogeneous target group of the bank was, in fact, attitudinally diverse and heterogeneous. To assess this hypothesis, Yankelovich used its Mind-Base system to assign each of the customers in the target group selected by the bank to a MindBase segment. To do this scoring, the bank sent the names and addresses of each of these customers to a third-party list company that had scored its complete database of names with MindBase. The list company matched each of the customers with the corresponding MindBase segment. A file with the names, addresses and MindBase segment codes for each of the customers was then returned to the bank.

The analysis by Yankelovich showed that the customers in the bank's target group were disproportionately likely to be found in 11 MindBase segments. This validated the Yankelovich hypothesis. Looking only at demographics and behaviors, the bank regarded these target customers as the same; hence, the bank was going to treat them in the same way. Yankelovich suggested a different approach.

The bank's plan was to send the same direct mail piece to all target customers. The piece was developed in accordance with the best industry practices. The envelope was personalized. The benefits were clearly stated near the top of the letter and, in this case, bullet-pointed to stand out. The letter was personalized, too, and the opening sentence involved the reader with the word you. The letter was written in ordinary language with short sentences and active, power words. It listed six financial benefits and promised some additional "extra advantages." It also asked for the sale and provided clear, simple and easy-to-use contact information.

But the personal connection in the opening sentence was weak: "Because you've been such a loyal customer, you are a prime candidate for membership in [the name of the new checking account service]—our exclusive fraternity of those who receive extraordinary financial rewards." In effect, this sentence said that because you've done business with the bank in the past you ought to do more business with the bank in the future. That has more to do with the bank than with the customer. It's as if doing business with the bank is what's special in a person's life rather than the bank being the means by which someone can get or do something special in life. But this reflected what the bank knew about its customers—their bank relationships, not their personal lifestyles needs and aspirations.

With MindBase, though, the bank had access to Addressable Attitudes that provided a connection to the attitudes of each individual person. The Addressable Attitudes were used to develop 11 different versions of the direct mail letter for the premium checking account service, one for each of the 11 MindBase segments found among the customers in the bank's target group. Each person received a letter that was personalized on the basis of the attitudinal insights from MindBase.

Three elements were varied across the 11 versions of the letter to focus the relevance of the message on each person's individual lifestyle interests and preferences (Fig. 9.1). The opening paragraph was written to have a stronger emotional resonance with people's individual values and attitudes. The six benefits listed were varied to coincide with people's personal interests and priorities. And the suggested response channels varied according to individual technology attitudes—either a Web site and a toll-free telephone number or just a toll-free telephone number.

With MindBase, the bank was able to talk to its target customers about their lives in addition to their finances, thus striking a more resonant chord. MONITOR also identifies emerging lifestyle trends, so for some segments the bank was able to connect with attitudes of growing importance, keeping its message on the cutting edge ahead of its competitors.

To measure the incremental impact of the MindBase letters, the bank executed this direct mail campaign with a control group that received a generic direct mail piece. Most of the target customers received one of the 11 MindBase versions while the control group received a generic direct mail piece. When the final results were analyzed, the MindBase mailings generated a response rate that was 44 percent higher than the generic direct mail piece. In other words, the letters written on the basis of lifestyle resonance persuaded 44 percent more people to open a premium checking account with the bank. Additionally, the amount of money that people put into the new checking account when they opened it was 47 percent more among people receiving a MindBase letter and opening an account compared to people receiving the generic letter and opening an account.

In short, the direct mail pieces with personal attitudinal relevance

Figure 9.1: **MindBase Message Personalization**

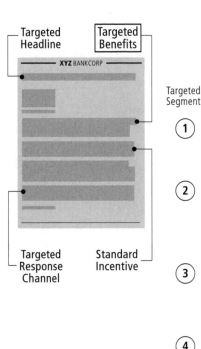

Standard Opening:

"Because you've been such a loyal customer, you are a prime candidate for . . . "

MindBase Targeted Benefits:
(Selected Examples)

(1) "You work hard to provide for the ones you love. So when you're considering professional advice about your household's finances . . . "

(2) "You're at a point where you deserve to kick back and watch the world go by. And you're probably set to do it because you've saved wisely or perhaps purchased some bonds. Well, now it's time to consider . . . "

(3) "When you're out fishing or enjoying nature, does your mind ever drift toward more serious matters? Perhaps financial decisions? Next time, take a quiet moment to consider . . . "

(4) "The next time you're discussing the market, hot stock or other financial matters with your co-workers, you might discuss the subject of . . . "

(5) "As your children grow older, perhaps you'll find more time to poke around the garden or watch the news at night. You'll probably be spending more time thinking about your savings . . . "

(6) "Perhaps you only have an average interest in financial matters. But I have news that could excite you as much as your favorite musical group . . . "

generated a 44 percent increase in the number of new customers and a 47 percent boost in revenue per new customer. These results were achieved with only slight modifications from one version of the letter to the next. The offer to each group was the same; the only changes were in the benefits communicated to each individual customer. The power of messages that are personally relevant is so enormous that even a modest use of these insights for crafting marketing campaigns generates a substantial improvement in response rates.

Another Yankelovich MindBase client is a large national retailer of household products. The retailer maintains a database of customers that, among other things, is used for direct mail announcements of special promotions and store events. The retailer's database contains demographic data on each customer as well as information about past purchases at the retailer.

The retailer was working with a leading manufacturer in a certain category to send a promotional piece in support of that manufacturer's brands to a large group of the retailer's customers. The objective was to promote the manufacturer's brands in order to get customers of the retailer who had never bought that category of products from the retailer to do so by purchasing the manufacturer's brands.

The customers chosen to receive the direct mail piece were selected because they shared the same MindBase attitudinal profiles as other customers of the retailer who had bought products in this category in the past. So, the lifestyle attitudes of individual people were used for target selection.

Additionally, the MindBase Addressable Attitudes were used to create the direct mail piece itself. Seven distinct attitudinal groups were represented among the target customers. Each piece emphasized the particular benefit that would resonate most strongly with each group and each piece showed different lifestyle scenes that would have the strongest connection with each group. No incentives or offers were included in the mailers; only the attitudinally based marketing message.

To assess the incremental impact of crafting direct mail promotional pieces on the basis of MindBase Addressable Attitudes, a generic direct mail piece was sent to a control group of customers who matched the demographics and attitudes of the MindBase group of customers. Once again, substantial gains were realized because of the ability to do some modest, attitudinally based personalization of the direct mail pieces using MindBase Addressable Attitudes.

The overall marketing ROI after 12 weeks was 215 percent. In fact, customers receiving one of the MindBase direct mail pieces were not only more likely to buy in the category of interest, they were more likely to buy in other categories as well. The average increase in total store purchasing was $24 per customer for those customers receiving a Mind-Base mailer.[1]

Relevance makes a huge difference in marketing productivity, and relevance is going to matter more than ever in the future. New technologies are being introduced for both cable TV and the Internet that promise to deliver marketing messages to individual people. The problem with these technologies is that the systems on which they are based lack any attitudinal information about individual people. While these technologies can deliver individually targeted messages, they offer no insights about what to say to people. Addressable Attitudes fill in that gap and make it possible for any system, old and new, to deliver messages of genuine relevance to the people receiving them.

McMINE

McDonald's understands that a new approach to personal relevance is the key to success and marketing productivity. In a keynote luncheon speech at the Third Annual *AdAge* AdWatch Conference on June 16, 2004, Larry Light, Chief Marketing Officer for McDonald's, declared an "end" to brand positioning as it exists today—and not just that, but an end to mass marketing and advertising-centricity as well.

Larry Light has long been a thought leader in the marketing profession. He began his career at BBDO Worldwide before joining Bates Advertising as the chairman and CEO of its international division. Larry helped pioneer the concept and methods of brand equity measurement as the first chairman of a joint, industrywide group known as the Coalition for Brand Equity, and he put these ideas into practice as the founder of Arcature, a well-respected boutique branding consultancy. Light is steeped in traditional marketing. So is McDonald's. Yet, both are walking away from the fundamental concepts that have defined marketing practice for decades.

Light's message to the advertising community in his luncheon keynote was simple: The world has changed but McDonald's has not, so the time has come for McDonald's to catch up. In particular, the dynamism and diversity of today's lifestyles and tastes make a single positioning overly, if not fatally, "simplistic." McDonald's is a big brand, Larry concedes, but not a mass brand. Customers will not accept the "monotony" and "repetition" of a mass brand. Instead, people want a brand that is "creative," "dynamic" and "multifaceted." Meeting the challenges of the new marketplace means practicing marketing in a new way, a way that reflects the ideas of concurrence marketing.

Light introduced the new approach for McDonald's marketing called Brand Journalism, which is a better way for McDonald's to tell its story to people. Instead of a single message bearing down on people everywhere they look, McDonald's is now looking to communicate many messages about the brand, each of which tells just one part of a multi-dimensional story about the brand. From this multi-part story, individual people will be able to find a connection with the brand that has personal relevance.

As a complex brand that means different things to different people, no one positioning will do justice to the McDonald's brand. The task of Brand Journalism is not to drill one positioning into consumers' heads but to "chronicle" all of the different things that are happening with the brand. McDonald's doesn't want to advertise, it wants to report all of the interesting and compelling stories that make up the "tapestry" of the brand. As McDonald's weaves this story together, individuals will be touched by the particular messages that resonate especially well with them.

Each vignette in the chronicle of McDonald's will offer "a different insight" into the brand and what it means to people. Note the word that Light used. He put *insights*, not marketing processes or customer relationships, at the center of the McDonald's marketing organization. That's what the best journalists do: Collect all the facts, distill them down to their essence and then report the story that tells what the facts mean. Journalism is all about insights. So is Brand Journalism.

Only by abandoning the hard selling that goes on in 30-second TV ads for the story-telling that is the style of brand journalism can McDonald's ensure that it offers something personally relevant to everyone in a way that generates engagement, not resistance. McDonald's is not accumulating an audience for a single positioning; it is compiling a variety of messages that will speak in relevant ways to many different localized audiences.

The focus on variety and localized relevance extends to every aspect of how marketing is practiced at McDonald's. Local ideas are championed. Local agencies are all equal partners, each the expert in its part of the world. Specific customer groups are invited to find ways in which the brand can meet their specialized tastes and needs. Relevance is not only how the message is developed, it is how marketing itself is practiced and organized. Everything is done to make McDonald's relevant in all of the varied and multifaceted ways in which the brand is experienced by individual people.

The emphasis on insights also means that McDonald's is looking for new ways to connect with people, many of which will involve new forms of interaction and exchange. McDonald's sees a new marketplace and a need for new forms of relevance. Doing this in an optimal way will send McDonald's in search of new tools to facilitate the delivery of diverse messages to individual audiences.

Already, Light noted, the McDonald's marketing research group is working to pioneer ways of testing marketing communications programs when there is no one brand positioning against which to gauge success. This is perhaps the most telling thing that Light said in his luncheon keynote. Judging creative in terms of its fit with a brand positioning statement is an internal process focus that puts the brand first. The alternative that Light has brought to McDonald's is to make those judgments in terms of a fit with people's lifestyle needs instead. That puts insights at the heart of the business and looks for marketing productivity improvements from better relevance, indeed, from P&R^2 as a whole.

THE NEW HARMONY

Relevance is different than it used to be. What used to ring true with people doesn't resonate anymore. People's attitudes about their lifestyles have changed and so the things they want from the marketplace have changed, too.

While the underlying dynamics of the lifestyle changes occurring today are broad-based, they do not have a uniform effect. In fact, inherent to the nature of these dynamics is an ever-greater diversity and multiplicity of marketplace needs and interests. Not only is relevance different in substance, it is different in style. It is no longer possible to stay relevant just by keeping current with emerging trends. Now, staying relevant means keeping current at an individual level of specificity. Broad-based emerging trends will have many different manifestations and implications. Addressable Attitudes offer the only way to put these emerging trends in proper perspective.

Authenticity is one of these lifestyle trends. People want to surround themselves with things that are real and true, things with character and integrity, things with genuine roots and legitimate values. The desire for authenticity is not so much about honesty, although that's part of it, as it is about integrity of character. Public figures, institutions and brands that make no apologies for what or who they are and that are true to themselves without hype, disingenuousness, double-talk or hard sell are authentic.

The hype and exaggeration of the last 30 years, which grew to a fever pitch during the dot-com frenzy and hysteria of the late 1990s, has given way to a new and growing desire for authenticity. Less hoopla and more aplomb. Less blowing your own horn and more keeping your own counsel. Less pretension and more reserve. Less promise and more results.

Yankelovich MONITOR results show an increasing percentage of people who say they identify more with integrity than success. Not that the two are mutually exclusive ideas, but asking people to say which one they identify with the most reveals which idea has the strongest resonance. Only 58 percent said they identified more with integrity than success in 1999. For the last three years, 73 percent have said so. People want things that are redolent with integrity and authenticity.

The explosion of demographic diversity intensifies the desire for authenticity. People are celebrating their racial and ethnic roots, defending their sexual preferences, and setting up house in all kinds of different ways. Social forces have made difference the norm, and in a world of difference people look more for what rings true to themselves than for what's expected by the group. In the midst of diversity, authenticity becomes even more salient.

Just as people want authenticity in their lifestyles, so, too, do they want authenticity from brands. As people return to what's true of themselves, they want brands that remain true to their essence, no matter how quirky or imperfect. People want brands that can be enjoyed in authentic ways in authentic settings. It's not about brands with roots necessarily; it's about brands that are grounded, brands that are more than skin-deep.

Coke has tapped into this vein with its recent "Real" campaign. These ads are not about self-promotion or beauty shots of the product. Instead, these ads show vignettes of genuine, real moments in people's lives. Coke just happens to be there, too, but not because Coke is blowing its own horn. Coke is there because that's how things work in real life. Coke is a genuine part of the scene. Coke is a part of life so it's always around in authentic moments. Coke isn't bragging that it's the real thing anymore, it's showing people that their lives are the real thing. Coke is authentic because it is always there as a part of the authentic moments in people's lives. Like McDonald's, this is more storytelling than selling.

McDonald's is zeroing in on authenticity, too, as it seeks to chronicle the many ways in which McDonald's shows up in people's lives. In Brand Journalism, what makes McDonald's genuine is its ability to connect with people in ways that really matter to them, rather than demanding that people connect with McDonald's in ways that only matter to McDonald's.

What Coke and McDonald's see is that authenticity is at least as much personal as it is interpersonal. Something feels authentic when it strikes a chord of legitimacy. What's valid and true for one person will seem hokey or faux to someone else. Rappers and soccer moms both drink Coke and eat at McDonald's, but the authentic nature of these experiences is different for each. Indeed, given the nature of the emerging marketplace, authenticity is more personal today than ever before.

As authenticity settles in as a basic part of the structure of the post-accumulation marketplace ahead, the need will grow for marketers to understand the individual nuances and subtleties of an authentic connection with people. In this marketplace, Addressable Attitudes will be essential for establishing genuine relevance.

Connectedness is a similar lifestyle trend. Interest in connections is on the upswing. After four decades of increasing atomization and self-containment, there is a rising interest in relationships and community. People want to live where they can enjoy the comforts of family, friends and neighborhoods. This is not a relinquishment of self-rule but a reawakening to the individual pleasures of the company of others.

Many factors are at work. Aging Baby Boomers want to look outside their four walls now that their kids have left the nest. And thirty-something GenXers are maturing into the lifestage of household formation with a desire to safeguard their families from intrusions and sacrifices.

Two-thirds of GenX women today agree that having a child is an experience every woman should have, compared to only 45 percent of Baby Boomer women at the same age in 1979. Half of Boomer women in 1981 believed that people should live for themselves rather than their children versus 33 percent of GenX women today. Two-thirds of all GenXers vow that they will do a better job of raising their children than the generation before them.

Among young parents, family is more sacrosanct than it has been in a generation. This is not a criticism of Baby Boomers, who had no choice but to make certain family sacrifices as women fought their way back into the workplace and as all Boomers struggled through the four recessions that occurred between the early 1970s and the mid-1990s. It is only to say that times have changed.

Indeed, the push towards individualism and self-fulfillment has taken on a paradoxical character as people have begun to realize that the best and most self-indulgent thing they can do for themselves is to reach out and connect with others. Lisa Berkman, currently the Norman Professor of Health, Social Behavior, and Epidemiology at the Harvard School of Public Health, led an intensive nine-year study of 7,000 adults in Alameda County, California.[2] Her research found that people who were disconnected from others were roughly three times more likely to die during the course of her study than people with strong social ties. The kinds of social ties didn't matter. What mattered was being nested in some network, such as family, friends, church, volunteer groups, and marriage, even after taking into account other risk factors such as smoking, drinking, obesity, or little exercise.

Michael Resnick, a professor in the Department of Pediatrics at the University of Minnesota School of Medicine and Director of the National Teen Pregnancy Prevention Research Center, led an in-depth study of 12,000 adolescents in grades 7 through 12 called the National Longitudinal Study on Adolescent Health. One of the important findings was that a sense of connection at home as well as one at school were the two conditions most protective of a child's well-being.[3] In fact, it was a child's perception of connection that was key, not any specific program or situation. Kids are best protected when they feel caught up in a web of community connections.

Everywhere you look, people are coming together in new and interesting ways. Book clubs are booming to such an extent that publishers now offer many titles in book club editions. Talk radio yammers away up and down the dial. The Internet ties people together at light speed with instant messaging, chat rooms, personals and social networking Web sites. People are flocking to the communal settings of micropolitans and revitalized downtowns. Road racers must now step aside to make room for so-called penguin brigades of walkers who come along more for camaraderie and celebration than to set a personal best. Musicians are adding home concerts to their tour schedules as fans turn their living rooms into intimate performance spaces and sell a small number of tickets to one-night shows. Poetry slams are reviving interest in the communal experience of the spoken word. From support groups to coffee bars to volunteering to adult education programs, people are actively pursuing contact and connection.

Yankelovich MONITOR results show a burgeoning, nearly universal craving for connections and relationships. Ninety-one percent say that they are looking to find more time for the important people in their lives. The percentage of people saying that they get a lot of satisfaction from the primary personal relationship in their lives was second to one's home in 1999. Now, it tops the list with 70 percent saying so, up from 53 percent in 1999. Eighty percent of parents say they wish they had more time to talk with their kids, up from 68 percent in 1999. Seventy-three percent of people say they are looking to do things that make them feel closer to others rather than things that make them feel different from others. Nearly everyone wants to leaven his or her individualism with some communalism.

Neighborhoods reflect this growing interest in connectedness, too. The lifestyle innovations in the cutting-edge communities being built today provide a greater density and quality of connections. These so-called lifestyle villages are designed as walk-able neighborhoods that bring people together in environments that combine residential and commercial buildings. These communities have a bit of an urban feel to them, albeit with a suburban gloss and sheen. Even many suburbs built on the outskirts of town to escape urban life are now incorporating many of the lifestyle elements found downtown. Connections are what matter most. So, people are remaking their suburbs to emphasize a new harmony—no less of the material achievements of place and property but far more of the spiritual fulfillment that comes from the company of others.

It's not just neighborhoods, it's home, too. People are refashioning their homes into hives in response to this craving for comfort and connection. *Hiving* is the term coined by Yankelovich to describe how people are returning to home today.[4] Hiving is the embrace of others in a safe setting abuzz with engagement and activity. Since 9/11, media reports about the return to home have described it as the new cocooning. But the renewed interest in home pre-dated 9/11 and cocooning is no longer the appropriate way to describe what people are doing.

Cocooning is the term coined by futurist Faith Popcorn to describe the ways in which people were returning to home during the late 1980s and early 1990s. This was the victimization era—recovered memories, the jobless recovery, the Menendez brothers hung jury, reports of Satanic rituals at daycare centers, OJ Simpson, downsizing at GM and IBM, the crack epidemic, the broken promise of "Read my lips," and more. People felt exposed, at risk, victimized. So, people wanted a retreat, an escape, a refuge—a cocoon, said Faith, or a place where people could withdraw and wrap themselves in a protective shell, and then pamper their battered psyches with soothing indulgences.

The current return to home is about reaching out, not about retreating—about others, not about oneself—about finding comfort through connection, not through isolation. Nowadays, people don't feel victimized so much as they feel challenged. People want to meet today's challenges head-on. To do that, people need the support and help of others. So, a different metaphor is needed—not a cocoon of isolation but a beehive of activity and engagement. In a special MONITOR OmniPlus survey conducted for the 2003 PCBC Trade Show and Conference of the California Building Industry Association, Yankelovich found that when asked directly, 64 percent preferred that their homes feel like a beehive full of activity connecting them with others.

The pockets of strength in the otherwise sluggish economy in the two years after 9/11 were products, big and small, that facilitated home-centered connections with others, many of which were new products that skyrocketed to success notwithstanding the troubled economy: DVD players. HGTV. *Better Homes & Gardens.* The Food Network. Home renovations. *Trading Spaces.* The family plans of T-Mobile and Cingular. Microwavable pot roasts. Lifestyle villages. Driving family vacations. Even ping-pong tables and board games.

A story in the *New York Times* in early 2003 reported that the generation of thirty-somethings raised on video games and the Internet is now embracing board games as a way to reconnect.[5] Games like Monopoly, Risk and Scrabble along with new games like Settlers of Catan. Board games create the opportunity and the means by which people can get together face to face in a home-based setting. This is what hiving is about—engaging and reconnecting with others through home-based activities.

The challenge of connectedness and community, though, is that people want to preserve their individuality even as they re-engage with others. People do not want to replace the extremes of individualism with the extremes of collectivism, yet they now see that they are most at peace with themselves when they are most connected with others. This is why the newfound desire for connection will last. Because people have come to realize that their own selfish satisfactions are tied directly to their own acts of selflessness and sacrifice.

All of the new forms of community that are thriving allow people to preserve their individuality even as they participate in a communal experience. People can have individual style, self-expression and personal opinions, all within the supportive context of a group experience. People see community as a part of, not apart from, their own individuality. People are not looking to lose themselves in a faceless crowd; rather, they want to complete themselves through a union with others.

In a recent interview, Larry Light of McDonald's echoed what Yankelovich sees in the marketplace.[6] Light referred to it as "the age of I," in contrast to the age of me that gave rise to the me generation and the me decade. Light noted that the people who only cared about "me" have gotten lonely and, lately, have come looking for the company of others.

The integration of self with others is crucial. Marketers cannot customize and personalize to the point that people feel no connection with others through the brand. People will abandon brands that intensify the isolation they are fleeing. Indeed, this is the flaw in one-to-one marketing.

People want customization, but not to the point of losing connection with others. There was a time not too long ago when customization and personalization to the point of isolation was in better keeping with what people wanted. But in the marketplace of today and tomorrow, brands must provide people with an experience of one-with-many not one-to-one. Personalization is not the same thing as personal. What people want is something with personal relevance, and that means a connection with others as much as something for themselves alone.

Brands are social anyway. Brands represent ideas that people can share in common. Brands are powerful only to the extent that they bring people together, at the very least to buy the same thing. What's personal about brands is the individual meaning and resonance that the shared meaning of a brand has in someone's lifestyle. Brands can't dictate meaning, though. Brands must provide unity while respecting and facilitating individuality. Relevance does not come from one or the other. It only comes from both at once.

This balance is what McDonald's is trying to provide. McDonald's provides a common theme for people, but enables people to make that common theme relevant in a personal way. This adroitly masters the challenge of offering both individuality and connectedness. Light said that the reason McDonald's continues to advertise on TV in the age of nano-diversity is to provide that common, unifying link. At the same time, McDonald's is experimenting with numerous alternative marketing activities that appeal to individuals and that enable people to make their own statement about McDonald's. As an example, Light mentioned that McDonald's is opening McKids stores to sell McDonald's toys, clothes and videos. Fashion is a statement of personal style that bubbles up from the street more often than it trickles down from the runways these days. So, even as McDonald's is sustaining its overarching image, it is developing ways that allow customers to personalize what that image means to them.

Like authenticity, the new sense of connectedness is as much personal as it is interpersonal. The paradox of community these days is that its relevance and meaning are more individual than social, so resonating with the connectedness that people want will confound mass appeals. Even self-invention is ultimately rooted in community, for the things that make each person capable of setting his or her own course are the networks, tools and infrastructure provided by others.

People can only be united one by one, on a name and address basis.

Individual attitudes, not social norms, are defining the bonds of community. For marketers to join the circle, relevance will have to be defined individually. The one tool that can enable marketers to do this is that of Addressable Attitudes.

Indeed, every development in the marketplace ahead points to the need for Addressable Attitudes. In the midst of changing lifestyles, marketing must work harder to ensure its relevance. New insights are needed to understand what's happening because the shared expectations and ambitions of the past have given way to a world in which even communal interests are individually defined. In this marketplace, Addressable Attitudes are the only way to speak to people with genuine relevance.

SUMMING UP

- Marketing productivity can be dramatically increased by improving marketing relevance as well. Addressable Attitudes facilitate the delivery of messages with personal relevance at the level of individual names and addresses.
- People's lifestyles are changing rapidly, and so, too, are the things they want from the marketplace. Inherent in these changes is an ever-greater diversity and multiplicity of marketplace needs and interests.
- Authenticity is a key lifestyle trend. The desire for authenticity is about integrity of character.
- Connectedness is another key lifestyle trend. An important manifestation of that is hiving, which is home-centered reconnection with family, friends and community.
- The desire for community and connection does not mean that people are giving up individuality and difference. People want both. In particular, people do not want marketing customization to the point of isolation. People want brands that provide unity while respecting and supporting individual self-expression.

NOTES

1 The details of this program were outlined in greater detail at the 9th Annual Fred Newell Customer Relationship Management Conference, June 5, 2003, in a case study presented by Craig Wood, president of Yankelovich MONITOR.

2 Lisa Berkman and Lester Breslow, *Health and Ways of Living: The Alameda County Study*, (New York: Oxford University Press, 1983).

3 Michael D. Resnick, P. S. Bearman, R. W. Blum, K. E. Bauman, K. M. Harris, J. Jones, J. Tabor, T. Beuhring, R. E. Sieving, M. Shew, M. Ireland, L. H. Bearinger and J. R. Udry, "Protecting Adolescents From Harm. Findings from the National Longitudinal Study on Adolescent Health," *Journal of the American Medical Association*, September 10, 1997.

4 See the entry in Word Spy at http://www.wordspy.com/words/hiving.asp.

5 Seth Schiesel, "The PC Generation, Back to the Board," *New York Times*, April 10, 2003.

6 Michael Arndt, "Marketing In The Age of 'I'," Interview with Larry Light, *Business Week Online Extra*, July 12, 2004.

Insights Integration for Consumer Power

Marketing is the last frontier for consumer power. Since marketers have been slow to give consumers power over marketing, other services have been invented to give people the power to avoid marketing altogether. Consumer power means creating a process by which consumers can be involved and can have a say. This kind of marketing will generate engagement, not resistance, and thus will be more productive.

The Toyota Scion hit the market in June 2003 with a bold declaration to buyers: "We relinquish all power to you."

The Scion is targeting Echo Boomers, and for the generation that came of age with the refrain, "All your base are belong to us," the Scion's pronouncement sounds familiar. It's almost in the same meter. In effect, Scion is saying, "All our cars belong to you." Echo Boomers will have it no other way.

WHO'S IN CHARGE HERE?

The power that Scion buyers are being given is the power to invent for themselves the cars they want to drive. The Scion Web site encourages buyers to "[s]tart building your personalized Scion." Standard equipment for the Scion includes a six-speaker audio system, air conditioning, power windows, door locks and mirrors, and sport seats. Everything else is up to the buyer. A bit more flair? More performance? A certain style? Buyers have the power to decide.

Dealerships have been refurbished to make support tools available on site to help buyers explore Scion options, including an information wall displaying optional engineering and interior accessories, a color and trim stand and self-service Internet kiosks. Toyota calls this the discovery zone, which can be augmented by help from certified salespeople in a separate consultation zone. The overall objective, Toyota noted in a November 6, 2002 press release, is to create "highly interactive surroundings [that] will deliver a customer-controlled atmosphere." Customers, not salespeople, are in charge.

Buyers are responding. As this book was going to press, 14,793 cars were sold in July 2004, the fifth consecutive best-ever sales month for the Scion. 2004 sales are projected to be in excess of 75,000 cars, and 2005 sales, above 100,000 cars. Sales of personalized accessories have averaged $1,000 per car, about three times what Toyota expected.

Besides giving buyers the power to invent their own cars, the Scion resonates with the motive of self-invention in two other ways. First, the Scion is outfitted with a Pioneer sound system. Control over music, especially the elements of mobility and access, is a key cultural element for younger people. Designing the Scion to be an "Apple iPod on wheels"[1] taps directly into a generational interest that is all about participatory power and control.

Second, the Scion was introduced in California, its first market, without the customary deluge of marketing and promotion. Jim Farley, vice president of the Scion division, has noted that the two most common ways in which people in California discovered the Scion were seeing it on the street and finding it on the Internet.[2] Marketing for the Scion was in keeping with the ways that people are looking to regain control over their experiences in the consumer marketplace.

And this is not just about Echo Boomers. In a February 3, 2004, Toyota press release, Farley said, "For Toyota, Scion is a laboratory for change." Toyota is closely watching what happens with Scion as a way to "ensure continuous improvement of the entire brand experience." In other words, Scion's success might soon have all of Toyota relinquishing power to its customers.

Bank One thinks this is a good idea, too. "Create your own card" is Bank One's proposition. On its Web site, dozens upon dozens of different credit cards are available—cards that differ by organization supported, rewards earned and interest rate charged (sorted by low introductory rate or low everyday rate). People can even choose among a wide array of cards with special artistic designs. Bank One is offering people the chance to fashion a credit card that signals to others the causes or institutions they care about and that gives something back that is valuable to them. Bank One is empowering its customers to invent for themselves the credit card they want to carry.

Motorcycle manufacturer Ducati invites customers to provide online feedback about prototype designs. MTV recently ran a promotion called MPEG Us in which people could come to the MTV Web site and use the music available there to make their own music videos for possible airing on MTV. The tagline at Reflect.com is "True Custom Beauty. Active Ingredient: You." Women customize their own cosmetics to fit their personal color, skin and hair. And Reflect.com uses a so-called Heart & Souls Process to collect personal information from each woman in order to create a customized Signature Fragrance for her.

People can personalize Nike footwear, backpacks and watches at NIKEiD.com. At Dell.com, people can configure a computer that is customized for their needs. The Honda Element, designed for younger buyers, and the Nissan Quest, designed for young mothers, have modular interiors that can be easily reconfigured at the touch of a latch to accommodate personal needs and preferences.

People want power. Good marketers are selling it to them. Brilliant, insightful marketers are just flat out surrendering it to them, thereby gaining control over future success by ceding control to customers.

In some circles, this trend has been referred to as an open-source business culture. Proponents argue for a business approach in which consumers are an active part of the process, helping to invent the products they buy rather than just choosing from among the products made available to them. Well-known open-source initiatives like Linux and Wikipedia are cited as archetypal successes. Even so, many businesses worry about the loss of control over trade secrets and production processes. But customers are assuming control anyway, so sooner or later, companies are going to have to face up to this transfer of power.

Better to step up now and embrace customers as teammates than to oppose them and be forced to make an expensive peace with them later.

TEAMMATES

Many companies are empowering customers to take control, even if it means showing competitive brands. In October 2001, General Motors (GM) launched AutoChoiceAdvisor, an online advisory service that collects information about tastes and preferences from a person and then instantly provides a rank-order list of recommended cars that would meet his or her needs. Oftentimes, none of the recommended cars are made by GM. AutoChoiceAdvisor empowers people to assess alternatives and learn about new options free from the dreaded hard-sell pressure of car buying that they do not trust or appreciate.

GM has created a system that will build goodwill for itself over time, but it has immediate value as well. When a GM car fits a person's profile of tastes and preferences, it is able to introduce that person to one of its cars, which may well be an option that many people would not have considered on their own. When no GM cars fit a person's profile, a link is displayed that offers to show people GM cars that come closest to their tastes and preferences. No one is required to click on this link, but it is another chance for GM to introduce people to its cars.

Most importantly, GM is able to collect consumer data that gives it a competitive edge in the marketplace. The information provided by the tens of thousands who visit AutoChoiceAdvisor each month gives GM an early warning system for the waxing and waning of consumer tastes. When GM sees shifts of interest in certain types of cars or in various aspects of performance and styling, GM can modify its car designs before competitors. Plus, GM gets indirect feedback on its brand image based on the choices people make between GM and competitors when its cars match competitors on all key features.

Progressive Casualty Insurance Company offers a similar service for its insurance products for automobiles and other vehicles. People fill out a profile online that includes basic information about demographics and driving record. Based on that information, Progressive provides insurance rates for its own products as well as those of competitors. In many cases, Progressive is not the least expensive insurance product.

Progressive gets value from its service in several ways. It is building goodwill from its independent comparison service, just as GM is building goodwill from AutoChoiceAdvisor. This service increases visitation to the Progressive Web site, which raises the likelihood that people will click on other links to learn more about Progressive's line of products and services. And it is better able to manage its business by ensuring that it is matching people to the right rate.

Advisory services such as these have been studied by Glen Urban, the former Dean and a professor of marketing at the MIT Sloan School of Management, Fareena Sultan, an associate professor of marketing at Northeastern University, and William Qualls, a professor of business administration at the University of Illinois. In the late 1990s , Urban and his colleagues built a prototype online advisory service for pickup truck buying called Truck Town.[3] The independent information of Truck Town was highly trusted and was much more likely to stimulate buying interest than a traditional dealership setting. From this initial work, Urban has now developed a more detailed framework for trust-based marketing.[4]

Based upon the growing power of consumers, Urban notes that the traditional strategies no longer work. Marketing saturation, or pushing harder as Urban characterizes it, worsens consumer distrust and is increasingly ineffective. Customer relationship management usually devolves into nothing but marketing saturation on a name and address basis. The alternative identified by Urban is a strategy of customer advocacy in which marketers put their customers' interests first. The key to this strategy is building trust so that customers believe that marketers are on their side. And the best way to do this is to relinquish the control that has traditionally been monopolized by marketers.

eBay is perhaps the best example of what can happen when a business makes consumer power the backbone of its entire value proposition. The apocryphal story of eBay's beginnings is well known. Peter Omidyar, a French-Iranian American who immigrated to the United States from Paris in 1967 at age 6 and graduated from Tufts with a degree in computer science, had already made his first million starting and selling one technology firm when his fiancée Pam groused to him one night in 1995 that since moving with him to San Jose from Boston, she was having trouble finding fellow collectors of Pez dispensers. Omidyar, who was working at the time in developer relations for the mobile communications start-up General Magic Corporation, spent Labor Day weekend developing an auction Web site that Pam could use to buy and sell her Pez dispensers. He called it AuctionWeb and announced it to other early Internet users on a couple of online bulletin boards.

For a time, Omidyar ran AuctionWeb as a hobby and offered it to users for free. But its popularity caught fire. In February 1996, Omidyar had to start charging a percentage of the final sale price as a fee in order to cover the costs of maintaining the Web site.[5] From the first month fees were charged, AuctionWeb turned a profit. As the popularity of AuctionWeb grew during 1996, the fees generated enough money for Omidyar to quit his day job, incorporate his company and hire his first employees.

In September 1997, the company changed its name to eBay.[6] Its growth continued to skyrocket. The number of eBay users and auctions quickly jumped from the hundreds of thousands to the millions. In March 1998, Harvard Business School-educated Meg Whitman joined eBay as CEO. She came from Hasbro, where she was the general manager of Hasbro's Preschool Division. Prior to that she was president and CEO of Florists Transworld Delivery and president of Stride Rite.

In September 1998, eBay went public and, in keeping with the tenor of the times, its stock price had nearly tripled by the close of the first day of trading. eBay's market capitalization during the height of the dot-com boom enabled it to further solidify and strengthen its position in the marketplace. In 1998, it cut a deal with AOL to be its official auction site and to get prominent placement on the AOL Web site. The next year, eBay bought Butterfield & Butterfield, one of the largest and best known auction houses in the world, as well as Alando.de, Germany's largest online auction house, and Kruse International, one of the largest auctioneers of collectible cars.

By the turn of the millennium, eBay had established itself as a transformative business. Its success was virtually unparalleled. eBay leaped into the top tier of American business by breaking all of the old rules about power, control and dominion.

From the beginning, Omidyar's central concept was to let users manage themselves and their online relationships. Sometimes disputes arose between buyers and sellers that forced Omidyar to step in and mediate. But even as mediator, Omidyar encouraged people to work things out on their own. He constantly reminded disputants that other people are basically good and that most disagreements probably arise through misunderstandings. As a way of enabling users to police eBay on their own, Omidyar created the Feedback Forum in February 1996. This was the start of eBay's famous rating system by which buyers and sellers can give each other marks that are made available to other eBay users. A person who is consistently unreliable or untrustworthy is quickly identified to the eBay community at large.

This kind of customer-controlled evaluation system creates added value in the transactions. People will pay more to buy from sellers they trust because of high ratings. In a controlled experiment on eBay, a team of researchers found that buyers were willing to pay 8.1 percent more to buy from sellers who had high ratings than from unknown, unrated sellers.[7]

In a December 2001 interview with *Business Week Online,* Omidyar elaborated at some length on his philosophy of empowering customers to be in control.[8] He was explicit in this interview: "I wanted to give the power of the market back to individuals. . . . [T]he best ideas came from the community. . . . Our success is really based on our members' success. They're the ones who have created this, and they're the ones who will create it in the future." For eBay, control of its success has come from relinquishing control to its customers.

On eBay, customers provide the ratings. Customers find community and build relationships. Customers negotiate all the prices. Customers control their own inventory and shipping. Customers spread the word to other customers. Customers buy and sell directly from one another.

There's nothing new about the story of eBay's success with its peer-to-peer or customer-to-customer business model. The story has been told many times. So why repeat it here? Because the lesson has yet to take.

The most interesting observation that Omidyar made during his *Business Week Online* interview was in answer to a question about how eBay schools new managers in the revolutionary principles of customer control. Omidyar noted that in a traditional retail environment, companies have the ability to maintain control over inventory, merchandising, training, and the like. But not on eBay. eBay can only "influence" the customer experience; it can't control it. So, when eBay hires managers with traditional backgrounds and training, "[I]t sometimes take months of deprogramming for our new marketing people to get rid of that instinct [for control]."

AVOIDANCE OR ATTRACTION?

The Internet has spawned a surfeit of Web sites that enable people to take control of nearly every aspect of what and how they buy. The options seem virtually limitless.

- LendingTree.com enables people to apply for loans and then receive competing offers from different financial institutions.
- People can make fast, direct price comparisons for competing airlines at Expedia.com, Orbitz.com or Travelocity.com. People can do the same for automobiles at Edmunds.com, Autobytel.com or KBB.com (for Kelly Blue Book).
- eRealty.com and ZipRealty.com provide online alternatives to traditional real estate agencies.
- Buying comparison services such as BizRate.com, Shopping .com, Productopia.com, NextTag.com and Froogle.com give people in-depth comparative information about options and alternatives for products of interest.
- Epinions.com, ConsumerReview.com, and ReviewCentre.com are product review sites where people can exalt or disparage the products they have used. Amazon.com's reader and listener reviews do the same. CNET.com offers the same service, plus technical reviews and shopping comparisons, for technology products.
- Social networking sites like Friendster.com and Tribe.com facilitate instantaneous access to the recommendations of others.
- Vault.com gives people the inside scoop on potential employers with company facts as well as employee feedback.
- WebGripeSites.com and TheComplaintStation.com give people a place to air their dissatisfactions for others to read.

These are a mere smattering of examples. The ability of online technologies to put people in greater control of cultural experiences, political activities and personal relationships is no less powerful.

People are better users of technologies than marketers. People use technology to out-smart whatever technologies marketers deploy. Marketers need to become as skilled with technologies as their customers. The best way to do this is to use technologies to give people the power they want. Otherwise, people will always look to technologies as a way of resisting marketers rather than engaging with marketers.

Urban has grouped the empowering effects of information and Internet technologies into five categories. Alan Mitchell, author of *Right Side Up: Building Brands in the Age of the Organized Consumer* (Trafalgar Square: 2001) and co-founder of the Buyer Centric Commerce Forum, has identified five areas of empowerment, too.[9] Mohanbir Sawhney, the McCormick Tribune Professor of Management at Northwestern's Kellogg School of Management, has identified five points in the business process where companies have used the Internet to move to collaborative creation.[10]

But, however these online services are described and categorized, the impact that all of them have is of one sort. In various and sundry ways, these online services enable people to avoid marketing. Marketing avoidance is the common thread.

While many marketers have taken steps to give consumers power over design and access, few marketers have given consumers power and control over marketing. Marketers have not made marketing more transparent, nor have they made it less intrusive. In fact, even as marketers have involved customers in design and distribution, marketers have moved in the opposite direction when it comes to marketing. Instead of relinquishing control over marketing, marketers have developed systems to make marketing even more widespread and invasive. Marketing is the last frontier for consumer power.

Traditional marketers who rely on saturation, intrusiveness and dominion are finding themselves surrounded by a large and growing number of online services and competitors seeking to give people the power to avoid marketing. Marketers may get their messages through, but these new services are diluting the impact of these messages. This is only going to escalate.

A graduate student at the MIT Media Lab has invented a handheld device with a scanner and a memory chip that he calls the Corporate Fallout Detector. It's set up to sound off like a Geiger counter: A person scans the bar code on a product and the worse that company's history of pollution and ethics violations, the more furiously the Fallout Detector clicks. A research sociologist at Microsoft has invented something similar. His device uses a scanner, a handheld computer and a wireless Internet connection. A person scans the bar code on a product, and the device searches the Internet for information about any dangers or hazards.[11]

Imagine a person on a shopping trip once these devices are commercialized. Browsing items on the shelf, he or she would scan the bar codes to learn which products contain ingredients that would trigger his or her allergies or are not on his or her diet. Advertising claims could be second-guessed. People concerned about the environment could set up their devices to scan environmental databases for an instant rating of how a company stacks up. Indeed, this could be done for any issue: third-world labor practices, trade with certain nations, product safety, workplace safety, labor relations, contributions to political parties, support of charitable organizations, presence of women or people of color in top management, truth in advertising, and more. The only requirement would an accessible database of pertinent information. But that's not likely to be a problem.

For people concerned about more than one issue, there could be a multidimensional score of acceptability. And people wouldn't have to sort through complicated reports to make a decision. In all likelihood, their handheld devices would show something like a green light for buy, a red light for don't buy and a yellow light for buy only if nothing more acceptable is available.

Just as marketers use the information in their databases to figure out whom to target, so, too, will people use these devices to make decisions about what brands to consider and what products to buy. Technologies like handheld scanners and online shopping services are shifting the balance of power completely in favor of consumers. These technologies are going to take all of the bite out of marketing because no matter what marketers do or say, people will have the means of getting another perspective, both before and at the point of sale. But this doesn't mean that all is lost. It just means that starting now, marketers need to put consumer power into the ways in which they do business.

A POWER SHIFT

Insights Integration is the organizing strategy for consumer power. The question to ask of every marketing activity and system is whether it serves to empower consumers. The presumption should be that anything taking power away from consumers is allowed only as an exception. The reasons for keeping power from consumers must be clear and overwhelming.

When it comes to consumer power, the One World Cafe in Salt Lake City makes no exceptions. There are no prices on the menu. Customers pay on the honor system. Some of the regulars pay in other ways. One pays the water bill. Another donated a quarter-acre of a vegetable garden. Some wash dishes; others repair the equipment. Most, though, pay. And the restaurant is breaking even. It's an idea that seems to be catching on. The landlord of the building in which the One World Cafe is located lets the restaurant owner set her own rent. The president of the Utah Restaurant Association said that many restaurants have already moved to "menu-free, size-optional" formats.[12]

But the integration of insights must go farther than simply dumping all power into the laps of consumers. The insights must recognize the nuances and degrees of power that are appropriate in particular situations for particular individuals. With Addressable Attitudes in place, these differences in preferences about power can be handled individually. There are many options available to marketers. The objective is to practice marketing in a way that gives power to consumers.

Let people participate in the creation of meaning. Icehouse Beer, brewed by Miller, was introduced in 1993 without a slogan. Its first print ads asked readers to suggest a slogan and in its initial TV ad, that first aired during the 1994 Super Bowl, a character named Paul was shown sitting next to an empty billboard waiting to paint the Icehouse slogan on it. Viewers were given a toll-free number to call with suggestions. Hundreds of thousands of calls came in. Icehouse wound up with so many good slogans that it more or less adopted them all. A visit to the Icehouse Web site today shows many different slogans fading into view, one after the other, each credited to the person who sent it in. Over the years, Icehouse billboards have also rotated through many of the slogans sent in by people.

In 2001, Icehouse ran a contest called, "We'll Make the Icehouse. You Make the Ads." People were asked to send in homemade TV ads for Icehouse. Thousands of entries were received, from which eight were selected and aired during 2002. The nature of the contest itself was the most important message, though, for it communicated that Icehouse wanted to welcome its customers into the creative process for shaping the marketing that they would see. Icehouse invited people to help it present the brand in its advertising, thereby sending the kind of message about empowerment that gives people a sense of ownership for the brand.

In the run-up to the 2003 Super Bowl, Pepsi set up a Web site where people could come and view two alternative endings to the Sierra Mist ad that was scheduled to air during the Super Bowl. They could also register to win prizes at the Web site. Tens of thousands of votes were cast.

Gap ran a similar event in November and December 2002 called the Gap Casting Call. People were encouraged to place themselves in consideration for possible inclusion in a 2003 Gap print ad by submitting a photo and a bio online or at any Gap store. From the 200,000 entries, Gap selected 24 finalists, four in each of six categories (men, women, boys, girls, baby boys and baby girls). The photos and bios of these finalists were then posted online at the Gap Web site. For nine days in late January and early February 2003, people could log on and vote for their favorites. The six winners were selected on the basis of the 500,000 votes that were cast.

Like Icehouse and Sierra Mist, the Gap Casting Call gave people a direct opportunity to participate in the creative process. People were given the power to have an influence on the marketing that they would see. Icehouse, Sierra Mist and Gap offered people the same opportunity to participate in the creation and personalization of marketing that Scion, Bank One, Ducati, NIKEiD.com, and Dell.com offer people for the creation and personalization of the product itself.

In early 2000, Kellogg's Canada selected 21 kids between the ages of 11 and 15 to be part of the Jacks Pack team for Apple Jacks breakfast cereal. The team worked as part of the marketing group, with specific responsibilities for developing and introducing three new package designs, selecting a new color for the cereal, and updating the product's Web site. The team attended a kick-off summit in August 2000 and then, for the next nine months, met online or by phone for about three hours every other week. Jacks Pack members were also featured in TV advertising for the brand and helped develop a new ad as well. As the *Toronto Star* noted at the time, with this effort, Kellogg's was, for the first time, turning "over a cereal brand to its target consumers."[13]

Some critics dismissed the Kellogg's Canada effort as little more than a publicity stunt. Others opined that while it might be a legitimate effort, it was nothing but a dressed-up focus group with kids. These critics missed the point. The real value came from giving power over key marketing decisions to these kids. It was a signal to consumers that Apple Jacks wanted to practice marketing in a way that would share control over its marketing with the people to whom the marketing is directed.

Movie studios have begun to share power, too.[14] After some initial struggles, studios have learned that special-interest Web sites have enormous influence over which movies people go to see, especially fantasy, horror and comic action movies. These sites are run by movie buffs and frequented by millions of interested Internet users. Initially, studios battled these sites over copyright infringement, but they soon came to learn that creating ill will with these Web sites could, and in some cases did, cost them millions in lost ticket sales.

Not only do these special-interest movie Web sites have the power to hurt a movie, they have the power to help it as well. Good reviews and positive word-of-mouth can make a movie a runaway success. In some cases, these Web sites have influenced how movies were made—a character cut from a scene in "Lord of the Rings"; the Hulk filmed with, instead of without, his trademark purple shorts; the visibility of a character reduced in "Star Wars Episode I: The Phantom Menace."

Movie studios now see that active consultation with these fan Web sites is good marketing. Giving people a role in how a movie is developed and produced not only enhances the marketing of a movie, it is, in fact, a form of marketing the movie—not infrequently, the most effective marketing that can be done for a movie nowadays.

Ask for permission over and over and over . . . and over again. Never stop asking for permission. There are two flaws in the way permission marketing is practiced today. First, once permission to send marketing is granted, the character of the marketing that follows tends to be exactly what people were hoping to escape by granting permission. Second, once permission is asked and received, the question is never asked again.

So, having granted permission, people find that, de facto, they are back in the opt-out world they were trying to escape. Permission may seem like a new type of relationship, but when it entails the same marketing as before and when it puts people back in an opt-out position, permission is just more of the same.

People don't want to have power only to lose it the instant they exercise it. Yet, that's what permission marketing does when permission is asked only at the outset. Unless permission is subject to renewal, then permission is not really empowering. The way to give people control over the marketing to which they are exposed is not to ask for permission but to ask for provisional permission that periodically must be affirmatively re-extended.

Provisional permission is better for marketers, too, because it creates the opportunity for a continuing dialogue between marketers and customers. It also enables a brand to stay fresher in people's minds because it is not something that a person can deal with once, then file away and forget.

Allow customers to define the when and where. What's convenient for marketers is a function of processes, not of insights. It is convenient for telemarketers to call people during the dinner hour because that's when they have the greatest likelihood of catching people at random. It is convenient for customer service agents to read a sales script in the middle of a service call because that's when they have people on the line. It is convenient for TV advertisers to interrupt a show to run an ad because that's when they have people's attention. Convenience for marketers has little to do with when people might be in the right frame of mind. For marketers, it's mostly about a certain point in the process.

Similarly, marketers try to herd people with technology systems. A live operator is rarely needed on a service call, but when one is needed, figuring out how to get through the system's menu to reach one can be like working one's way through a maze. It's an uncooperative game of hide-and-seek that has gotten to be such a problem that Bob Chatham, a principal analyst at technology consulting firm Forrester Research, has said that if it doesn't improve soon, "companies may be (legally) forced to disclose to consumers how to reach a human being."[15]

Ultimately, the question is one of how to deploy technology. Business strategy consultant and one-to-one marketing guru Martha Rogers has warned that "[n]ew technology gives companies the ability to treat people the way they *don't* want to be treated faster and more effectively than ever."[16] There are two rules-of-thumb worth remembering. First, don't deploy technology in place of valued relationships. ATM's, airline check-in kiosks and self-service checkout lanes work well because the essence of the experience is functional, not emotional. On the other hand, Webvan failed to catch on because people want to go to the grocery store. Its technology and delivery system worked well.[17] The problem was that even though people complain about grocery shopping, what they want is a better shopping experience, not a technology replacement. Webvan had good research on people's complaints, just poor insights about what it meant.

Second, use the microwave model for deploying technology. Most people do not want technology per se. People want solutions. The first bulky, noisy microwaves involved a series of steps to use them. Hit the power button. Set the level. Hit the timer button. Select the time. Hit start. Check the food at the end and be prepared to run it for a few more seconds to finish the cooking. Today, microwaves are more powerful, more compact, and more convenient to use: All it takes is to hit the popcorn button, so to speak. As the technology has gotten more powerful, the user interface has gotten much simpler. Always move in the direction of simpler interfaces that are benefit oriented, not process oriented.

Make the media more empowering. When marketing appears in a setting over which people have more control, the marketing itself benefits by association. As a corollary to this, the marketing should not be delivered in such a way that the empowering aspects of a medium are negated. This is a particular problem for the Internet. The empowering experience of the Internet is often defeated by Web sites that won't release one's browser or pop-up ads that materialize uninvited or Web pages that require registration so that marketers can collect email addresses.

TV has experimented with steps to make it more empowering. Viewers could vote by cell phone on *American Idol*. Newscasts, true crime shows and historical documentaries display Web addresses for more information.

Mitsubishi has had success with a TV campaign called "See What Happens." In one ad, a Mitsubishi Galant GTS is shown racing against a Honda Accord EX across a partially constructed bridge. Both cars reach

70 mph and then brake at the same point. Only the Mitsubishi stops before the drop-off at the middle, at which point the ad breaks and gives viewers a Web site address to see what happens.

The first ad in this campaign broke during the 2004 Super Bowl. It showed a Mitsubishi Galant GTS and a Toyota Camry XLE dodging bowling balls, barbeques, trashcans and other cars being thrown in their way from vans ahead of them. Against a punk rock soundtrack, the Mitsubishi outperforms the Toyota, and the Web site address to see what happens is shown at the end. In the 6 hours after the ad first aired, the Web site recorded 11 million hits. During the 24-hour period after the ad first aired, the Mitsubishi Web site got more unique visitors than it does in a typical month. Two-thirds of these visitors watched the 50-second ad twice. More people downloaded follow-up information than do so in a typical month.[18]

This campaign is being hailed as a triumph of integrated marketing. But it's more than that. It is the conversion of TV into an empowering medium by combining it with the Internet. A TV ad has more impact when it connects with people in a more empowering way. People have the power and control to do something with the ad.

Ford did something similar with a promotional campaign it ran in 2004 called "What will Phil do next?" The witty ads in the campaign featured golfer Phil Mickelson trying his hand at all kinds of new activities, like playing hockey with Wayne Gretzky, singing with Toby Keith, and talking shop with Dale Jarrett. In one ad, Mickelson is on the phone with Jarrett inviting him to play golf with himself and Gretzky. When Jarrett asks who's the fourth, Mickelson replies that he's working on it, at which point viewers are invited to go to a special Web site to register for the chance to play in that foursome.

All media need to introduce elements of empowerment and control into the experience, which may mean merging and partnering with elements of other media. The mass and micro-media are approaching the limits of their abilities to reach small, specific audiences. The next steps forward are not more channels, more versions, more sections or more formats. The way to move ahead is to make media more empowering so that people can self-select themselves into content and marketing of relevance to them rather than being hunted down by media vehicles desperate for audiences.

One quick solution is for marketers to make their own Web sites an empowering medium. A company's Web site should be a place for community where customers come to connect with other customers and share ideas, stories and even complaints. Let the community figure out how to solve the problems. It should be a place for people to get fast feedback from companies and to hear more about lifestyle solutions, not more product pitches. P&G has created such a place with its Web site, that it calls "[Y]our home for everyday solutions" in personal and beauty care, house and home, health and wellness, baby and family, and pet nutrition and care. P&G uses its Web site as a source of information and tips to give people more control over their lifestyles.

Offer service guarantees with no questions asked. People find rules, restrictions and hassles enervating. Process gets between customers and brands because, in the experience that people have with a brand, policies override insights.

Some automobile companies have taken steps in this direction. Saturn's Vehicle Exchange Program guarantees that if a customer isn't completely satisfied with his or her car, he or she can return it for another Saturn vehicle within 30 days or 1,500 miles. Carmax has a five-day, no questions asked, money-back, full-refund guarantee on its used cars. And for certain eligible vehicles, GM offers people a 24-hour test drive.

Hotels are being even more aggressive with guarantees. As part of a "Make It Hampton" renovation and upgrade program completed and announced in January 2004, Hampton Inns and Hampton Inn & Suites reaffirmed its commitment to the 100% Hampton Satisfaction Guarantee by putting a silver plate on the front counter of every inn that reads: "Friendly service, clean rooms, comfortable surroundings, every time. If you're not satisfied, we don't expect you to pay. That's our commitment and your guarantee. That's 100% Hampton."' As Hampton reiterated in a January 28, 2004, press release, this guarantee is "unconditional." If a customer is not satisfied, "that night's stay is free."

Sheraton announced something similar in September 2002 called the "Sheraton Service Promise," which reads: "If you're not entirely satisfied, we'll take care of it. And we'll make it up to you with an instant discount, points for our rewards program, even money back. And that's a promise." Sheraton overhauled its customer service programs to ensure the immediate resolution of any problem that might arise. As print ads at the time said, "Something not perfect? Just say so." A September 6, 2002, Sheraton press release noted, "No matter what the problem, guests need only tell a hotel associate and they will automatically receive compensation." Like Hampton, the guarantee comes with no questions asked.

THE GRADATIONS OF POWER

Consumer power does not mean turning over the whole business to consumers. It means creating a process by which customers can be involved and can have a say. Most especially, it means giving customers veto power. When customers have the power to say no, then marketing will be sure to improve because the only way customers will say yes is if the marketing is precise, relevant, empowering and reciprocal.

Relinquishing all power means different things for different products, customers and circumstances (Fig. 10.1). Not every person will want the same kind of power, so there is no one-size-fits-all way of empowering people. The key variables are the interest, familiarity and skill that a person has in a category. When all three are high, as with online movie buffs, marketers should offer tools but not interfere. When all three are low, as with many commodity products or with technology products for technophobes or with automobiles for people indifferent to cars, then marketers should take command.

Figure 10.1: **Empowering Customers**

		Interest			
		High		Low	
Familiarity		High	Low	High	Low
Skill	High	Tips & Tools	Introduction	Macros & Programs	Supervision
	Low	Oversight	Instruction	Automation	Management

There are no hard-and-fast rules about how to share power with people, but a few general guidelines are pertinent. For people with higher levels of skill, marketers should be in more of a facilitation role. People who know what they are doing want tips for doing it better and tools that make them better. But they don't want to be told what to do.

For people with higher levels of interest, marketers should stay in the background. Trying to do more would compete with people for center stage and highly involved customers want the spotlight to themselves. Marketers can play a role as agents and stage managers, giving people a chance to be involved and making sure that people find their involvement to be rewarding. People with low interest don't care as much about the limelight, so they are willing for marketers to do more and save them the trouble.

For people with higher levels of familiarity, marketers don't need to do as much. People who are very familiar with a product or category don't need much help, although their overfamiliarity might make them prone to overlooking things, much as people are more likely to have an accident close to home because the route is so familiar that they pay less attention to the road. For people with high familiarity, marketers can offer protection and automated tools. For people with low familiarity, marketers should provide education and control.

There are different ways of empowering people. The bottom line is to make customers feel more in control in a particular situation. The only way to know for sure what would make a particular person feel empowered in a given situation is to understand that person's attitudes about the situation. And the only way for marketers to do that is to practice marketing on the basis of Addressable Attitudes.

THE PRINCIPAL: POWER
THE WAY YOU LIKE IT

The Principal Financial Group (The Principal®) is a global financial institution headquartered in Des Moines, Iowa, that offers a wide range of financial products and services, including mutual funds, annuities, investments, life, health, dental, vision and disability insurance, online banking and retirement products and services. The Principal is one of the top administrators of employer-sponsored retirement plans in the United

States. Financial advice is one of the strengths of The Principal, and has been a key part of its overall success.

The Principal gets the bulk of its customers through companies using it for benefits and retirement services. Building upon the brand recognition it establishes as a company's benefits provider, The Principal communicates directly with employees to market additional services and offerings. Even with this advantageous starting point, the company must still sell itself to employees since many have had no exposure to the company other than what they have gotten through their employer. By and large, marketing to employees is no different than any other sort of new customer acquisition—the most important step is figuring out whether or not a particular employee is a good prospect for services.

The Principal is most interested in customers who have the potential to do an increasing amount of business over the long term. Hence, life cycle growth potential is a key consideration in prioritizing prospects. Companies like The Principal use a wide variety of techniques to segment prospects in order to identify high-potential targets. These methods work with financial and demographic data, and the company has made successful use of these methods in the past, but it has long known that a particular attitude is also very relevant to the fit between its customers and its services. Facing a growing need to boost its marketing productivity and to solidify its competitive position, The Principal recently decided to build a more robust marketing system that included attitudinal information.

The power people are looking for in their relationships with marketers is not just the ability to do everything for oneself. There are several varieties of empowerment. For many people, empowerment comes from having the right team behind them, especially in financial services. Having the right team is how many people feel they have power and control. The Principal has discovered that the more it can provide tools, support, advice and guidance, the more empowered, confident and secure its customers feel. The company does particularly well with customers whose notion of power with respect to financial services is the power to delegate, approve and evaluate as opposed to the power to be completely independent and self-contained. More specifically, the less "self-directed" the individual, the more likely he or she will find value in advisory services—a core strength and competitive advantage for The Principal. These are the kinds of people who will respond to marketing and thus become more valuable customers over time.

Attitudes about power and self-direction have not been part of prospect screening at The Principal in the past because attitudes have not been available in customer and prospect databases. But the innovation of Addressable Attitudes pioneered by MindBase provided a promising solution.

Not only did MindBase offer the company a rich, diverse set of attitudes to link to each name and address in its database, MindBase had a specific measure of self-direction. Thus, MindBase enabled the company to prioritize individual people on the basis of each person's attitudes about self-direction.

Prior to installing MindBase, The Principal conducted an exercise to validate the accuracy and power of MindBase. From past research, management knew the attitudes about self-direction for a portion of its customer base. MindBase was merged with a sample of this group and tested to see if it could correctly identify which people preferred more self-direction and which preferred less. The MindBase attitudinal match proved to be much stronger than traditional syndicated segmentations, providing The Principal with the marketing system it needed.

Derived directly from attitudes and lifestage, MindBase enables the company's marketers to more accurately prioritize individuals in its database on the basis of self-direction. Prospects can now be screened on financial, demographic and attitudinal criteria. Those with appropriate financial and demographic profiles who are also less self-directed now receive mailings or calls from the company's financial representatives. The Principal is delivering a particular kind of power to the people who want that kind of power the most. The company reports that by providing names of the best attitudinal prospects to its financial representatives, the overall productivity of its investment services marketing has been improved.

With MindBase in place at The Principal, other business groups, Principal Bank in particular, are utilizing MindBase to improve the precision and relevance of their offerings. More importantly, The Principal is working to ensure that all of its products are being matched to customers in ways that fully and exactly satisfy the kinds of power people are looking for in each sort of product and financial services category. Addressable Attitudes provide the foundation on which these insights into customer power can be integrated into all of the ways the company interacts with people in the marketplace.

SUMMING UP

- Marketers have been slow to give customers power over marketing. But those marketers who have invited customers into the marketing process have enjoyed big successes.
- Many services have sprung up to give customers the power that most marketers are unwilling to share. These services enable people to avoid marketing and thus make it even more difficult for marketers to engage people in the marketplace.
- Giving power to customers means giving customers the ability to control their participation in the marketing process. This can be accomplished in several ways:
   —Allowing people to help create the marketing itself.
   —Asking for permission. Not once, but regularly, thereby creating a dialogue.
   —Letting people decide when and where they want to receive marketing.
   —Making the media more empowering. Tying old and new media together is a good way to do this.
   —Offering service guarantees with no questions asked.
- Not every consumer will want the same kind of power in every situation. What people want depends on their individual levels of interest, familiarity and skill. Addressable Attitudes are needed to give each person the power that he or she prefers.

NOTES

1 Michael Jordan, "The Rise of the Scion Nation," *Automobile Magazine*, March 2004.
2 Ibid.
3 Glen Urban, Fareena Sultan and William Qualls, "Design and Evaluation of a Trust Based Advisor on the Internet," MIT Center for eBusiness Papers #123, July 1999.

4 Glen Urban, "Customer Advocacy: Is It For You?" MIT Center for eBusiness Papers #175, October 2003.

5 eBay calls these "success fees." Now, eBay also charges "placement fees." Sellers pay both fees.

6 Short for Echo Bay, a name symbolic of nothing that Omidyar simply liked but which was taken by the time he tried to register it as an Internet domain name.

7 Paul Resnick, Richard Zeckjhauser, John Swanson and Kate Lockwood, "The Value of Reputation on eBay: A Controlled Experiment," March 12, 2004, http://www.si.umich.edu/~presnick/papers/postcards/.

8 Robert D. Hof, "Q&A With eBay's Pierre Omidyar," *Business Week Online Extra*, December 3, 2001.

9 Alan Mitchell, "The Buyer Centric Revolution: The Rise of Reverse Direct," *Interactive Marketing*, April/June 2004.

10 Mohan Sawhney, "Rethinking Marketing in a Connected World," January 2003, http://www.mohansawhney.com/registered/content/presentations/RethinkingMarketing.pdf.

11 Will Wade, "A Good Corporate Citizen? This Scanner Can Tell," *New York Times*, August 28, 2003.

12 Paul Foy, "Utah Restaurant Bets on Honesty," *Associated Press*, AOL News, July 13, 2004.

13 "Apple Jacks Ad Deal A Sweet Deal for Kids," *Toronto Star*, August 2, 2000.

14 Scott Bowles, "Fans Use Their Muscle To Shape The Movie," *USA Today*, June 20, 2003.

15 Bruce Horovitz, "Whatever Happened to Customer Service?" *USA Today*, September 26, 2003.

16 Ibid.

17 Joanna Glassner, "Why Webvan Drove Off A Cliff," *Wired News*, July 10, 2001, http://www.wired.com/news/business/0,1367,45098,00.html.

18 Joseph Jaffe, "Case Study: See What Happens," *iMedia*, February 18, 2004.

Insights Integration
for Consumer Reciprocity

People want every moment to count. If the experience that people have with marketing is consistently unrewarding, then marketing won't pass muster. Today, most marketing is seen as irrelevant, disempowering and non-reciprocal. Marketing must start to give something back. Marketing must offer reciprocal value.

A platinum credit card is not the top of the line any more. The most exclusive card is black. It is the American Express Centurion™ Card. Introduced in October 1999, the Centurion Card is so exclusive that no one can apply for it. American Express offers it to its super-elite customers who charge more than $150,000 each year and who are willing to pay the $2,500 annual fee.

The black card arrives in a black box and comes with no credit limit. In addition to many perks, each cardholder is assigned a personal travel counselor and a personal concierge. Whether it's planning dinner for two or a wedding for hundreds, cardholders need only ask and it gets done.

Urban legends abound, some undoubtedly true, about the things that people have bought with their black cards or have arranged through their personal concierges.[1] A Bentley. A charter on a private jet. The horse that Kevin Costner rode in "Dances with Wolves." A handful of Dead Sea sand for the school project of a child in London. An audition to work as a member of the crew for a weekly soap opera.

The black card is rich with status, yet the people able to qualify for it don't need it as proof of their success. They have plenty of standing already. What the black card gives them is different. As American Express noted in the October 14, 1999 press release announcing its introduction, the Centurion Card "offers customized personal service to help ease the busy and demanding lifestyles of cardmembers." Time is what people get from the black card.

In a story on "Marketplace," a daily show on National Public Radio, Gordon Smith, president of American Express Consumer Card Services, noted that Centurion cardholders lead "such incredibly busy lives that they need some time back." [2] That's what the black card provides.

Giving people something of value isn't just about big spending, though. The simplest and quickest way to give people time back is to get rid of the fine print. Eliminate the hassles and irritations that frustrate and annoy people and that take up a lot of time. Not only is that a benefit sure to please everyone, it's a good way to give people something to talk about. No more nuisances would be such a radical change from business as usual that the people who like to spread the word would be thrilled with the opportunity to talk.

Circuit City did just that by using its database of customer transactions as a service tool. And it was big enough news to advertise. Print ads showed an entrance to a Circuit City store with a floor sign announcing, "No shirt. No shoes. No service. No receipt, however, is no problem."

Offering customers a little something extra is nothing new. The newest twist is to give people time, whether it's a concierge or no more fine print. Many retailers are streamlining their browsing and purchasing processes in order to be more efficient, from Amazon.com's patented 1-Click ordering system to self-checkout aisles in grocery stores. Time well spent is what people want most.

FEELING COMMITTED

While giving people time back is a good thing to do in a time-pressured world, doing so in a way that takes time away from the overall interaction people have with a product is not. The double-bind facing marketers is that people won't do business with them if takes a lot of time, but they are less likely to become loyal customers unless they spend a lot of time with a company's products and marketing. This paradoxical challenge arises because of a psychological phenomenon that Arizona State University psychologist Robert Cialdini calls the commitment principle of persuasion.³

Simply stated, psychological research has shown time and again, across a wide variety of settings and interpersonal situations, that when people make an initial commitment to something, they will strive thereafter to act in ways that are consistent with their prior commitment.

Marketers already employ this principle in a variety of ways. It is no accident that car salesmen always start by asking a person if he or she is ready to buy that day if the price is right. That small initial commitment dramatically increases the likelihood that someone will buy a car in order to be consistent with his or her stated commitment of being willing to buy. In sales and marketing circles, the psychological principle of commitment is perhaps best known as the foot-in-the-door technique. Initial compliance with a small, innocuous, inexpensive request greatly increases the likelihood that someone will agree later to a larger, more expensive request.

The most persuasive type of initial commitment is when someone does something. Behavior, like writing something down, is the most effective kind of initial commitment. As Cialdini notes, for decades, marketers have sponsored contests asking people to write and send in short testimonials about why they like a product. In addition to the publicity that is generated, these contests have the added, more important benefit of creating legions of customers who have committed themselves to a product in writing.

Sometimes, the commitments required are big, like tribal initiation rites, fraternity hazing, and military basic training. But big commitments work best when people undergo the effort on their own initiative, not because they are being forced or enticed to do so. In effect, big threats or rewards reduce the commitment people have to put forth.

Perhaps it's nothing but a coincidence, or perhaps it's not, that as companies have taken steps to reduce the effort required of customers to do business with them, customer loyalty has plummeted. Certainly, it would be silly to suggest that companies should make it difficult to do business with them. But if initiatives to make it easier to do business with companies wind up freeing customers from having to make any commitments at all, then relationships are definitely weakened because the psychological process by which associations are cemented into lasting relationships has been short-circuited.

This is one reason why loyalty marketing initiatives are disappointing so much of the time. The objective is to reduce churn and turnover by boosting retention rates—a significant need in many categories like telecommunications and magazine subscriptions. The difficulty is that the commitment required for someone to be a customer in the first place is not very large, usually because the initial subscription was heavily discounted, which means that marketers are trying to get subscribers to be consistent with a commitment they have never really made. In customers' minds, nothing has been invested.

The growth of marketing saturation has paralleled the declining productivity of marketing. Again, it's probably a coincidence, but maybe not, that as marketers have increased the pressure to force people to buy, people have become more fickle and less dependable customers. The bigger threats and rewards of high-pressure, high-saturation, highly intrusive marketing are less likely to inculcate a strong sense of brand commitment. Even though people can be pressured to buy, and to buy more than before, a weakened sense of allegiance to the brands in the minds of the people who have bought the brands means that marketers have to work harder and harder and have to spend more and more to get people to buy the next time.

As Robert Levine, a professor and the former chairperson of the psychology department at California State University at Fresno, points out in his book *The Power of Persuasion: How We're Bought and Sold* (John Wiley & Sons, Inc.: 2003), when it comes to force, less is more. A gun to the head will make someone obey, but it won't make someone believe. The least amount of pressure that can get someone to take the next small step along the way is the most effective form of persuasion because it leaves people feeling that they're being motivated not coerced. And with each small step, people will have made another commitment that will continue to steer them in the right direction.

If the only response of marketers to the time pressures faced by customers is to make marketing less time-consuming, then marketing productivity will continue to decline because marketing effectiveness will be undermined by the paucity of the commitment required. The solution for time pressures is not for marketing to disappear but for marketing, as well as for shopping as a whole, to become more compelling: The time spent must be worth the effort.

At the same time, marketing can't be an imposition on people's time, no matter how compelling. Marketing works best when it fits seamlessly into people's lifestyles so that it is not something that has to be dealt with in addition to everything else. This is what Steve Heyer, the former President and COO of the Coca-Cola Company, meant when he declared at the 2003 inaugural *AdAge* Madison & Vine Conference that brands must enrich people's lifestyles. Heyer said that marketing must be a natural part of people's lives, something that people encounter in the course of everyday life. Heyer said that people must see Coke in more places than just TV commercial breaks. Marketing is least time-intrusive when it is integrated into the other things that people are doing, not when marketing itself is yet another thing to do.

There are many ways to get people to make a commitment, some devious, roundabout or coercive, others straightforward, honest and sincere. The best way to get people to make a commitment is to offer them something in return. When people believe that their commitment will get them something of value, they become engaged on the basis of the psychological principle of reciprocity as well as that of commitment. In fact, marketers have no other options for getting people to make commitments to brands. Compared to even the recent past, people today are smarter, more skeptical and suspicious, better educated and informed, and more experienced and better schooled in how marketing works. Absent something of value, as recent trends and Yankelovich MONITOR research make clear, people are not going to spend time with marketing.

The problem today is that people don't expect that time spent with marketing will generate sufficient reciprocal value to be worth the time or effort. Rewarding people for their time is not a question of the amount of time; it's a question of the quality of time. If marketing is worth it, people will gladly make the time.

CONSUMER RECIPROCITY

Marketing must offer value per se, not simply promise the value of something else. Product pitches are passé. The marketing for a product has become as big a part of a product's value to customers as the product itself. When it does, it creates a sense of reciprocity that helps marketers sell.

Reciprocity works because of a general social ethos of cooperation and consideration and an aversion to inequality and exploitation. Reciprocity creates a shared feeling of mutual dependency. We want to help others because we feel indebted by the help they have provided to us, even if the person creating the indebtedness is unwelcome or disliked and even if the debt or gift is unwanted or uninvited. This builds social ties and strengthens interpersonal relationships. Trust is rooted in reciprocity. All societies have norms that govern and prescribe social interchanges and exchanges.

Marketers are not unfamiliar with the psychological principle of reciprocity.[4] Uninvited gifts of free samples, free gifts, flattery, service, kindness and even cash, have all been used by marketers in various and inventive ways to persuade people to buy. The commonly used negotiating strategy of starting high then going low is a concession strategy that works because it taps into reciprocity (i.e., we feel obliged to reciprocate when we are given the "gift" of a concession).

Interestingly, small gifts tend to work better than large gifts because the debt created by large gifts is usually too big for people to comparably reciprocate. So, the recipients engage in a process of rationalizing why they deserve it, which means they come to feel no sense of obligation and, hence, no need to reciprocate. On the other hand, small gifts are entirely sufficient to induce people to reciprocate in a larger or more valuable way. So, free samples not only give people a taste, they are a small gift that motivates people to reciprocate by buying the product.

The weak reciprocity that people feel for marketing is evidenced by the declining productivity of marketing. A stronger sense of reciprocity would give the same marketing dollar or commercial exposure more impact.

Additionally, giving people something back for the time spent with marketing makes it less likely that people will dodge marketing as a way to get time back in their time-starved lives. Most marketing is seen as irrelevant, disempowering and nonreciprocal. Marketing must give something back.

When reciprocity is central to the practice of marketing, precision and relevance are better assured. The process of paying people to spend time with marketing provides a more overt reminder to marketers that clutter wastes money. If marketers have to pay for the privilege of getting people to look or listen, then marketers will want to make the most of the opportunity. This is not to say that marketing isn't costly now. It's only to say that reciprocity puts things in sharper focus.

Reciprocity also forces marketers to offer things of real value. Handing out cheap watches as promotional premiums or subscription give-aways doesn't measure up in a marketplace of luxury parity. Reciprocity has to entail a meaningful exchange of value.

Different people want different kinds of value from marketing, which also varies by category and brand. Nevertheless, these differences can be identified in an actionable way through Addressable Attitudes because attitudinal data can point to the sorts of value that matter most to specific people.

Insights Integration is the means by which marketers can provide consumer reciprocity. The standard by which to judge every marketing initiative is whether it adds value to people's lifestyles in and of itself—not whether it promotes a product that adds value but whether the marketing does so as well. Obviously, the marketing will not provide the same value as the product, but for the product to be considered for purchase, the marketing must add enough value to command the attention of the audience.

The sales message must still be delivered in a marketing campaign. Value must be added but not in place of the sales pitch. Yet, the sales pitch will have an easier time getting through when people have first gotten something of value from the marketing. When the marketing is worth it, the product is, too.

MAKING MARKETING WORTH IT

In recent years, TV advertisers have been fretting about the eventual impact of digital video recorders (DVRs). Studies have shown that people who own DVRs like TiVo skip the ads in the TV shows they watch.

But the picture is not quite that clear. Online research firm InsightExpress and publisher Media Post released the results of a thought-provoking study of DVR usage called "Demystifying Digital Video Recorders" at the AD:TECH conference held in San Francisco in May 2004.[5] When DVR viewers skip commercials, they are usually fast-forwarding through the ads, which means that viewers are seeing the ads, albeit in a way reminiscent of silent slapstick movies. When fast-forwarding, 15 percent of DVR viewers "always" notice the ads going by and 52 percent "sometimes" notice the fast-forwarded ads. This research also found that 54 percent of DVR users have rewound or paused an ad to understand it better. Even with TiVo, when people think that there is something worth watching in an ad, they will spend time with it.

The biggest complaint that people had about ads in this research, mentioned by 70 percent, was that they were too repetitious. The best way to fight DVRs may well be something as simple as making ads more compelling so that people think that it's worth the time and effort to stop the recording to watch them. There are several things that marketers can do to deliver more value to consumers.

Make marketing a form of entertainment. Marketers have long thought in terms of entertaining people. Funny characters, cartoons, clever jingles, rock music, animals, babies, rhymes, alliteration, allusions, wordplay, euphemisms, sight gags, sarcasm, surprise endings, spoofs, and more, have always been a part of marketing. Indeed, it often seems as if the silliest ads are the most memorable.

But making marketing a form of entertainment doesn't mean making entertaining marketing. It means that marketing must become another form of entertainment, something that people turn to when they are looking for diversion and fun. Perhaps a day might come when marketing is such a rousing form of entertainment that people will be willing to pay to watch. In the meantime, marketing must deliver the same kinds of emotional and aesthetic experiences as other forms of entertainment.

BMW has already taken this to heart. In April 2001, BMW announced the release of "The Hire," a series of five eight-minute films available for downloading at BMWFilms.com. In 2002, three more were released to complete the series. To make the films for "The Hire," BMWFilms assembled an A-list of directors and actors, including David Fincher, John Frankenheimer, John Woo, John Carnahan, Ang Lee, Guy Ritchie, Mickey Rourke, Madonna, Don Cheadle, Ray Liotta and James Brown.

The series follows a character known only as The Driver, played by British actor Clive Owen, who undertakes a variety of perilous missions to help people and in the process has to use his expert driving skills to extricate himself from the treacherous situations he faces. In each film, The Driver is driving a different BMW. Obviously, the car is the real star of the show, although the car takes a severe beating in some of the films.

The films are pure entertainment, not car commercials. The BMW is simply the car that the central character drives, like any of the cars driven by James Bond in the 007 movies.

In late 2002, BMW and Microsoft announced that as part of a promotion of new media technologies, they were sponsoring a traveling show of eight independent films that would be shown in digital format at theaters in 25 cities. Prior to each movie, one of the BMWFilms short films would be shown. The entire series of eight films was later shown on DirecTV and the Bravo cable channel. A DVD collection was announced at the 2002 Cannes Film Festival. The films and the DVD collection are still available online.

Response was overwhelming. Over 30 million people have downloaded these films. Millions of these people registered on the site, the majority of whom requested additional information about BMW cars.[6]

At the same time that BMW was releasing and promoting its films, Ford was doing the same thing to promote the Ford Focus. Ford teamed up with Atom Films to produce three short films directed by young, hip independent filmmakers in which the Focus was featured. The films were available online for a period of time at a special Web site, and can still be seen at the Atom Films Web site. In each film, the Focus plays a supporting role as the characters display the kind of creative, innovative and edgy sensibility that Ford wanted to associate with the Focus brand image.

By making films instead of commercials for their cars, BMW and Ford made marketing into a form of entertainment. The buzz of interest created was far greater than anything that a mere TV ad might be able to stir up. And this interest has a much greater chance of persisting over time. Ads come and go; movies endure. Films can be seen over and over again. Critics continue to review them; fans continue to watch them. Films have a place in popular culture that ads do not. Films create movie stars who attract adoration and emulation. Even as movie stars age in real life, they remain forever young on screen.

BMW and Ford have turned their cars from products to be pitched into movie stars to be cast. Even as the cars change over time, their appeal in these films will carry over to later models and designs. People will have more access to these cars in films than in ads because films remain available while ads do not. Plus, the production of these films in a length and format suitable for the Internet means that people will have even greater access to these films than to regular feature-length movies.

This kind of entertainment is the sort of marketing for which people are willing to make the time. It enriches people's time rather than imposes on people's time. People get something in return at that moment for spending time with marketing. The value that people expect from viewing these product movies motivates them to make an initial commitment of time, effort and interest that will further shape their actions down the line.

American Express followed suit in early 2004 with a series of webisodes available at special Web site, starring comedian and American Express pitchman Jerry Seinfeld called "The Adventures of Seinfeld & Superman." Co-written by Seinfeld and directed by Barry Levinson, these five-minute webisodes feature Seinfeld and Superman in different comic situations that end with the American Express card saving the day. In the first webisode, entitled "A Uniform Used to Mean Something," the card's purchase protection plan is featured. In the second, "Hindsight is 20/20," the Roadside Assistance service is featured.

The Web site itself has the texture and character of a DVD. It shows the living room of an upscale apartment in New York City with a view of the Empire State building. The clock on the wall keeps real time. The fireplace embers are glowing. A statue of Superman is on the mantle next to a photograph of Superman and Seinfeld. By clicking on the photograph, a person can send one of three different e-cards to friends telling them to visit the site.

In the foreground is a table with a Playbill, a stack of film cans, a remote control and a green American Express card. Each of these can be clicked on to activate some feature of the Web site. For example, clicking on the card enables a person to apply for an American Express card. For each of the film cans in the stack, there is something different to watch: The TV teasers. Behind the scenes clips. Each of the webisodes.

The webisodes have proven so popular that NBC aired the first one in the break between back to back prime time episodes of "Friends." TBS also aired the first webisode following each of its premiere episodes of the HBO series "Sex and the City."

American Express did not develop these webisodes as entertaining marketing. Instead, it's all about marketing as a form of entertainment.

John Hayes, the chief marketing officer for American Express, said, "[W]e're trying to create media content where people actually opt in to watch."[7] Not ads to promote the brand. Rather, entertainment that attracts people to the brand. This is brand charisma.

Entertainment is a powerful form of reciprocity for marketers to offer people. *New York Times Magazine* consumer columnist Rob Walker wondered how the Burger King Subservient Chicken could be so popular if the Yankelovich data on marketing resistance were true.[8] SubservientChicken.com is a nutty Web site that enables visitors to make a chicken do anything they command. The answer is that it is not an ad; it's entertainment, however silly one might think it to be. The only promotion of Burger King is a small link to another Web page, but the power of this entertainment to promote Burger King has been substantial. As Walker himself concludes near the end of his essay, "these little films and games don't really count as advertising."

Approaching ads as entertainment content is not without precedent. Ads have been successfully packaged as entertainment in the past, albeit in a more traditional way than what BMWFilms and American Express are doing today. CBS has had repeated success with hour-long specials of old Super Bowl ads called "Super Bowl's Greatest Commercials." ABC has had similar success with nine different hour-long specials called "The Best Commercials You've Never Seen (and Some You Have)." Even as people are less interested in ads as marketing, they remain interested in ads as entertainment. When ads are all about fun, people will tune in.

People are desperate for fun these days. Fun has become hard work. Fun means making a list, squeezing it into one's schedule, buying all of the right equipment, mastering the necessary skills, dealing with the risks, and coping with the inevitable complications and minor disasters. When time for fun comes, the pressure is on. Fun had better happen. There is no choice. So, a person must work at it to make sure that he or she gets it while it's there to be had. Marketers can help by showing people how to have fun again.

Marketing itself should be fun, but fun is not something that always comes to mind when people always think of marketing, particularly the activities associated with marketing. In a Yankelovich MONITOR OmniPlus study on the state of marketing research conducted for the 2003 Annual Convention and Trade Show of the Advertising Research Foundation, fun was the one thing found to be missing from the experience people have with marketing research.[9] The overwhelming majority said that they try to give honest, accurate answers when participating in surveys and that they understand the importance and necessity of research studies. But only 37 percent said that they liked and enjoyed participating in research.

Not only is fun missing from marketing research, fun is important to the integrity of marketing research. Compared to people who did not enjoy participating in research surveys, people who did enjoy participating were far more like to say that they answer questions with their full attention and concentration—91 percent vs. 67 percent—and that they answer questions candidly—93 percent vs. 68 percent. It's likely, too, that if research surveys were more fun, response rates would be higher.

The biggest challenge facing marketing researchers is not methodological, it's psychological. Research instruments work well as long as people are having fun. Making research more fun is the number one issue facing the marketing research industry. And so it is with marketing as a whole.

Entertainment has long been one of the things that people like most about advertising. The 1964 study of people's attitudes about advertising sponsored by the American Association of Advertising Agencies found that people say that information is the best thing provided by advertising. However, when people were asked why they had given high ratings to certain specific ads and not to others, the most common reason was that those ads were more entertaining. Generally speaking, people want information from ads, but that information had better be presented in an entertaining manner. And today, that means making marketing a form of entertainment.

Make marketing informative. But not about products; about lifestyles. Even though people want entertainment most, they want information, too. But people want more than just product information. They can get that from many places that they trust more than marketing. Instead, people want lifestyle information.

The world is in a whirl. Things are changing fast and there is more to learn about and keep up with than ever before. Yet, people don't have time to dig into all of the options available to them. Marketers can build a relationship with people by being the source that people can turn to for lifestyle tips and hints.

Procter & Gamble (P&G) provides these kinds of "Everyday Solutions" on its Web site. As P&G says, "Innovative products, smart tips, samples, and offers to help simplify your life." Clinique does the same thing on its Web site, but goes a step further by giving people the opportunity to email personal questions to a beauty consultant.

Spiegel now offers fashion advice in its catalog and on its Web site. In short prefaces to item descriptions and in brief introductions to categories of items, Spiegel offers tips, hints, and insights. Instead of just describing an item, Spiegel first mentions why a particular item makes sense or when it is appropriate. Spiegel details the kind of look that certain items will give and suggests how they can be worn. By reading and considering the products in the catalog, a woman gets free fashion advice.

The information that people want is lifestyle information about ways to live, not product information about ways to buy. The problems people have nowadays are not product or shopping problems. They're lifestyle problems.

Word-of-mouth is the most common source of lifestyle information, but it has to be informed by something. Marketers who make their marketing communications a repository of lifestyle information will become the source that people turn to for the advice and guidance they offer to others. This boost to a marketer's reputation and standing will give all of its communications a bigger, more receptive audience.

Marketers are in constant communication with customers, so there are numerous opportunities to help people with useful information. Direct mail pieces could include nuggets of interesting facts and ideas as well as links to Web sites with more information—and not just a marketer's own Web site, but any pertinent Web site maintained by any type of organization. Telemarketing calls could open and close with tips and advice. Emails could provide links to other sources of information or objective product comparisons. Instead of sending nothing but coupons and flyers, marketers could send personalized information, product updates and consumer safety warnings. If people thought that the marketing communications they received might contain useful or interesting information, consumer resistance would melt away.

Beautify marketing. The notion is to make marketing itself into something decorative or ornamental, something so well crafted and artistic that people want to experience it or even collect it. This is not about creating collectibles. This is about bringing an artistic sensibility to marketing so that it becomes a lifestyle enhancement that people want to associate themselves with in some way. By making marketing itself into a beautiful object or a delightful experience, marketers are offering people of all means the chance to have a luxurious interaction whenever they spend time with marketing.

Pottery Barn sends out catalogs that are so exquisitely beautiful they're more like coffee table books. In this way, it is giving its customers an attractive complement to their lifestyles through its catalog marketing. Browsing and buying have become small luxury experiences.

Many retailers have aggressively experimented with experiential retailing environments. REI, Land Rover, Bass Pro Shops, and Virgin Megastores, among others, have been leading the way.

A variety of automobile dealerships have invested millions in recent years to make car buying into an experience more like an afternoon luxury getaway.[10] Planet Honda in New Jersey features the new color and logo schemes common to all Honda dealerships, along with New Age music and soothing aromatherapy fragrances that fill the showroom. Not to mention the play area for children and the coffee bar for adults. At Planet Ford near Houston, salespeople in golf carts greet customers with bottled water and service crews wear uniforms like NASCAR pit crews. Planet Dodge in Miami wants to give every customer the "Ritz-Carlton" experience, including a concierge who greets every customer by name.

The owner of The Collection in Coral Gables, which sells Audis, Porsches, Ferraris, Maseratis, Aston Martins, Jaguars and Lotuses, also compares his showroom to a "luxury hotel." The Collection has a concierge, a cafe and a specialty shop that sells items like a Ferrari beauty case, Porsche watches, and an Audi pen and pencil set.

The need to make marketing into a beautiful experience goes beyond retailers. It even includes white goods manufacturers like Whirlpool and KitchenAid. They joined together to open Insperience™ Studio in Atlanta in November 2002. Situated in the heart of trendy Buckhead, Insperience has seven fully functioning laundry and kitchen areas stocked with the latest Whirlpool and KitchenAid appliances. Insperience is a place for people to come and try out new appliances in a low-key, non-sales environment. No appliances are for sale there. Insperience is just a hands-on marketing environment where people can learn more about the product lines or meet with their builders, designers and architects.

Insperience maintains a full calendar of events, seminars and demonstrations. People are even encouraged to bring in their laundry or come cook a meal just to get a feel for how the appliances work. According to David Provost, Whirlpool's Director of Purchase Experience, one man even brought in a bag of trash to test the trash compactor.[11] Not only is Insperience a place where people can learn more, Whirlpool and KitchenAid are hoping that Insperience will teach them more about people's needs and interests as well.

Embed marketing in the content in a way that makes the content better. Too often, embedded advertising is nothing but a gratuitous placement in a TV show or a movie. The product gets seen but the product adds little, if anything, to the content of the show. On the other hand, if products were embedded in a way that contributes to the plot or adds an extra dimension to the content, then the product would get an even bigger boost because it actually plays a part. For people to feel like they have gotten something of real value, products must make a contribution, not a mere appearance.

This is how the products were used by BMW, Ford and American Express. The storylines weren't about the products, but the products played a natural role that added to the content.

Enriching the experience of watching a TV show can even be done without product placements within the shows. The contributions can be embedded by taking a different approach to advertising. This is what P&G did during the Friday night prime time movies on the Lifetime cable channel during the summer of 2004.[12] P&G bought all of the advertising time for the Friday night Lifetime movies that ran between the first week of July and the first week of October. Three of the two-minute ad breaks told a story about a woman being made over by a Glam Squad using P&G products. The other ad breaks showed regular commercials for P&G products. To see the makeover from start to finish, viewers had to watch the entire movie.

The P&G products weren't peripheral to the makeover; they facilitated the makeover. Not only was the story entertaining, it gave women lifestyle information about beauty tips and advice. This sequence of ads told a story that combined all of the different ways in which to give people something in return for their time and attention—entertainment, information and an indulgent experience, albeit vicariously. As Tina

Glahan, manager of media and marketing for P&G, told the *Wall Street Journal* when the deal was announced, "Consumers want to be educated, and they want to enjoy themselves when they watch TV."[13] The P&G ads did more than just pitch a product; they enhanced the enjoyment of the movie while providing lifestyle information at the same time.

This is the way that "Movie and a Makeover" works on TBS. Host Mia Butler introduces the Saturday morning movies and then during small segments between the movie and each commercial break, she works with a team of experts who give a makeover to someone. The makeovers range from fashion to beauty to home and garden projects, involving experts like stylists, landscapers, nutritionists and designers. For certain makeovers, branded products of companies like Home Depot and Sears are included.

The success of "Movie and a Makeover" comes from the fact that it creates a bigger experience than just the movie itself. The value of the entire program is greater than that of the movie alone. The makeover segments are both informative and entertaining, and viewers have to stick around to the end of the movie to get all of the relevant tips and advice and to see the outcome of the makeover. The products used in the makeover directly contribute to its success and thus offer people something much more enriching to watch than just another product pitch.

Practice marketing with more politeness. This seems obvious, but regrettably it is not always the case that marketing is practiced with politeness. Offering civility would give people an experience with their time that is not common, yet much desired.

In a Yankelovich MONIOR OmniPlus survey completed in July 2003, 81 percent agreed that people are not as polite to one another as they should be, a figure virtually the same as the 79 percent in a 2002 Public Agenda survey who agreed that the lack of respect and courtesy is a serious problem in need of attention.[14] In the Public Agenda survey, 61 percent said that the problem had gotten worse in recent years and 41 percent admitted that they themselves were part of the problem. In the Yankelovich MONITOR, roughly half report that they are willing to live by stricter rules if everybody else would do the same. The problem is taking the first step. Marketers can provide the needed leadership.

There is an untapped market opportunity for products designed to facilitate politeness by eliminating the annoying things that people consider rude: Silent candy wrappers and snack packaging for the movies. Volume meters on cell phones to let people know when they're talking too loudly. Two horns for every car, one that means excuse me or I'm sorry.

Toyota is already revving up to do this. On July 26, 2004, the patents column of the *New York Times* reported that a team of four inventors at Toyota had just received a patent for a car design that is able to communicate human emotions by imitating human facial expressions for glaring, crying, laughing, winking and looking around. Information about the state of the road, the car and the driver change the car's outer appearance and color.

But beyond products, marketers can set an example in their marketing practices: Unsolicited telephone calls just to say thank you. Direct mail letters and telemarketing scripts that are as aggressive about civility as they are about closing. Ads that showcase courtesy as a competitive advantage. Marketing that always asks permission. Politeness guarantees. Money back for impoliteness. Marketing that somehow always manages to say please and thank you.

It may seem silly to insist that marketing say thank you but Citi Card believes in the power of politeness. In June 2004, Citi Card consolidated all of its various credit card reward programs into a single program called the ThankYou Redemptions Network.[SM] On its Web site, Citi Card says that the program is meant "[a]s a special Thank You for our customers." The program includes new, faster ways to earn points to redeem rewards, and if Citi Card does not offer the reward item that someone wants, he or she need only request it and Citi Card will make that reward available under a feature of its program known as "Your Wish Fulfilled." With this new program, Citi Card has given its customers a product incorporating every element of P&R². And from a marketing standpoint, every time an ad for this program appears on TV, viewers hear Citi Card say, "Thank you."

Being polite means deliberately adopting a different tone and approach to marketing. It means having a deeper empathy for consumers and understanding them as people not as target segments. It means looking at people from a lifestyle perspective, not from a marketing perspective. It means caring about whether a marketplace transaction makes consumers better people instead of better shoppers. It's easy to be cool, detached and dispassionate when dealing with consumer marketing constructs. They're statistics in a report. They just don't seem like real people. But they are real people who are actively resisting and pushing back against marketing practices that don't treat them with respect.

Admittedly, taking up a new rhetorical style is a tricky proposition in today's shrill political and cultural environment. Even news reporting has become relentlessly breathless and belligerent. Every sentence from every public voice seems to end in an exclamation point these days. It's all about verbal finger jabs in the chest, whether it's politicians berating their opponents or cable sports commentators going around the horn on the latest controversy. People learn how to speak and what to expect of others from what they see and hear in the public domain. Civility has become the casualty of the strident tone of public life.

But perhaps this is where marketers can provide leadership for the public good even as they capture competitive advantage for themselves. For there is a marketing opportunity available to marketers willing to practice marketing with more courtesy and respect. People want something in return for the time they spend with marketing. Politeness is a form of reciprocity that will reward them for their efforts. Civility is also the first step in building greater trust.

IN EXCHANGE FOR TRUST

Trust is key to reciprocity. Unless people trust marketers to deliver value in exchange for time spent with marketing, efforts to provide reciprocity will fail to have an impact. Unfortunately, trust in business has plummeted in recent years.

This is not to suggest that people are in revolt against business. However, it is to recognize that interacting with people has gotten harder and more expensive as a result of the distrust that people feel. Distrust affects business and marketing productivity in many ways. Customer service becomes a bigger cost of doing business. Marketing isn't as persuasive. People take their business elsewhere. And it is harder to convince people to share information and data with businesses.

To better understand this widespread distrust of business and to diagnose exactly what needs to be done, Yankelovich fielded a special MONITOR study on trust in partnership with research firm FGI among a nationally representative sample of its SmartPanel of MindBase-coded Internet panelists.[15] This research confirmed the severe levels of distrust that people now feel towards business and underlined the severe implications for privacy.

Privacy concerns are the biggest consequence of distrust in business. Seventy-one percent of the respondents in the Yankelovich/FGI Trust Study said that protecting personal information and privacy is more of a concern than it was just a few years ago. Only 11 percent felt that retailers are doing everything they should be doing to protect personal information and a mere 12 percent expressed confidence that government will ensure that companies take steps to ensure privacy. When people don't think that government or business will protect them, then they have no choice but to take matters into their own hands. As a result, resistance becomes even stronger.

Ninety-seven percent are doing one or more things as a consequence of losing trust in business. Most of these actions are negative, like buying less, shopping less, canceling a credit card or filing a complaint. If there is any good news in these results, it is that only 49 percent report shifting their spending to a competitor. But the bad news is that 44 percent of those who report that they don't shift their spending say that it's because competitors can't be trusted either. Even worse, when people lose trust in a business, their spending with that business declines by 87 percent.

Glen Urban of MIT has outlined eight things that must be done for a business to build and maintain trust with consumers: transparency of information; product and service quality; honest product comparisons; correct alignment of sales incentives; partnering with customers and giving them self-help tools; cooperative design with customers; ensuring trust throughout the supply chain; and, making a comprehensive organizational commitment to trust. [16]

Urban's eight steps recognize that for trust to take hold, a company must integrate insights about trust into the heart and soul of how it operates, but Insights Integration is just the first step. Even with this, there is yet more to be done. The Yankelovich/FGI Trust Study identified three things in particular.

First, the personal encounters of customers must be completely trustworthy. When asked what fosters trust, personal experiences, both positive and negative, topped the list. Independent ratings, recommendations from family and friends, a company's reputation, and the lack of a privacy policy followed. While these other things are important—many of them the things identified by Urban—personal experiences were first.

Trust can only be rebuilt one small promise at a time. Big corporate pronouncements trumpeting honesty and integrity won't restore trust. People want to experience it every time they interact with someone at a company, so companies must ensure that their people act with unfailing integrity. Every interaction should be turned into a chance for a company employee to make a small promise to a customer and then immediately fulfill it. Every customer request should be responded to with a promise that is instantly kept. Every customer service operator should be scripted to answer inquiries with small promises that can be carried out right away. Every marketing communication should carry a promise, even if implicit, that will be kept each time a person interacts with the company.

Asking employees to make promises to customers engages the desire that everyone has to be an honest person. No one wants to break a promise, so transforming customer interactions into promise-keeping opportunities will connect employees more closely to customers. When employees are trained to make and keep promises, they will come to see the importance of committing to customers. Companies that reward promise-keepers will soon find that their employees are working harder to give customers what they want. After all, that's what they've promised to do. Or, to put it another way, when employees make a commitment to something, particularly a promise, they are much more likely to act in ways that are consistent with that commitment.

Companies themselves need to keep their promises to people, especially promises about privacy. Privacy policies must be unambiguous, easily accessible, and irrevocable. Rebuilding trust in business means restoring the public confidence in the motives and aims of business. Marketers are the most visible part of a company. In an era of marketing databases and information management, privacy is the most important thing affecting confidence and trust. Keeping promises about privacy is thus one of the biggest responsibilities that marketers must shoulder.

The second thing that needs to be done is to give people power. The Yankelovich/FGI Trust Study asked respondents what would cause them to be willing to share personal information with a company (Fig. 11.1).

Figure 11.1: **Willingness to Share Information**

Influence on decision to share personal information with a retail company:	Agree
Gives me control of how my information is used	**58**%
Keeps customer information safe	**55**
They are open and honest in their business practices	**50**
Customer service	**47**
Company reputation	**47**
Has a straightforward privacy policy	**45**
Good rating by consumer protection third-party (e.g., BBB)	**45**
Length of time as a customer	**42**
Provides best value	**41**
Testimonials from other customers	**23**
Involved in the community	**19**
Has a trustworthy CEO	**17**

Source: Yankelovich MONITOR OmniPlus / FGI SmartPanel Trust Study 2004

Topping the list was control over how personal information is used. Second on the list was security.

Businesses have focused most of their time and energy on information security. Certainly, consumers want security, but that is not enough. People want to have a say in how their information is handled. It is not enough to inform people about what might or might not be done with their information. People want to be involved in the decisions. Customer control must be a major factor shaping how businesses manage people's personal information.

Finally, companies need to provide reciprocity for the information that people share. The failure to do so to date is the biggest reason why people are worried about the privacy of their personal information. Privacy is not an all-or-nothing proposition. For the right price, people are willing to share any information, even the most unflattering information. One need only watch daytime TV talk shows to see that people will confess to the most outrageous and uncomplimentary things in exchange for their Andy Warhol 15 minutes of fame on a syndicated TV show. The value exchange is fair to them.

So far, marketers have not engaged in a value exchange for the private information of people. People learn about the information practices of marketers serendipitously and then feel exploited because they had no say in the matter and received nothing in return, except more marketing saturation. Reciprocity is the missing ingredient. If marketers were to negotiate with people for access and use of personal information, then a fair price could be struck.

The Yankelovich/FGI Trust Study examined what it might take to motivate people to share personal information. A number of shopping incentives were assessed, including greater convenience, early notification of sales, bonus reward points, access to special account representatives, more customized products and services, and price discounts. Nothing but price discounts had more than a modest impact (Fig. 11.2). Money, though, made a big difference.

Figure 11.2: **Price Discount Necessary to Share Information**

	From a company you **haven't** bought from before				From a company you **have** bought from before			
Amount of discount:	**5%**	**15%**	**50%**	**75%**	**5%**	**15%**	**50%**	**75%**
Gender	56%	58%	78%	68%	59%	65%	63%	73%
Name	42	49	65	60	54	58	56	64
Interests / Hobbies	37	40	63	56	42	51	51	62
Email address	34	33	54	54	39	46	52	59
Mailing address	27	34	54	50	46	47	46	58
Date of birth	31	27	54	48	31	41	43	51
Telephone number	19	22	34	29	24	30	35	43
Household income	15	20	34	28	17	29	25	42
Credit card #	11	9	20	18	13	17	18	20
Medical history	7	3	10	5	5	8	9	10
Social security number	1	2	3	5	1	4	4	7
Average of all items	**25%**	**27%**	**43%**	**38%**	**30%**	**36%**	**37%**	**44%**

Note: Figures shown represent the percentage who would share
that type of personal information at that level of price discount.

Source: Yankelovich MONITOR OmniPlus / FGI SmartPanel Trust Study 2004

For a company unfamiliar to people, it takes a 50 percent price discount to get people to share their private information. For a company that people know and have bought from in the past, only a 15 percent price discount is needed. While these results are by no means definitive about specific categories or brands, they do show that reciprocity is the key to having a productive privacy relationship with customers.

These findings do not suggest that trust is for sale, but they certainly show that reciprocity plays a big part in the trust that people feel for a company. The more that reciprocity characterizes the interactions that people have with a company, the more that people feel good enough about that company to trust them with private information. Reciprocity gives people assurance that a company is not trying to get the better of them.

Money is not the only form of reciprocity that will satisfy the exchange that people want. But it is a form of reciprocity that works and thus a cost of doing business that marketers must account for as they look for ways to re-engage resistant consumers.

The biggest part of the solution to the challenge of marketing resistance is the revolutionary new tool of Addressable Attitudes. But people will feel uncomfortable even with something that is non-invasive and privacy-neutral like Addressable Attitudes unless they get more power and reciprocity. Piecemeal efforts won't raise marketing to the next level. It takes a full-blown commitment to Precision, Relevance, Power and Reciprocity supported by Addressable Attitudes and Insights Integration. With that commitment, marketing will be ready at last for the 21st Century.

SUMMING UP

- People today know more about how marketing works and so they want more from marketing. No one is going to spend time with marketing unless there is some value associated with the time it takes.
- By avoiding marketing, people are not making a commitment to brands. The lack of a commitment of time and effort makes it harder for brands to win people's patronage and loyalty.
- When people believe that their commitment to marketing will bring them something of value, they will seek out an opportu-

nity to be engaged. Thus, the best way to reconnect with resistant consumers is to offer some form of reciprocity in exchange for their time and effort.

- Different people will seek different kinds of reciprocity. Addressable Attitudes provide the tool for linking specific forms of value to individual names and addresses.

- Marketers can deliver reciprocity to consumers in many different ways:

    —Make marketing into a form of entertainment so that people will seek it out just as they do other forms of entertainment.

    —Make marketing informative, with information about the lifestyle issues of importance to people

    —Make marketing itself into an object or an experience that people value and want to enjoy.

    —Embed marketing in content in a way that makes the content better.

    —Practice marketing with politeness and civility.

- Reciprocity is key to trust. Trust is key to privacy. For marketers to obtain the information that is needed to deliver the best value to customers, there must be a fair exchange of value. Reciprocity reassures people that companies want to be fair and responsive.

NOTES

1 See http://www.snopes.com/business/black/blackcard.asp.

2 Lisa Napoli, "Keeping Credit in the Black," *Marketplace* on NPR, April 26, 2004.

3 Robert Cialdini, *Influence: Science and Practice* (Allyn & Bacon: 2001, 4th Edition).

4 Nor is the CIA. In his book, Levine described the recently declassified 1963 CIA interrogation manual *KUBARK Counterintelligence Interrogation* as "100 percent applied social psychology." No torture, just persuasion. The KUBARK manual is available for purchase at www.parascope.com.

5 InsightExpress Press Release, "Digital Video Recorders Offer Advertisers Opportunities, Not Threats," May 25, 2004; Joe Mandese, "Study: DVRs 'Recapture' 96% of TV Ad Zapping," *Media Post's Media Daily News,* May 25, 2004; and Robyn Greenspan, "DVRs Not Necessarily Ad-Killers," *ClickZ Stats and Applications,* May 25, 2004.

6 Tony Hespos, "BMW Films: The Ultimate Marketing Scheme," *iMedia Connection,* July 10, 2002.

7 Rick E. Bruner, "Amex Launches 5-Minute Seinfeld Webisodes," *MarketingVox News,* March 31, 2004.

8 Rob Walker, "Poultry-Geist," *New York Times Magazine,* May 23, 2004.

9 This study was a telephone callback of 600 Yankelovich MONITOR respondents conducted February 28 to March 9, 2003 among a nationally representative sample of adults, 16+, who had participated in at least one research survey of any sort during the past year (other than the MONITOR survey).

10 Phil Patton, "Buy A New Lexus, Get A Massage," *New York Times,* January 31, 2003.

11 Kathy Lamancusa, "Trend Talk: Experiential Retailing," *Realty Times,* October 2, 2003.

12 Brian Steinberg, "P&G Breaks Out of 30-Second Mold," *Wall Street Journal,* June 30, 2004.

13 Ibid.

14 Steve Farkas, and Jean Johnson with Ann Duffett and Kathleen Collins, *Aggravating Circumstances: A Status Report on Rudeness in America,* April 2002, A Public Agenda study funded by Pew Charitable Trusts.

15 The results of this research were first presented by Craig Wood, president of Yankelovich MONITOR, in a presentation entitled "A Crisis of Confidence: Rebuilding the Bonds of Trust" at the 10th Annual Fred Newell Customer Relationship Management Conference, June 3, 2004.

16 Glen Urban, "Customer Advocacy: Is It for You?" MIT Center for eBusiness Papers #175, October 2003.

Getting Concurrent

The future purpose of marketing must be to sell more stuff with precision and relevance so that more people will have the power to reciprocate more often for more money. Otherwise, marketing that sells more will be winning a losing game because profitability and productivity will continue to deteriorate.

Sergio Zyman, the brilliant and outspoken ex-Chief Marketing Officer at Coke, named by *Time* magazine as one of the top three pitchmen of the 20th Century and founder of the Zyman Marketing Group, has this to say about marketing: "The sole purpose of marketing is to get more people to buy more of your product, more often, for more money."[1] In other words, marketing is about selling. Everything else, from creative to concept development to customer relationship management, is just a means to an end. Bottom line, marketing had better sell or it's good for nothing.

Marketing has to do a lot of things along the way in order to sell, like build awareness or create a positive brand image or get a product into a shopper's consideration set, but none of these things are the purpose of marketing. The purpose of marketing is to sell. The tactics appropriate to marketing are whatever it takes to sell more products to more people more often for more money. As long as marketing can do so at a profit, that is.

While Zyman doesn't mention it explicitly, he certainly takes it for granted that marketing is supposed to sell at a profit. Furthermore, it is generally assumed that marketing should be productive in a scalable way, which is to say that the rate of return on marketing spending should improve over time. Yet, increasingly, marketing is falling short on all three grounds. It doesn't sell as much and when it does, it often does so unprofitably and at a declining level of productivity.

The conventional practice of marketing isn't in trouble so much as it is behind the times. What worked in the past no longer fits the contemporary marketplace. Making marketing sell more stuff profitably and productively means practicing marketing differently. No more dominion, saturation and intrusiveness. Concurrence is needed instead.

The need for concurrence is rooted in the changing dynamics of consumer lifestyles. People want different things than they did in the past. The only way to understand this is to study people's attitudes because their past behaviors reflect a different set of needs, wants, values and preferences. And the only way to understand attitudes today is on a name-and-address basis because that's how marketing execution systems now operate. Only Addressable Attitudes enable marketing organizations to be centered on these important insights.

People want less clutter and more value. Less clutter means Precision and Relevance. More value means Power and Reciprocity. Less clutter because of agreement and synchrony. More value because of cooperation and collaboration. Altogether, these are the components of P&R², the four cornerstones of Concurrence Marketing.

To paraphrase Zyman, the future purpose of marketing must be to sell more stuff with precision and relevance so that more people will have the power to reciprocate more often for more money. Otherwise, marketing that sells more will be winning a losing game because profitability and productivity will continue to deteriorate.

ATTITUDES FIRST

The fundamental shift required to improve marketing productivity is to put attitudes first. Insights must rule everything. Process-centricity must give way to insights-centricity. The problem of marketing productivity is now being tackled as a process problem. This is seen most clearly in the flurry of efforts being made to shift marketing dollars from mass media vehicles to micro-media vehicles in order to find the eyeballs that no longer watch TV or read general-interest magazines. The objective is not to better connect with what people want; the objective is just to get in front of people. This is all about marketing processes and the search for new ways of doing the same old marketing.

There are many reasons why people are migrating away from mass media to micro-media, but chief among them is flight from clutter, saturation and intrusiveness. People hope that new media will give them more control over their marketing experiences as well as more offers and communications that correspond to their specialized interests—interests which drew them to these niche media in the first place. Unfortunately, the character of the marketing practiced in micro-media is usually little different than that practiced in mass media.

If a marketing organization were centered on attitudes, then marketing processes would be marshaled and utilized only as appropriate for satisfying what people want. The logistics of where people are found would be secondary to insights into what people want. Indeed, people are not turning away from mass media because of anything to do with how the mass media operate or sell space to advertisers. After all, in many ways, the mass media look the same to people as micro-media. The way people now receive network TV, for example, is just like any other cable channel. Network stations are one choice among hundreds of others from which people choose what they want. The reason that people are turning away from mass media is because mass media no longer provide what they want.

Internet media are generating lots of interest because they offer marketers the chance to place marketing offers and communications in more relevant environments. Some search engines sell higher placements in search results or sponsored links. Most search engines list ads for products related to the search topic next to the search results. This kind of placement gets marketers in front of people who have expressed an explicit interest in a particular area.

Internet contextual advertising also links ads to content. Some contextual ads are delivered by software that deciphers the topic of the Web page that a person is viewing. Other contextual ad placements are worked out directly between Internet advertisers and online publishers. Unlike search engine ads that work from a specific topic specified by a user, contextual ads infer interest in a particular topic from the content of the Web page.

Collaborative filtering systems, such as the recommendation system used by Amazon.com, utilize both types of information. These tools consider what is specified by a user as well as what can be inferred from the content of interest to a user. For example, a collaborative filtering system would make a book recommendation based on the books that a person has bought before or is considering buying. To do this, the system looks at people who have bought the same book in the past and then examines the other books that these people have bought. From this analysis, the system would make a book recommendation. The notion is that people who share the same taste in one book are more likely than not to share the same tastes in other books as well.

These sorts of Internet systems offer marketers the ability to get their products seen and considered by people whose behavior signals a specific interest in something. Presumably, the marketing is more precise. But it is not necessarily more precise nor is it guaranteed to be more relevant.

Digital delivery systems are just more sophisticated ways of using demographic and behavioral data to execute marketing. The breakthrough they offer comes from the fact that these systems are being used for personal media, so the audience is essentially an audience of one. Traditional mass media have not been personal media. But digital technologies are in the wings to transform many mass media vehicles into personal media devices, digital TV in particular. As all media vehicles become personal media systems, the advantage that many micro-media have today, particularly Internet media, will contract. At which point, clutter may even be worse as people make their way through a world like that of Tom Cruise's character in the Steven Spielberg movie "Minority Report" in which everyone is personally inviegled by every billboard and media screen to buy things recommended to them on the basis of databases of information about their demographics and past purchases.

But all media systems, new and old, lack an understanding of attitudes. Just because an ad is delivered in context online doesn't mean that it is any more relevant, empowering or reciprocal. It certainly doesn't mean that it talks to people in an appropriate way about the subject matter defining the context. All context can do is provide an opportunity for an ad, but that ad will still be clutter unless it has something suitable and motivating to say.

Digital media systems are nothing but a better address book. The best that digital media systems can ever do is to make better use of demographic and behavioral data. These systems will never get past the performance ceiling inherent to the weak correspondence of descriptive data and purchasing attitudes. Past behaviors offer no insights into buying motivations, so the productivity improvements from attitudinally based precision and relevance are no more available to the new personal and micro-media than they were to the traditional mass media.

Certainly, context matters for precision and relevance, but context is not something new that is unique to personal or micro-media. Advertisers already make rough guesses about context in the past based on audience demographics and program content.[2] The new digital media systems eliminate much of this guesswork, but the new media have not introduced a catalyzing element that will set off sweeping changes in the practice of marketing. All that the new digital media systems have done is provide a means of executing the old model more efficiently. Certainly, performance improvements have been realized and should not be underestimated. But the real revolution in marketing awaits new fundamentals based on a new model.

Concurrence Marketing is that breakthrough. Addressable Attitudes make Concurrence Marketing possible.

PUTTING ADDRESSABLE ATTITUDES IN PLACE

Each marketing organization will find its own path to becoming an Insight-Centric Organization practicing Concurrence Marketing. But in every case, Addressable Attitudes are required. There are several things to keep in mind as Addressable Attitudes are used to reshape an organization's marketing practices.

Get the Right Information

Addressable Attitudes are not a catchall for any and every type of attitudinal data. Only the attitudes that matter should be gathered and compiled.

1. Lifestyle information. Typically, marketers have lots of information about product attitudes but little if any information about lifestyle values and preferences. And lifestyle information is a necessity given that the marketplace is shifting from product-based considerations like quantity, tangibles and money to lifestyle-based considerations like quality, intangibles and time. People don't want product satisfactions so much as they want products that provide lifestyle experiences.

2. Attitudinal drivers. Not all attitudes matter. The attitudes of greatest interest to marketers are the ones that drive or motivate consumer behavior in the marketplace. Identifying attitudinal drivers involves modeling the relationships between attitudes and key behaviors.[3] Successful models will be selected on the basis of statistical results as well as expert knowledge of the marketplace. The drivers identified from this modeling process are the key variables for inclusion in a system of Addressable Attitudes.

Attitudinal drivers are most reliably estimated as constructs composed of multiple, related variables rather than single variables alone. Individual questions are not as stable as multivariate constructs nor do they fully capture the many nuances that characterize most attitudinal factors.

Typically, it takes more than the drivers alone to make sense of consumer interests, motivations and preferences. So, additional attitudes must also be included to provide the context, perspective and elaboration needed to generate meaningful customer insights.

3. Power and reciprocity. These are two crucial dimensions for Concurrence Marketing. But different people will want to receive and exercise power and reciprocity in different ways. This will vary by category and brand as well.

4. Demographics and behaviors. Just as demographics and behaviors are not a substitute for attitudes, neither are attitudes a substitute for demographics and behaviors. The fact that attitudes have more breakthrough potential than demographics and behaviors does not mean that attitudes should be used in place of them. Demographic and behavioral data play an important role and provide a necessary foundation. Concurrence Marketing can be practiced with nothing more than Addressable Attitudes, but the combination of the three is the most powerful platform for highly productive marketing.

Various kinds of modeling require detailed demographic and behavioral data. Attitudinal drivers are modeled by looking at the relationship between key behaviors and attitudes. Attitudinal improvements can't be made to lifestage and geodemographic models until those models are first built with demographic data.

Deploy Attitudinal Information

Attitudinal information cannot improve marketing execution unless it is deployed in a way that makes it compatible with and usable by databases and quantitative marketing metrics. Attitudes must be included in all marketing execution systems.

1. Develop linkage models. Linkage models are the way in which attitudes are deployed for marketing execution. Addressable Attitudes are created by models that link attitudes to individual names and addresses.

Syndicated systems such as MindBase or Lists With Attitudes have already developed linkage models, which have been used to deploy Addressable Attitudes to third-party compiled lists. Individual companies can overlay Addressable Attitudes by sending a file containing names and addresses to an allied third-party list company. Names and addresses will be matched and the Addressable Attitudes from either MindBase or Lists with Attitudes will be scored onto individual records.

Proprietary systems require custom development of linkage models. The first step is to complete an attitudinal research project that includes all of the variables from the database to be scored with Addressable Attitudes. At the conclusion of this research, two sets of models need to be built. First, a segmentation model will be built to assign people to tightly clustered attitudinal segments. Twenty or thirty segments are not uncommon since many segments are needed to ensure a high degree of attitudinal consistency within each group.

Second, linkage models will be built from the database variables in order to score people into segments without the attitudinal information. The performance of these models must be rigorously tested against holdout sample groups. These models work better if it so happens that the attitudinal segmentation also included non-attitudinal data in the final solution. So, as a rule of thumb, it is smart to look for segmentation solutions that have a mix of attitudinal, demographic and behavioral data. Good linkage modeling work can yield assignment accuracy rates as high as 90 percent.

2. Create an insights repository. The value of Addressable Attitudes is best captured by means of a formal structure that accumulates and stores insights for use by the entire organization. This is different than just sharing data. Already, most marketing organizations make all types of data freely available to every group within the company. Each group makes its own use of the data, though, often without benefit of insights that other groups have developed from that data. These insights are much more important than the data per se.

An insights repository is a meta-database that functions as a large-scale cross-referencing system. Each bit of data is tagged with a number of additional links and identifiers that connect it to other key facts and descriptors, such as:

- Other pieces of data correlated with a particular bit of information.
- Predictive models making use of a piece of data, and the sort of use made.
- Prior marketing applications involving a data element, and the success statistics for those programs.
- Reports that include a piece of data and the conclusions and implications drawn that make use of that bit of information.
- Age and quality of a data element.
- Internal experts who have made use of certain kinds of data in the past.
- Creative and strategic ideas associated with various sorts of information.

This last element of an insights repository is the most crucial. Insights Integration refers to the organization of marketing around ideas rather than processes. These ideas are connected to attitudinal insights, so it is important to preserve that connection in an insights repository.

3. Link to other systems and databases. Addressable Attitudes must be incorporated into the execution systems used to run marketing. Prospecting lists must be scored with Addressable Attitudes so that prospects can be targeted and communicated with on the basis of attitudes. Media buying databases must be scored with Addressable Attitudes so that media can be bought on the basis of attitudes. Marketing tracking systems must be scored with Addressable Attitudes so that performance can be tracked relative to attitudes. And so forth.

4. Maintain self-optimization systems. The match of attitudes with individual names and addresses should be constantly upgraded and improved. Original assignment accuracy should be improved as necessary.

But the most important factor is that the dynamics of the marketplace are fast moving, so a system to ensure accuracy and consistency will keep a system of Addressable Attitudes up-to-date.

Different approaches can be used to update and refine the match of attitudes to individual names and addresses. Questions can be asked during marketing or service contacts with individual customers to determine how well their answers match the scoring of Addressable Attitudes, from which corrections can be made and linkage models can be refined. Survey work can also be done to make the same kind of assessment and model refinement. Responses of individual customers to marketing programs also provide an indicator about the match of the Addressable Attitudes.

Use Addressable Attitudes and Insights for Marketing Execution

The purpose of Addressable Attitudes is to make it possible for attitudes to be used directly in marketing execution.

1. Conduct a profiling analysis. The first thing to do is to profile key customer groups with attitudinal information. Transactional data should be included so that the attitudes of high-value customers can be identified and contrasted with those of low-value customers. A relevant baseline of comparison is needed, such as total category or total U.S., in order to show the extent to which a customer group is different or unique. These differences are the basis for more precise targeting and more relevant communications. Key insights should be distilled from data patterns apparent in the profiling and then used to develop plans for marketing initiatives.

2. Enhance targeting models. Addressable Attitudes can be added to target selection models just like any other data element. The relevant test will be whether the Addressable Attitudes improve the predictive validity of the targeting models. In many cases, Addressable Attitudes provide a statistically significant incremental improvement in models for target selection.

Attitudes can also be used to generate a list. In this case, the attitudes themselves are the basis for target selection, so there is no test of model improvement. Instead, the response provided by a list based on attitudes is compared to the response generated by alternative lists. Almost all of the time, lists created on the basis of attitudes outperform other lists.

3. Build relevant offers and messages. The greatest value and impact of Addressable Attitudes comes from improved marketing communications.[4] When people receive an offer or a message that speaks directly to their lifestyle values and interests, the marketing is well received. Such offers and messages stand out against the background noise of clutter, so these communications get more notice. Not only do these communications generate business, they boost a brand's image because the marketing itself is so much better. Better marketing practice not only sells, it paves the way for the future by strengthening the perceptions that people have of a brand.

4. Advertise marketing practices. The shift in marketing practices made possible by Addressable Attitudes is an improvement worth publicizing. It's what people are looking for, so marketers should take credit for doing it. Marketing practices can be a source of competitive advantage and brand differentiation because nowadays, the value of a brand is tied to its marketing practices no less than to its product performance.

5. Test and re-test. Experimenting with alternative offers or variations on benefits and language extend and deepen the insights provided by attitudes. Marketing execution tests are an important way of optimizing the productivity gains generated by a marketing system based on Addressable Attitudes.

Re-center the Organization on Customer Insights

With Addressable Attitudes in place, a marketing organization has the information needed to unify all groups around a common set of customer insights. No longer must some groups work with attitudinal data and others with transactional data. Every group can have access to the same insights. The customer can now be heard by everyone in the organization.

1. Put attitudes at center of marketing. Marketing processes must step aside. Customer insights must rule. Processes must be used only to the extent that they serve the interests of customers. Every contact is a marketing opportunity if it is appropriate for what people want. New contacts should be pioneered, but old media should not be abandoned willy-nilly because in many cases mass media will turn out to be a better way of getting in sync with people's attitudes.

2. Adopt a new internal vocabulary. Addressable Attitudes bring individual people to life. Marketers can stop talking about customers in dry, scientific terms. Marketers can focus on the interests of particular people instead of the aggregate needs of a group of people. A vocabulary rooted in attitudinal insights instills a stronger sense of empathy throughout the organization and strengthens the bonds between customers and company service and marketing representatives.

3. Monitor impact. Marketers must ensure that Concurrence Marketing is having an impact. Marketing clutter should be reduced if not eliminated. Customers should perceive more precision and relevance as well as more power and reciprocity. Customers should be able to notice and articulate improvements in their lifestyles. Marketers must monitor these dimensions to ensure that their marketing is showing specific improvements in the areas that matter most. Marketers should also see a measurable and significant improvement in the productivity of their marketing investments.

4. Engage customers. Customers want to be involved, so marketers should look for more and more ways of giving people access to brands and marketing. This should be an on-going search that is constantly informed by customer suggestions. Wherever possible, customers should be allowed to manage the process themselves. And marketers should be on the look out for new forms of reciprocity. Dissatisfactions as well as new lifestyle interests are opportunities for more reciprocity.

Customers can never be too involved. Marketers should look for every opportunity to hand something over to customers. The job of brand management should be to obviate the need for brand management.

5. Do less. Get more. Precision means zeroing in on people who have the right attitudes. No money wasted on those who don't. Relevance means talking to people in ways that are personally meaningful and motivating. No wasted words. More precision and reciprocity mean re-engaging resistant consumers. Concurrence Marketing is all about boosting marketing productivity by getting more while doing less.

6. Use new media to make old media better. The new media are not a replacement for the old media. Never in history has an existing medium been eliminated by the emergence of a new medium. The roles of media change as technologies and lifestyles evolve, but accumulation, not substitution, is the pattern that media show over time.

Already, word-of-mouth and the Internet are being used to make TV more involving. Integrated uses of new and old media provide better opportunities to deliver empowering messages that offer people something interesting and entertaining in return for their time and attention. Besides, people have become experts at multitasking across multiple media formats. Media blending is smarter marketing.

7. Appoint a Chief Insights Officer. This is more than just a new name for a strategic planning officer or a head of research. This is someone to oversee the development of the insights that drive breakout success. This is hard to get from other C-level officers because of their day-to-day operating responsibilities. Yet, it's insights that now matter most.

The addition of Addressable Attitudes brings new opportunities. Not just a better way of doing the same old things but entirely new things to do. Marketing systems are different and marketing insights are improved. At the highest levels of the organization, Concurrence Marketing must be embraced.

BACK ON TRACK

The basic template for marketing is pretty straightforward: Insights to Strategy. Strategy to Tactics. Tactics to Results. Three basic transitions that entail a number of components and systems. Concurrence Marketing improves all three.

The basic insights that drive marketing are improved when Addressable Attitudes are used to create a repository of knowledge around which the organization can integrate its thinking and its activities. The net result is a better link to strategy.

Strategy is improved when it is developed around the insights-centric principles of P&R² rather than the process-centric elements of the 4P's. Insights-driven strategies have a tactical connection when consumers are involved in making things happen and when the attitudes behind the strategies are built into the marketing execution systems. The net result is a better link to tactics.

Tactics are improved when attitudes are part of the systems used to run marketing programs. The net result is substantially better performance.

In years past, marketers have done a very good job of working with demographic and behavioral data to create value for their businesses.

But the point of diminishing returns has been reached. Further improvements are only going to be incremental, and they will come at great expense. Productivity gains will be smaller and smaller. Something new is needed, not new ways of doing the same old things. Attitudes are the next opportunity for big leaps forward in marketing productivity.

Marketing has been buffeted by a gale force of change over the past decade. Many pundits have wondered if there is a future for advertising and advertising agencies. Make no mistake, there is a bigger role than ever. Insights are the stock-in-trade of ad agencies and insights are the essential requirement for success in the future.

But agencies have developed and delivered these insights within the framework of a media environment that no longer exists. The future of agencies must be about the creative use of insights in the context of the new media environment, which means integrating insights, attitudes specifically, into the marketing execution systems that have operated without attitudes in the past. Insights are no less important just because the mass media are fading away. Indeed, they are more important than ever. Ad agencies are, too.

It's been said that marketers now operate in an "attention economy," a marketplace in which people's attention is the scarcest resource and the most valuable media inventory. Information overload is said to have created an economy driven by a new currency, which is the attention that people are willing to pay to things. In this economy, marketers have no control over the most precious resource and inventory. Marketers cannot negotiate with one another to get more access to or better prices on people's attention. Customers control what marketers need most.

Actually, though, the attention economy is no change at all. Marketers have always pursued people's attention. Marketers have always looked for new ways to get in front of people. Marketers have always coveted people's attention. And even with less information in the past, people have always had more things to attend to than they had the time or energy to devote to them. The attention economy is at least as old as marketing itself. There's just a lot more information these days, and a much stronger perception of a time famine. But to at least some degree, attention has always been scarce.

What's new is marketing resistance. Attention is not just scarce. Nowadays, attention is being actively, intentionally and often maliciously withheld from marketing. While more information than ever competes for people's attention, that fact, in and of itself, is neither good nor bad for marketers. It all depends on how marketers operate. By and large, marketing today operates in ways that create more overload with less value, so people have turned away in annoyance and disappointment.

There is a different way to operate, however, and that way is Concurrence Marketing and the principles of P&R². Concurrence Marketing is not a magic bullet that will cure marketing overnight. But it is the way to improve the fortunes of marketers struggling to boost marketing productivity in the face of consumer resistance and a rapidly changing marketplace. Concurrence Marketing makes marketing worth it. And when marketing is worth it, people will pay attention.

NOTES

1 Sergio Zyman, *The End of Marketing As We Know It* (HarperBusiness: 2000).

2 For example, in a story entitled, "Campaigns Use TV Preferences To Find Voters," Jim Rutenberg reported in the *New York Times* on July 18, 2004 that the Bush and Kerry Presidential campaigns were concentrating their advertising spending in different TV programs. Bush was focusing on crime shows and Kerry on late-night comedy, women's shows and shows featuring minorities. Other shows with heavy concentrations of women and elderly viewers were being targeted by both campaigns. The different emphasis of each campaign reflected a strategy of placing ads in shows with a context compatible with the message and of connecting with people who would find the ads relevant in that context and pertinent to their political beliefs.

3 Yankelovich utilizes a suite of Precision Analytics™ to perform this modeling work.

4 Marketing programs properly designed on the basis of MindBase have shown positive improvements in marketing ROI, with incremental lift relative to a control group ranging from 10 percent to 60-plus percent.

About Yankelovich Partners, Inc.

www.Yankelovich.com
www.ConcurrenceMarketing.com

Yankelovich Partners, Inc. is a marketing services consultancy providing information, database and segmentation solutions that deliver breakthroughs in marketing productivity. Its clients include Fortune 500 companies in the retail, financial services, agency, consumer products, technology, automotive, media, entertainment and insurance industries, among others. Yankelovich offers a full suite of Concurrence Marketing solutions and Addressable Attitudes products. For over 30 years, The Yankelovich MONITOR® has tracked and forecasted consumer values and lifestyle trends. MindBase® links the MONITOR information on why people buy directly to databases of customers and prospects. The Segmentation Company®, a division of Yankelovich, provides high-end analytics for proprietary segmentation solutions that support Addressable Attitudes. Yankelovich is headquartered in Chapel Hill, NC, with offices in Norwalk, CT and Atlanta, GA.

Chapel Hill, NC Headquarters	**Norwalk, CT**
400 Meadowmont Village Circle	20 Glover Avenue
Suite 431	2nd Floor
Chapel Hill, NC 27517	Norwalk, CT 06850
919.932.8600	203.846.0100
919.932.8829 (fax)	203.845.8200 (fax)

J. Walker Smith is President of Yankelovich Partners, Inc. He is the co-author, with Ann Clurman, of *Rocking the Ages: The Yankelovich Report on Generational Marketing* (HarperBusiness: 1997), a highly regarded assessment of generational marketing strategies, and *Life Is Not Work, Work Is Not Life: Simple Reminders for Finding Balance in a 24/7 World* (Wildcat Canyon: 2001), a collection of short essays and personal reflections on work/life balance that was picked by the *Wall Street Journal* as one of the ten best work-life books of 2001. Described by *Fortune* magazine as "one of America's leading analysts on consumer trends," Walker is a much sought after speaker and authority on social trends in America whose quotable insights appear regularly in the national media and business press. He does a weekly commentary called "City Views" for "Smart City," an award-winning public radio program about cities and community life that is hosted by Carol Coletta on WKNO-FM in Memphis. He also writes a regular column for *Marketing Management* magazine and for *DIRECT* magazine with Craig Wood. Walker serves on several corporate and academic boards and holds a Ph.D. from the University of North Carolina at Chapel Hill.

Ann Clurman is Senior Partner at Yankelovich Partners, Inc. She is the intellectual force behind the Yankelovich MONITOR, the firm's unparalleled, on-going 30-plus-year old study of consumer attitudes that tracks and forecasts consumer lifestyles and behaviors. *U.S. News & World Report* described Ann as "one of the best researchers and generation-watchers" in America. She is a nationally recognized authority and lecturer on American consumers, particularly women and youth. Ann is a knowledgeable and spirited speaker who regularly appears before diverse client, industry and government groups. She is often quoted in the business and popular media. She is the co-author, with J. Walker Smith, of *Rocking the Ages: The Yankelovich Report on Generational Marketing* (Harper-

Business: 1997). She is a former regular columnist on social and demographic trends for *Marketing Research* magazine. Ann holds a B.A. with Phi Beta Kappa honors from New York University and an M.A. from Brown University.

Craig Wood is President of the MONITOR division of Yankelovich Partners, Inc. In this capacity, Craig oversaw the introduction of MindBase, a pioneering product that was the first database enhancement service able to merge attitudinal data into behavioral and transactional databases. Craig is a nationally recognized authority on data solutions and consumer motivations. He is a frequently requested speaker for conferences on privacy, trust, CRM, loyalty, database marketing and a wide variety of vertical industries. Craig serves on several corporate and trade boards and planning committees. He is a regular contributor to leading marketing periodicals, including a monthly column for *DIRECT* magazine that he writes with J. Walker Smith. Craig was the President and COO of Businessmodel.com, a Web analytics and consulting firm, and EVP at KnowledgeBase Marketing, an integrated information consultancy that is a division of Y&R/Wunderman. Craig holds a B.S. from the University of Virginia.